COUNSELING TECHNIQUES THAT WORK

COUNSELING TECHNIQUES THAT WORK

Dr. Wayne W. Dyer
Dr. John Vriend

FUNK & WAGNALLS

New York

Manufactured in the United States of America

Library of Congress Cataloging in Publication Data
Dyer, Wayne W
  Counseling techniques that work.
  Includes index.
  1.   Personnel service in education.   I.   Vriend,
John, joint author.   II.   Title.
LB1027.5.D9   1977   371.4′044   77-607
ISBN 0-308-10300-9

10 9 8 7 6 5 4 3 2 1

To
Susan and Butch Barry

Contents

0384340

They conquer who believe they can. He has not learned the lesson of life who does not each day surmount a fear.

—Ralph Waldo Emerson

If this is the vision of the future—if this is the direction in which we want to move—the next thing we must consider is how we propose to get there, and what obstacles lie in our path. For such a vision is never self-fulfilling. We cannot stand idly by and expect our dreams to come true under their own power. The future is not a gift: it is an achievement.

—Robert F. Kennedy
Promises to Keep

"The best thing for being sad," replied Merlin, beginning to puff and blow, "is to learn something. That is the only thing that never fails. You may grow old and trembling in your anatomies, you may lie awake at night listening to the disorder of your veins, you may miss your only love, you may see the world about you devastated by evil lunatics, or know your honor trampled in the sewers of baser minds. There is only one thing for it then—to learn. Learn why the world wags and what wags it. That is the only thing which the mind can never exhaust, never alienate, never be tortured by, never fear or distrust, and never dream of regretting. Learning is the thing for you. Look at what a lot of things there are to learn—pure science, the only purity there is. You can learn astronomy in a lifetime, natural history in three, literature in six. And then, after you have exhausted a million lifetimes in biology and medicine and theocriticism and geography and history and economics, why, you can start to make a cartwheel out of the appropriate wood, or spend fifty years learning to begin to learn to beat your adversary at fencing. After that you can start again on mathematics until it is time to learn to plough."

—T. H. White
The Once and Future King

Introduction

Just as a writer is one who writes, not one who labels himself or herself a writer and then merely talks about writing, a practitioner is one who practices, who does. It is the practitioner who was always foremost in our minds as we compiled, organized, and wrote this book. The practicing counselor, the trainer of counselors, and the committed beginner seek greater effectiveness and results that make a difference in the world of real people. These are empiricists, pragmatists, hypothesis testers, whose theoretical constructs, skills and competencies, and behavioral practices are firmly lodged by virtue of their experience. Such ones are we, and such we imagine our audience to be.

Thus, what we present in this book is not for those who are interested in fanciful theoretical postulations about various schools of counseling and therapeutic philosophies. We do not attempt to satisfy those who seek sophisticated research designs and elaborate statistical procedures. The reader will find few quotations or references in this book. This is not another dreary or esoteric book written to gain professorial advancement. We are interested in contributing what we have learned about counseling to the everyday practitioner, to those engaged in the difficult struggle of becoming increasingly better at what they have committed themselves to do.

Although we recognize the value of the research process, we know that greater effectiveness in counseling comes from practice and hard work, not from reading such reports. The scientific knowledge commonly yielded by these reports is trivial because behavioral scientists insist on modeling research designs, methodologies, and procedures after those developed by physical scientists. But if research with people in real life contexts, that are always in a state of flux, is modeled after the physical world research designs, it is doomed to yield little valid or reliable knowledge. Since human behavior is neither fixed nor stable, it is not replicatable under the high standards of the research laboratory. Our concern is not with research designs but with effective performance, productive human interaction in the matrix of actual life situations.

Presented in this book are techniques that work. How can we make such an assertion? Because we have tried them. We have lived them over and over. They come from our own living as practicing counselors, from the thousands of hours of counseling in our own private practices and public service work roles, and from the hundreds of groups we have co-counseled. They represent some of the distillation of our experience. When many of the techniques and skills in this book were first used, they were inventions of the moment—and they worked. These counselor interventions made a significant difference, a behavioral change impact on the clients we were serving. They led to new insights and ultimately to new ways of behaving for clients in any of the several stages of counseling—not one time with one client, but time and time again with many diverse clients.

The techniques worked in that they fit into the total counseling process. As we employed the techniques in new settings, we altered them, refined them, and eventually built up our own repertoires of specific counselor behaviors that we could manifest in group and individual counseling. We know the techniques work because we have trained hundreds of counselors and allied professionals in our parent institutions and in endless consultancy assignments around the country, where the goals always included teaching existing staffs to upgrade performance levels in the delivery of helping services to various client populations.

We have been deliberately nonpedagogical in these pages. Our thought was that we could bring together under one cover a collection of related writings which spoke directly to the practitioner striving for professional development and personal effectiveness. Our theoretical ramblings are minimal. Our use of references is only for clarity or explication. Presentations of research designs are few, not because they have no value, but because these are notes from two successful counseling practitioners and trainers of counselors who are attempting to give away what they know works. This is the entire thrust of this book. We know that clients respond to the kinds of counselor behaviors we describe, that group members react positively, that counseling groups are exciting and productive when the leader can draw on a large selection of group techniques. We are sharing what we know because we are convinced of its value, we see it as timeless, and we are aware of its almost universal applicability.

Originally, this book was conceived and written for counseling professionals, and they loved it. The first printing sold out in under eight months. Then, an interesting phenomenon occurred. We found that all sorts of people outside the discipline of psychological counseling were scooping it up and using it in practical ways to help themselves get better at helping others. We saw no reason not to encourage such efforts. Humanity, on an individual as well as a mass level, needs all the help it can get. How can any human being be against helping people? It goes against instinct. Aware that our book was being used by so many nonprofessionals, we were pleased to be able to speak to them directly when the opportunity arose with this new printing. Therefore, we have added a section called: "So You Want to Help People: Notes for the Nonprofessional Counselor."

Beyond this, the book has two major parts. The first part emphasizes techniques that work in counselor training and in the practice of counseling an individual client. Chapter 1 leads off with a translatable-to-action definition of counseling and includes a rating scale for determining effectiveness of counselor performance in some selected competency dimensions. Chapter 2 follows with a detailed presentation of the composition of an effective initial counseling interview. The fifteen essential components of a first counseling session are laid out to provide a checklist for the practitioner, which will enable personal assessment of initial interview performance.

Chapter 3 deals with one of the most troublesome problems in the counseling field: how to understand and help chronic drug users. The chapter draws on internal/external notions of self-responsibility for emotional states and unfolds to the development of counselor strategies for effectively helping the addicted and preaddicted personality. Chapter 4 introduces the reader to various productive writing activities associated with increased counselor competency as part of a structured counseling practicum experience. This chapter presents specific instructions for counselor log keeping; an actual log along with the supervisor's running commentary; guidelines for writing meaningful case reports, including a model of an actual report; and, finally, guidelines for writing a self-evaluation of learning progress.

Chapter 5 is a reprint of an article which appeared originally in the May 1973 issue of the *Journal of Counseling Psychology*. It contains fundamental principles and operational strategies that any counselor must understand in order to be maximally effective in working with reluctant clients.

Chapter 6 involves the reader in an actual counseling experience. A technique for training counselors is explained and demonstrated wherein a supervisor creates a tape-of-a-tape, an audio record of supervisor intervention into the actual counseling interview. Chapter 7, the final inclusion in the first part of the book, appears to be a departure from the thrust of skill-building, of technique and strategy acquisition, but it provides the kind of essential background thinking out of which effective counselor behaviors emerge.

The second part of this book focuses on group counseling techniques that work. In Chapter 8 we again start with a translatable-to-action definition and provide twenty attendant assumptions upon which the definition of group counseling is founded. Chapter 9 details twenty group counselor behaviors every masterful leader of counseling groups will want to incorporate and gives examples of both effective and ineffective application of these. The chapter also contains a checklist of the twenty behaviors which the self-teaching practitioner can use for personal assessment of development leading to mastery.

In Chapter 10 we present nineteen special techniques and strategies that can enlarge the effective group counselor's repertoire of available interventions for helping members attain positive behavioral change goals. All are tried, tested, and refined strategies that work. They have application to virtually all counseling groups, and we feel that the practitioner will find this chapter to be provocative and exciting reading. Interventions for specific and appropriate times in the group counseling process are chronicled in Chapter 11. The chapter lays out ways to intervene effectively at signal junctures in the activity of the group and backs up such group counselor action with a cogent rationale in each instance. In Chapter 12 major barriers to effectiveness in group counseling are elaborated along with techniques for eliminating such barriers in the ongoing group.

Chapter 13 presents the step-by-step formulation and operation of a homogeneously organized experimental counseling group of chronically obese girls conducted in a high school and how the counselor actually was able to make a positive difference in the lives of one often-neglected special population of students by applying group counseling strategies. A host of practical suggestions, techniques, and methods for utilizing role working in counseling groups is offered in Chapter 14, the chapter which concludes the book.

Beyond these fourteen chapters, we have included four items in the appendix which group counseling practitioners and trainers will want to employ for increasing the productive impact of counseling group membership: instructions for log keeping for group members, guidelines for audiotape analysis of group counseling process variables, guidelines for the analysis of behavior in groups, and a "Group Counseling Scale for the Analysis of Fully Functioning and Self-Defeating Behaviors."

We trust that this collection of some of our accumulated learnings will help every serious reader and doer to make fresh differences in daily performance on the job. But even above such a welcome commitment to professional development, there is the promise and payoff of a happier, more in-charge kind of personal living for the counselor who works at skill and competency building. One can hardly show and teach others to be more in charge, more personally masterful in all phases of living, without knowing how to be so in one's own right. We've been there and we know, and in this book we share much of that knowing with you.

Part
I

1

Components of Effective Counseling

Counseling is an interpersonal helping procedure which begins with client exploration for the purpose of identifying thinking, feeling, and doing processes which are in any way self-defeating or which require upgrading. The client determines and declares to the counselor what the counter-productive behaviors are and makes decisions about which ones can be worked on. The counselor helps the client to set goals in which more positive thinking and feeling will lead to the acquisition of self-enhancing behaviors which had not previously been a part of the client's repertoire. The counselor helps the individual to identify significant self-logic and self-performance wherein thinking, feeling, and doing are evidently self-defeating. The counselor then helps to move the client toward self-understanding by examining with the client why such self-crippling behavior persists, as well as the psychological maintenance system for such behavior. This means fully answering to the client's satisfaction a key question: What is it (both positively and otherwise) that the client gets out of perpetuating the self-defeating behavior? The counselor then moves the client to explore possible alternatives to the self-defeating thinking, feeling, and doing. The next step in the process involves setting goals which are specific and realistically attainable for the client. After goal setting, the client tests proposed alternate behaviors in the counseling sessions, where helping interventions, structures, activities, or simulations are provided by the counselor. Psychological homework assignments are then mutually initiated and agreed upon, and the client tries the new behavior in his or her personal world—outside the counseling session where it truly counts. In subsequent sessions the client reports on the new thinking, new feelings engendered by the new thinking, and the new behaviors. This is followed up with revised behavioral goals, which are established as a result of analysis and evaluation in the counseling. Such reports go on through the life of the counseling. The individual either incorporates the new thinking and behavior or rejects it or gets recycled for additional exploration, self-understanding, and goal setting. The total emphasis is on the acquisition and incorporation into the self-system of productive new behaviors.

There are a number of assumptions in the above definition, the most significant of which are the following:

1. *Counseling effectiveness is judged by positive client change.* If there is no mental, emotional, or physical change in the client's behavior outside of the counseling, the effects of counseling are negligible.

2. *The client is the all-important person in the counseling twosome, the one for whom the activity and the relationship exist.* In this sense, all that goes on is client-focused. Everything that the counselor does is for the sake of the client. Anything that goes on for the sake of the counselor is not counseling, is unethical and nonproductive, and has the capacity to be destructive to the client in some ways. The counselor can personally profit from the experience by being paid or by increasing skill and competency development, the latter being an unscheduled gain, a by-product of some experiential counseling moments. The counselor serves the client, who is the sole reason for all time, energy, and effort expended in the relationship.

3. *The counselor cannot merely do what comes naturally, according to his own "style."* The counselor has learned specific skills and competencies which are employed in counseling for the results they are known to produce. The counselor has a rationale for each behavior, which can be shared with the client at any time. To the extent that the counselor can summon forth any part of past experience or personal resources at any given counseling moment for servicing the client, the counseling will be more or less effective. This includes everything that is in the counselor's make-up.

4. *Counseling is work, probably the most difficult and rewarding kind of work in which two people can engage.* The client works or doesn't grow. Essentially, the client is attempting to learn, and learning is self-activity. When this learning of new ways of thinking, feeling, and doing is in personally troublesome areas, then the work of counseling can be of the most humanly painful kind. Thus, many clients resist or avoid it. Discomfort and pain more frequently than not accompany the work in which the client engages. What the counselor does is work, often straining and draining work. Part of this work includes understanding the client's pain and discomfort and providing every kind of support possible within the counseling activity.

5. *Thinking, feeling, and doing have a causal relationship.* While the end sought in counseling is positive client behavioral change, the concept of behavior requires modifying descriptors to bring about real-life meaning. Thus, changes are sought in a client's thinking behavior, feeling behavior, and doing behavior. In each case, in each instance of a client's life, thinking, feeling, and doing behavior can be further delineated and specified with accurate descriptors. Doing behavior, and the feeling behavior which *always* accompanies it, is preceded by the thinking behavior which causes both. A person *thinks* herself or himself into both feeling and doing, whether proactive or reactive. Thus, clients are not hurt by others; they hurt themselves as a result of what they think about whatever stimuli others have provided.

6. *The counselor is the skilled and competent person in the relationship and the interpersonal helping activity, and to the extent that a counselor is less skilled or competent than the client in a given behavioral dimension, counseling will be unproductive, even abusive to the client.* Given this assumption, a counselor does not engage in or promote activity which is outside the realm of competence and meaningful service delivery. The counselor's repertoire of skills and competencies is always in need of enlarging. It includes every kind of possible learning. Thus, the counselor continually seeks greater personal mastery in order to become the more consummate expert in the delivery of counseling services. The counselor is perpetually in self-training, seeking to increase performance levels in every mental, emotional, and physical area. Thus, each of the following is of supreme importance: diagnosing another's reality data, learning how to be in touch with more behavioral options at any given time, learning how to remember more, to discriminate more effectively according to criterion sets, to concentrate, to focus, to communicate in more ways, to listen more acutely, and to feel in certain ways, at times when doing so, is enhancing to the ongoing counseling process. By this logic the perfect counselor would be that person who had incorporated an understanding of and the ability to manifest at will every mental, emotional, and physical behavior learned by any human being in the history of the world. Thus, being an "expert" is relative; it is a useful concept which describes an evolving counseling self; the enlargement of a counselor's essence, the summation of learnings at any given moment in time, never reaches completion and ends at death.

7. *Client self-enhancing behavioral change does not come about mysteriously.* People change their behavior themselves and they do so more with the aid of certain helpful stimuli and life-space reality variables than with others which are less helpful. Behavior is learned

and caused, in spite of the fact that the components of the learning process and the causes are not always identifiable or understood. For a counselor to ascribe results to some form of magic, divine intervention, or mysterious fate is to perpetuate, rigidify, and consolidate ignorance. If the light of a counselor's consciousness is not bright enough to illuminate the make-up of a particular reality, the counselor is not ready, and it is the counselor who is in the dark. He or she ought neither to accept nor curse the darkness, but to light another candle. Counseling, in the final analysis, is consciousness training for both client and counselor.

8. *All clients live in their own minds, bodies, time, and life-space, in their own relational and geographical circle. Each client's data are unique, personally owned, and of a particular character having personal meaning and value.* The counselor's job is to enter the client's world, to deal with the client's self-data, to understand it, make sense of it, and to be immersed in it consciously. Only by getting into and dealing with the being-time-space reality data of the client can a counselor be effective. Thus, all counseling activity is accepted or rejected by the client and either incorporated or manifested in a particular way in a particular living person's life, a life totally separate from the counselor's or that of any other person in the history of the world.

These eight assumptions are the most essential of those undergirding the given definition of counseling, though not the only ones. A communication to the client of what counseling is, how and why it works, what work (behaviors) will be engaged in by both client and counselor, and what outcomes can be reliably expected and realistically pursued—all in language understood by the client—is important to an effective launching of the counseling process and relationship. But more important are the unfolding reality exchanges through the course of any set of counseling sessions, because what counseling is in any given case is defined by what actually happens. All of the ideas herein noted have neither value nor meaning until some real people live them. In the living of them, their shape will change but their essence will be actualized. Such actualization, whatever its form with whatever twosome, is where one looks for a definition of counseling. The actualization of counseling will be effective to the extent that parts of this model definition are incorporated into the process.

If counseling success is measured by the new behaviors of a client now living a more personally masterful life, a final thought about this definition requires saying: The entire process seeks its own dissolution. A counselor who functions at similar or lower levels than does the client in any given life dimension whereon the counseling has focused is no longer useful to that client. It is the counseling process that has been vital not the particular counselor who has been the embodiment and instrumentalization of the process. But in every case, since without client work, without client self-activity, there can be no expectation of client growth, however hard the counselor might work and strain in helping, it can be unequivocally said that the client has done the job, not the counselor. The process is one of self-promotion, and the client can take all the credit. The client who leaves counseling and feels that the counselor deserves the credit, who feels the counselor has accomplished the seeming miracle of producing the more effective life-handler that she or he now has become, has met a counselor lacking effectiveness in what is probably the most crucial dimension of all: psychological and physical independency. A counselor gets paid and/or more skilled for working and delivering. Additionally, spurred on or supported by the counseling, a client achieves intrinsic and extrinsic gains. Neither need be grateful to the other.

There is more than an assumption, in the text above, that the counselor possesses numerous specific skills and competencies which can be manifested in any given counseling session depending on what appears appropriate to attainable counseling ends. Further assumed is the idea that every committed counselor is constantly engaged in increasing the number of skills and upgrading performance levels in any skill area. Either of these two counselor self-development goals requires that the counselor first clearly define the skill, technique, strategy, or competency in question in operational terms and then consciously begin to practice it, evaluate such practice, and finally incorporate it into the self-system. Behavioral mastery in any skill component comes with consciously evaluated use.

Counseling competency is a broader concept than counseling skill. It may be defined as informed judgment which helps a counselor to make accurate assessments of client reality data and what has gone on in the counseling process over the course of its short- and long-term existence. Such assessment-making is ongoing and coterminous with counseling. That is, whenever the counselor is in the presence of the client and has the option to take this or that action, greater or lesser competency is behind whatever counselor action is taken. Thus, counselor competency, judicial mental-processing of counseling reality data, accounts for the selection and initiation of self-behaviors which impact and advance counseling interaction purposively. Obviously, counselor competency is more difficult to define operationally than a counseling skill; it requires a higher order of mental functioning involving the use of accumulated knowledge, accurate perception, and diagnostic ability; it comes from the matrix of analyzed experience—the more the better.

At the end of this chapter, we present our effort at isolating and operationally defining fourteen specific counseling skills and so organizing them that their manifestation may be assessed by a counselor, a counseling supervisor, or an observer. (Since all of the skills listed, if incorporated, would help any person to live more effectively, the skills can be taught to clients and the scale can be used creatively in actual counseling; thus, the client could be the subject of skill evaluation rather than the counselor.) The Counselor Competency Behavioral Rating Scale (CCBRS) is presented here chiefly as a model for counselors seeking a way of conceptualizing and evaluating skills they are currently attempting to acquire or upgrade.

Since the CCBRS lends itself to a myriad of uses, it is pertinent here that the authors' experience with the scale be briefly recorded. We are currently in the process of further refinement and are working at establishing validity and reliability norms. It is not, therefore, a finished product. In its present form, its limitations depend on the use to which it is put. For example, if it is used to determine which counselors in training have grown the most in a practicum experience, such subjects cannot be compared to one another. Carl Smith might achieve a high overall Counselor Competency Behavior Rating (CCBR score) because a few particular skills were repeatedly used masterfully in the counseling sessions which were rated. If these skills were of a low order of ability or importance, Carl would appear to be a more competent counselor than was actually the case. Thus, Carl might effectively and frequently manifest counselor behaviors such as exploring, underscoring, encouraging, and restating, while ignoring or not manifesting any of the other skills in the scale. Most of the other skills are of a higher order of ability and importance to client movement. Tom Anderson, who manifested a broader range of skills at a lower level of performance could thus appear to be a less effective counselor than Carl when their CCBR scores were compared, when in actuality Tom was the more competent counselor. This problem of unequal importance of CCBRS items is being resolved by differential weighting of the fourteen skills and will be incorporated in scale revisions.

Another problem has to do with who does the rating. Raters must be trained to assess accurately each manifestation of a skill. We have learned that it is possible to train raters, even though the rater might not be able to demonstrate or actualize the given skill in question when personally asked to do so. This is extremely important in counselor self-ratings.

The scale has the greatest value when it is employed by counselors themselves to make assessments of their own growth in particular skill areas over the course of time and not when it is employed as an evaluation instrument by supervisors endeavoring to give a grade to a student in practicum. When the instrument is used for research purposes to compare mean CCBR scores between experimental and control groups, it serves a useful function, too. In this latter case, it appears now to yield data which is as valid as any other measure we have tried.

Counselor Competency Behavior Rating Scale*

Counselor: _____

Rater: _____

Interview tape # _____

Other than tape (explain)_____

The Counselor Competency Behavioral Rating Scale (CCBRS) is designed to assess specific counselor skills and behaviors. It requires the rater to identify and tally the occurrence of each manifestation of 14 defined counselor skills and to rate the efficacy of each. The scale is designed primarily to assess counselor performance as it is manifested in an audio- or videotape record of a given counseling session, but it can also be used (without the frequency tabulation) as a summary evaluation of a counselor trainee's level of performance in the component areas, or as one measure of a counseling practitioner's overall performance by a supervisor. The scale also lends itself well to use as a self-rating instrument by counselors seeking to upgrade their own performance levels.

Certainly all the skills and competencies which a counselor ought to develop are not included. The assumption is made, however, that the 14 behaviors defined herein are all important and necessary to acquire for effective counselor functioning. Indeed, higher levels of performance in each of the components can be built into any counselor training program as outcome goals. In such a case, the scale can be used to provide pretest, ongoing, and posttest data resulting from a content analysis of sequential counseling interviews.

Directions

Definition: An intervention refers to any given instance of counselor verbalization. Some interventions might be characterized by the rater as containing instances of more than one of the 14 skill areas which make up the scale. In this case, the rater should make a tally and assessment of performance in each of the component areas. Some interventions will resist categorization into any of the component areas. For example, a counselor may tell an irrelevant anecdote about himself. Such material, while of interest to a counselor trainer, should not be counted or evaluated.

An intervention may be long or short and may or may not contain interspersed client verbalizations. What the rater needs to identify in his

---

*Researchers, counselor educators, or others who wish to use the CCBRS may do so without permission in writing from the authors, as long as authorship is properly credited. If reproduction in a publication is desired, however, permission in writing from the publisher *is* required. The scale was created by John Vriend, Wayne W. Dyer, Robert W. Brown, Wilbert J. McClure, and H. Jon Geis.

analysis is whether or not a particular segment of counselor verbalization or segment of counselor-client interaction can be characterized as fitting into a skill component area as defined in the CCBRS. Counselor intent, or the implicitly or explicitly implied direction of the intervention, is the chief ingredient here: Was the counselor's behavior manifested in order to achieve a given end inherent in any one of the skill areas? Was he consciously (or unconsciously) exercising the skill in question?

Marking the Scale—Frequency: In the left-hand column of the CCBRS the rater should tally each intervention which fits into one of the 14 categories beside the category into which it fits.

Marking the Scale—Performance Assessment: Following each instance of a behavioral manifestation of a skill component, the rater should immediately analyze the behavioral unit, make an evaluation of it, and assign a numerical value to it by inserting appropriate checks on the scale which appears immediately below the skill definition. (Avoid checks between numbers.) The number of checks on a skill area scale should equal the number of frequency tallies for that area.

While the scale represents a performance continuum of 11 points, the value of 10 being the highest, only 5 descriptors are provided as follows:

10	9	8	7	6	5	4	3	2	1	0

fully effective	mostly effective	minimally effective	slightly effective, but mostly ineffective	completely ineffective

Scoring: The CCBRS yields a Total Frequency Score, attained by adding the tallies of component occurrence. It also yields a Total Performance Assessment Score, attained by adding all component performance assessment values scaled in each performance instance. The Average Level of Performance Score is attained by dividing the Total Frequency Score into the Total Performance Assessment Score. The result comprises the subject's Counselor Competency Behavior Rating.

In addition, should the rater so choose, an average measure of performance for each component skill area can be attained by dividing the frequency of occurrence into the total number of assessment points a subject earns in that skill area.

Counselor Competency Behaviors

1. *Questioning, exploring, drawing out, evoking problem-related material:* Interventions which expose and make clear for the counselee, not just for the counselor, life-space concerns and difficulties the counselee has.

10   9   8   7   6   5   4   3   2   1   0

2. *Information giving:* Introduction of information useful or necessary to the counseling at the appropriate time (counseling procedural matters, referral information, educational-occupational information, testing information, role-working instructions, etc.). Fully effective information giving includes a check on the counselee's understanding of the information and the reasons for its importance to him and the counselor's correction of distortions in client perceptions regarding the information.

10   9   8   7   6   5   4   3   2   1   0

3. *Nonverbal behavior:* Identifying and focusing on nonverbal behavior manifested by the counselee in the interview, labeling it, commenting on it, relating it to counseling content and process data, and using it to forward counseling movement.

10   9   8   7   6   5   4   3   2   1   0

4. *Goal setting:* Helping the counselee to establish realistic and attainable goals. Goal setting is effective when the goals have specificity, pertinence, attainability, accompanying criteria for determining goal accomplishment, and evidence of counselee commitment to taking a course of action.

10   9   8   7   6   5   4   3   2   1   0

5. *Emphasizing, accenting, or underscoring:* Placing stress on an intervention or on counselee data by differing voice tone or by isolating and repeating pertinent statements to heighten impact.

10   9   8   7   6   5   4   3   2   1   0

6. *Reassuring, encouraging, and supporting:* Use of psychological or emotional support when counselee's anxieties begin to inhibit rather than promote counseling movement.

10   9   8   7   6   5   4   3   2   1   0

7. *Establishing connections:* Piecing together for the counselee fragments of problem-related material that the counselee cannot see as connected.

10   9   8   7   6   5   4   3   2   1   0

8. *Hypothesis testing:* Formulating hypotheses about the counselee's behavior and testing them out with the counselee in order to specifically identify the behavior and/or clarify its causes and the meaning it has.

10   9   8   7   6   5   4   3   2   1   0

9. *Restating:* Putting what has been said into different words so that it is more concisely understood and more meaningful to the counselee.

10   9   8   7   6   5   4   3   2   1   0

10. *Identifying, labeling, clarifying, and reflecting feeling:* Interventions which expose and make clear for the counselee, not just for the counselor, what feelings are present in him during the interview or in other parts of his world and how they accompany or affect his behavior in self-enhancing or self-defeating ways.

10   9   8   7   6   5   4   3   2   1   0

11. *Confronting:* Straightforward presentation of the counselee's reality situation which he may wish to avoid.

10   9   8   7   6   5   4   3   2   1   0

12. *Interpreting:* Describing and formulating counselee's problem-related material and giving underlying meaning of an experience or statement.

10   9   8   7   6   5   4   3   2   1   0

13. *Summarizing or reviewing important material:* Drawing together the large bulk of what the counselee says in order to focus on essential aspects. Summarizing can additionally be of what happened in a given interview (or any part of it). Effective summarizing includes naming all the content parts, determining how and why each are important, and including the counselee in the process so that his perceptions of the material are gauged.

10 9 8 7 6 5 4 3 2 1 0

14. *Effecting closure:* Bringing the counselee's work on problems to a close when they have been worked through and capping a part of an interview, an entire interview, or all of the counseling. Effective closure leaves a counselee with a feeling of completeness regarding a given area, of problem status and/or resolution, and of understanding the whole with a minimum number of loose ends.

10 9 8 7 6 5 4 3 2 1 0

Total Frequency Score
Total Performance Assessment Score
Average Level of Performance Score (Counselor Competency Behavior Rating)

2

Vital Components in Conducting the Initial Counseling Interview *

Beginning behavior is crucial in determining future outcomes in virtually all significant human encounters. Any professional who is in greater demand as a result of a record of productivity and client satisfaction has learned that a first meeting with a prospective client is a time to collect, assess, and process a wealth of pertinent data. There is little or no time to waste. Such professionals know the value of having a repertoire of tried and tested beginning strategies. They have developed workable methods for guaranteeing transmission of components which are vital to initial contacts.

Proficient trial lawyers spend time and energy reviewing and mapping out strategies for their first courtroom appearances. Clarence Darrow, renowned for charismatic courtroom effectiveness, was keenly aware of the importance of first impressions on judges and juries. He creatively prepared himself for each new tack and role he decided to enact in any given legal case he was to argue in the theatre of the courtroom. Similarly, stand-up comedians know that early performance excellence is required if audiences are to be won over and their involved attention held. Actors and actresses know how important *one* audition or screen test can be; they win or lose a part on the basis of a single contact with decision makers. The list is endless. Campaigning politicians, sales personnel, advertising executives, consultants of every kind—all realize that unplanned and imprudently executed first contacts frequently result in failure.

*Reprinted with permission from *Educational Technology*, October 1974, Volume 14, Number 10, pp. 24-32.

Given the nature of such normative truths about significant human encounters, it is surprising that more emphasis is not given both in the literature and in training programs to the kinds of professional behaviors which effective counselors ought initially to exercise with each new client. Precisely identifying essential components of first sessions in counseling, therefore, seems germane to an understanding of how productive services may be delivered. Like the entertainer, politician, lawyer, or anyone engaged in providing services to the public or prospective clients, the practicing counselor loses options for being effective in later stages of helping if first encounters are bungled.

An initial session is successful if the client leaves with a feeling of confidence that he or she has come to the right place, a place where demonstrable help is forthcoming, where concerns can be alleviated or restored, where self-development is possible. Any client leaving the first interview soured by what has been experienced under the label of "counseling" is unlikely to return for more and, if forced to continue, is likely to gain little from the exposure.

The effective counselor knows what to do in the initial counseling session. Mastery of techniques, strategies, and productive behaviors enables the counselor to achieve beginning success with every client. This means that the client is committed to return and to become involved in the counseling process. This means that the counselor has followed a prescribed initial interview agenda, flexibly adjustable to variations in clients and the self-data they present; that possible counseling directions have been established; and that tentative early goals have been identified.

What follows is a chronicle in sequential format of significant high-priority components of initial interviews. The list is not exhaustive, nor are the components exclusive to first counseling sessions; indeed, some of them endure throughout the life of the counseling and others require frequent revisiting in subsequent sessions. The components lay a solid foundation. They comprise a comprehensive checklist that the counselor can use as a guide in first contacts with clients who are scheduled for ongoing counseling.

As specified in Chapter 1, counseling is professional activity engaged in by a trained expert whose authority derives from a proven ability to deliver predictable outcomes as a result of the application of masterful skills and competencies in each counseling engagement. Such a theoretical stance is implicit throughout this discussion. "Seat-of-the-pants" counselor behavior or "doing what comes naturally" or only that which might fit in with a counselor's "personal style" are seen as negative if not as totally unethical.

Basic Components of the Initial Interview

Opening the Interview

A counseling relationship is joined with the first verbal and non-verbal communication exchange between client and counselor. The tenor of what goes on in this setting is set at the very beginning. Initial statements are significant. They set the tone for what is to come in the counseling process.

Many beginning counselors ineffectively focus on trying to be overly friendly with their opening remarks, misguidedly seeking to establish "rapport," or compatibility, a goal which in most cases rests on the unwarranted assumption that without such counselor efforts disharmony or incompatibility will follow. Frequently the outcome of such overtures is client suspicion. "Why," asks the client, "is this person trying so hard to butter me up?" In the young, solicitous commentary from any adult who is not a significant other is frequently so outside of everyday experience as to be threatening.

Such utterances as "Well, what did you think of last night's ballgame?" or "Were the buses running on time?" or discussions about the weather are typical of an inane opening. While such statements are common in our culture as social ice-breakers, as informal conversational chit-chat, they serve little point in the counseling interview; if prolonged, they tend to retard rather than advance it. If the counselor behaves inanely and superficially from the beginning, the artificial climate can easily permeate what follows.

More supportable opening statements convey the real purpose of the visit to the counseling office. Preferably they are business-like and reflect the counselor's absorbing personal interest in delivering a service to his client. No pat opening statement is more appropriate than any other, but it is possible to suggest a few: "What has brought you here?" "I see you have been sent here by Mrs. Castle. Can you tell me how that came about?" "This is the counseling office, Mark. In what way can I help you?" "Someone seems to think you are having difficulty in school. Why don't you relate your side of that story?" "My understanding is that you're seeking help in making a decision about some important upcoming events in your life. If that's not accurate, correct my impression. If it is accurate, please elaborate on your concerns."

The opening ought to be devoid of stilted nervousness and as direct as possible about counseling expectations. The smiling sweetness of the tea room hostess or the overly solicitous demeanor of the chronically ineffectual do-gooder are disappointing to clients who look for knowledgeable confidence in a counselor. A down-to-business open-ing encourages the client to begin working on his concerns because here is a counselor who will deal "straight" from the outset.

Assessing the Reason for Coming to Counseling

Assessing why any self-referred client has come for counseling seems to be plain common sense. Yet many counselors do not effectively gather the whole of the story. Clients frequently put forth safe or weak reasons in order to be admitted to counseling on their terms. That is, they're "shopping" to see if this is the place where they can go to work on a deeper, more hard-to-handle concern.

Many clients have been referred by others and neither buy the diagnoses of others nor intend to do anything about them. It is important for the counselor to discover, therefore, who else besides the client cares about what happens in the counseling and what the expectations of these others are. It may very well be that none of the expectations for counseling held by those extraneous to the client-counselor relationship can be accomplished, and counseling goals built to these are foredoomed.

If counselor and client are unable to determine clearly who besides the client has a vested interest in counseling outcomes, there may be much fumbling and groping in the dark, and the client, instead of being committed to working hard on personal goals, not so secretely en-gages in sabotaging the counseling process. The clear delineation of the expectations of others helps counselor and client to choose whether or not these expectations are realistic and whether or not they have greater priority than those lodged exclusively within the client himself.

In counseling literature and practice the phrase "presenting prob-lem" is all but universally acknowledged as being an efficient and viable way of categorizing initial client data. It comes from medical practice where symptom analysis is followed by physical examination and treatment prescription, which hopefully then lead to symptom removal and health restoration. In counseling the use of the term "problem" is inappropriate because it is loaded with pernicious implications.

Problems have solutions, as in mathematics, physics, urban affairs, or a thousand other areas where thinking in problem units is produc-tive. In human behavior, people with problems are thought of nega-tively, as though they were less than whole, are sick, and need curing. People who have problems have something wrong with them. A client who is confronted with identifying problems is helped to be self-

32

judged as sick or disturbed in particular ways and given the simplistic impression that if the problem is corrected, the solution found or applied, then life will be improved and the client will be restored to acceptability.

Thus, a client says, "My problem is that I'm too short and people always see me as younger than I am," and the counselor, searching for a solution, suggests, "Have you tried associating only with people who aren't so tall and who *know* how old you are?" Or the client says, "I have a hot temper and it always gets me in trouble," and then goes on to document this self-definition with anecdotal data. Buying this, a problem-centered counselor responds with, "Okay, let's analyze what exactly sets you off, and you can learn to avoid such contacts," smugly feeling superior because he knows the answer, the solution.

But people don't have problems, and problem-centered counseling more often than not is trapped by being dependent on solutions. What people do have are difficulties, concerns, situations, and conditions with which they are living. And they currently behave, mentally, emotionally, and physically, in certain ways and at certain levels of effectiveness in response to whatever is in their lives. What is possible for any client as a result of counseling is that in any dimension of existence he can upgrade his level of performance or learn alternate behaviors which are more effective and self-enhancing. And the effective counselor helps clients to understand this kind of focus in the first interview, where counselor and client are joined, where erroneous thinking is labeled as such, where distortions about counseling expectations are eliminated, where it is made clear that the client can work on behavior upgrading and personally take charge in more and more life circumstances, which will result in greater happiness and personal effectiveness.

Assessing Previous Counseling Experience

It is important for a counselor to determine what exposure a client has had to individual or group helping attempts. Clients come to counseling with preset notions of what it is that they will find there, and these notions are the result of hearsay about counseling or of personal experience. Based on personal experience, they frequently are shopping for more of the same or looking for what decidedly will not be the same. Therefore, it is important for the counselor to determine not only with whom and when the previous helping experiences took place, how often they occurred, how long they lasted, and their causes, but also to learn what went on in those experiences and how the client views them. What the previous counselor did and what the client values or devalues about past experiences are vital for a new counselor to know.

There are many reasons for this. First, it provides the counselor with important historical data about a new client. Second, it helps the counselor to understand how the client views the counseling process. Third, it helps the counselor to know much about how the client characteristically functions. Many clients seek dependency relationships. Others are professional clients who seek out counselors as friends because they haven't learned friendship skills. Still others, like the Ancient Mariner, want to tell their stories over and over to anyone who will listen, seeking confirmation and reinforcement for maintenance of neurotic behavioral systems. But the most significant reason for the counselor ascertaining the amount and character of former counseling rests in the importance of clearly conveying what the nature of the present counseling will be. This will then lead to a clear statement of what the counselor will do as the helper, what the client will do in order to achieve results, and how this differs or is similar to what the client has experienced before.

Many counselors are ineffective in gathering data about former client counseling experience because they assume clients understand such a question as "Have you ever seen a counselor before?" A "no" answer closes the book on the subject for such counselors. Effective counselors determine whether a client has sought psychological help from any quarter: a minister, teacher, counselor, psychologist, psychiatrist, friend, relative, neighbor, or whomever. The counselor also determines whether the client has had involuntary encounters where others have decided that help or "straightening out" is needed, because the counselor knows that client perceptions are shaped by such experiences.

A thorough assessment, in short, of former client counseling experience may help to avoid many exploratory hours of counseling time and make clear the client's expectations for counseling.

Assessing Client Counseling Expectations

Every client has thought something about the impending experience before arriving in the counseling office for an initial interview. Whether it takes place in a school, agency, or private office, the counselor has some kind of reputation in general, and with any given prospective client that reputation is particularized into a personal vision. The counselor is rumored to be of a certain nature, or what it is possible to do or get in the counseling office has become unreliable information which has been traded about, and many clients may come to counseling looking for something that is undeliverable.

For example, an inner-city high school senior comes to a university counseling center as a result of a referral by his school counselor. At the center he encounters a counselor in training who, in classic nondirective pleasantness, explores the client's personal world, gets him to talk, and tries hard to be understanding, empathic, and authentic. The client, putting on his best demeanor, is cooperative, answers all questions, thinks he is "being good." Finally, in the sixth session, he can hold back no longer, and he gets down to what he is really looking for: placement help. He is chagrined to learn none is available: "You mean you can't help me get a job?"

This example is real, happens repeatedly, and is typical of the well-intentioned counselor's way of abusing clients and wastefully structuring valuable counseling time. Failure to thoroughly check out the counseling expectations of any given client certainly abrogates the much-touted admonition that counselors should be real, genuine, and honest. For the client to have different expectations than the counselor means that the counselor is presenting a false image.

Counselors who do not assess expectations lead a client down a thorny counseling path. Many clients have a host of absurd expectations about what constitutes counseling. It is not unusual for a client to believe that the counselor's function is to find out if he is really crazy, to get him a job, to tell him he is doing the right thing, or simply to be a friend who will be kind, warm, an understanding listener, and a person who cares. Without an early examination of a client's expectations, effective counseling can be impeded by the presence of false notions about counseling and the counselor's role; two individuals laboring at cross-purposes is the result.

Delivering a Clear Definition of Counseling

Surprisingly, many counselors, beginners in particular, overlook the importance of clearly specifying what behaviors will be manifested by the two participants in the upcoming counseling, or, if they don't ignore it completely, they tend to be global, fuzzy, or overly terse when they make an explanation. Such behavior constitutes professional shoddiness, because this component of an initial counseling session is of paramount significance to any and all achievements made in the counseling for as long as it lasts.

The components described above all lead to a more effective specification of what form the counseling will take. Until such time as the counselor knows what distortions are in his client's mind, he can hardly do an effective job of helping his client to eliminate them.

At some appropriate time during the first interview, the effective counselor focuses directly on the client's perceptions of counseling.

Almost always these are incongruous with those of the counselor. Having now an understanding of client perceptions and expectations, the counselor can provide a clear, well-thought-out definition of what counseling is and how it differs from all other forms of helping. Criteria for delivery of an effective definition include: (a) no mincing of words; (b) no promises that cannot be delivered; (c) no defining of a process that a counselor has read about but does not practice; (d) a delineation of counselor behaviors: what the counselor can and will do and how it will be done; (e) a delineation of what the client will do and how it will be done; (f) clear specification of the goals of the counseling in language and possibilities appropriate to this client (which is to say that client behavioral change, performing at higher levels or in different, more effective ways outside the counseling, are specified as possible outcomes); (g) explanation of the fact that counseling means "work" for a client, as well as of the inescapable corollary that behavioral change almost always involves difficult struggle and discomfort; (h) a check-out of client understanding of the definition through client play-back and counselor correction until such time as the client thoroughly knows; and (i) specification of how client progress will be assessed.

By providing a solid, buyable definition of counseling (see Chapter 1), the counselor teaches the client that counseling is a serious business, that the counselor knows what to do, and that both parties have particular responsibilities. Moreover, the territory which becomes so important to subsequent counseling activity is thus marked out. The question, "What has this got to do with what we said we were trying to accomplish here?" can be invoked at any time to give relevancy and productive focus to client counseling behavior which might be characterized as floundering or excuse-making.

Describing the Nature of Confidentiality

This important component of the initial interview is essentially an enlargement of the definition of counseling. Here the counselor states unequivocally who has access to any counseling content data, including what data the counselor might store in any kind of recordkeeping file. If tapes are made, the client has every right to know exactly what happens to them, who uses them, and for what purposes.

There are two points about confidentiality not commonly understood by counselors. First, over-talking and windy orations about the nature of privileged information tend to breed suspicion in clients. No amount of convincing will make a counselor more trustworthy in this or any other regard; how the counselor behaves in the counseling relationship will make the difference. Effective counselors know that trust builds as a result of their passing whatever tests arise in the minds of their clients. Matter-of-fact declarations about confidentiality that counselors know they will live up to under all conditions are all that are needed. This includes a statement about the specific nature of the feedback which the counselor feels ought to go to the referral agent, if such will happen.

Second, how clients handle their revelation of this or that piece of counseling content data about themselves to various others in their worlds often gets ignored. Counselors can do an immense service for most clients by checking out with them how they will report their experiences to others—parents, employers, marriage partners, friends, relatives, or whomever—by teaching them what about the counseling might be productively revealed, the kind of language to use, and generally what the meaning and virtues of privacy are. Here simulations, rehearsals, and role-working techniques (see Chapter 14) can be effective.

Searching for Meaningful Counseling Content

The necessary exploratory behaviors in which client and counselor engage during initial counseling stages, when they are efficiently manifested, do much to assure productivity. Sorting out client personal data in order to determine counseling priorities, to reach agreement and to settle on what will be accepted as a first, second, and third or more counseling charge, must be accomplished if the counseling is to become something more than just bobbing around on waves. Obviously, this process may go on for many of the early interviews, but a principal part of the first session is consumed by an active mutual exploration which will answer the question, "What will we focus on in the counseling?"

There are many important segments of a client's world to explore in this search for meaningful counseling content. These include (a) asking a client to provide a running account of how a day or a week was spent, an account of all movements and what generated them; (b) an assessment of the most significant people in the client's life and how they ought to change, by the counselor's asking, "Who are the people who control you?"; (c) finding out about the client's world of love: from whom does he get it and to whom is it given, and is the client skilled and satisfied in the giving and receiving of love?; (d) examining where the client is in the "pecking order" in this or that social enclave, such as the family, circle of friends, or work group; (e) checking out physical symptomatology, eating, sleeping, exercise, and medication habits; (f) exploring client's use of time, how much the client is externally controlled in it by outside pressures, how the client controls and uses it effectively; (g) some detailing of emotional behaviors, the patterns of ups and downs, their character and causes; and (h) looking at work obligations, including those which are self-imposed, and how these are managed. Exploration of these areas and a number of others helps the counselor and client decide together what it is that ought to monopolize counseling time.

Assessing Client Ability to Function

The counselor who treats all clients alike, as though each can use the counseling process similarly, has low appreciation for the wide range of differential functioning of which human beings are capable. Checking out clients' potential for using their own minds in every conceivable area, but most particularly in the likely-to-be-troublesome ones outlined above, is essential to counseling success. Counseling is a process aimed at changing a client's thinking about a given difficulty, which then results in the client's behaving differently, more productively.

School achievement records, test scores, and other formal assessment data seldom provide a counselor with the kind of accurate information about functional intelligence in a client needed to efficiently aim counseling efforts. The hard work of diagnosing functional intelligence is always necessary, and the effective counselor begins this at the very start by reading and judging all verbal and nonverbal client behavior. Should a counselor be able to collect other behavioral data on a client in contacts outside the interview, such as how this person interacts with others in a counseling group, this will immeasurably help to provide a more telling diagnosis. Lacking this, client self-reports and what is manifested in the counseling sessions are the most reliable resource material.

But every client reveals much which a trained eye can see and can be helped to reveal more by the counselor's studied presentation of selected stimuli. Does the client react to humor normally? Does he hang back or appear frightened, nervous, over-confident, detached from the reality of his own life? Does he initiate? Does he read the counselor well, pick up subtleties, have his antennae out? How does he use language? How effectively does he send his messages? Does he acquiesce on every exchange, yet appear to be indifferent, "tuned out"?

A multitude of clues give the counselor data for determining functional intelligence. Where a well-documented awareness of the client's ability to function is not gained, devised counseling interventions and strategies are usually fruitless. The use of abstract psychological logic with someone incapable of comprehending results in a client's feeling put down, reinforces judgments of low self-worth, or convinces the client that here is still another person "who doesn't understand me and the woes I have."

Many counselors bypass the work of determining client ability for intellectual functioning and find that their expectations for counseling success are too high; or they tend to blame clients as unable or unwilling to change, when in effect they have misread or failed to read client capacity for effective change.

Labeling What Feelings Are

The term *feelings* comes up repeatedly in all counseling interviews. In the initial session, the effective counselor teaches clients important concepts about feelings and how these are pertinent to the counseling that will follow. The counselor does this by asking what clients mean when they use the term. Client distortions are then corrected by specifying precisely what constitutes feelings and how they differ from thoughts and behavior. Since the term is used throughout the life of the counseling and many counseling goals take the form of generating positive feelings and eliminating negative and immobilizing ones, focusing early on the concept is crucial for counseling effectiveness.

At termination of the first interview, a client ought to have a clearer understanding of what constitutes feelings, how they are mentally caused physiological reactions, how to identify them and to know the forms they take, how they arise in a person, how they can and do stand in the way, and some preliminary notions about learning to control feelings and how feelings can work for rather than against a person in everyday living.

For the counselor to say that feelings are crucial and then not even know and show what they are or how they differ from mental or behavioral formulations is to be evasive and confusing to clients. Feelings are not ideas, though ideas cause them. That feelings are physical can be illustrated by the fact that tranquilizers don't work on a person's thoughts; they calm by their effect on physical properties. The implications for effective counseling permeate most of what a counselor does.

Determining Counseling Structure

In the very first contact a proficient counselor helps a client to accept responsibility for structuring the use of counseling time. The counselor knows the importance of teaching a client to do self-help things, how basic that is to the counseling process, how consonant that is with psychological health goals and the move away from all dependency.

At some point in the interview an analysis of its structure helps a client to know who has determined what has taken place. The counselor helps a client to know that events are not random or purposeless in counseling, that they are determined, and that the client can take charge of this in any given part of a counseling session. Nor are events random happenings in the client's own life outside the counseling; they, too, are determined, and the more of them that a client can control, the healthier and happier he or she will be. To this end, clients ought to be helped to structure at least some small part of the first interview and be aware of their success or lack of it in so doing.

Helping clients to structure their own time begins with the counselor's insistence that they establish priorities and plans. It is effective to have clients list their concerns and present an agenda of what they want to work on in the next interview. To the extent that clients can provide some of the structure, they are also saying what and where the focus will be. If this focus becomes tangential and diversionary, the counselor can intervene to bring it back to helping areas.

Obtaining a Commitment to Counseling

The client who is uncommitted to the counseling process can hardly be expected to do the hard work required for behavioral change. In all probability such clients will not return, or if they do, the chances are great that the counseling will flounder and bog down. But many if not most clients are sensibly reluctant to engage themselves fully in the process (see Chapter 5). Clients who are not self-referred can usually be expected to carry a high loading of resistance, if not outright antagonism or hostility, into the counseling encounter, and few of those who are self-referred have the kind of readiness to go to work for which a counselor might ideally hope.

The predominant reason for this client-set resides in the fact that effective counseling involves the removal or replacement of ingrained behaviors and attitudes that clients have lived with for long periods, perhaps over the course of their lives. Many defensive internalized strategies accompany such mental, emotional, and social behaviors, and as the counselor works at helping a client to think in new ways and behave in different patterns, the first natural inclination of the client is to shrink away and reject such invasions. Because self-defeating patterns are so entrenched and because giving them up is so painful, clients almost always want to reject counseling efforts to replace them. A strong commitment to counseling is necessary to help a client stay with the resolve to work at being a more effective, take-charge person, despite the discomfort which is inevitably caused.

How to go about insuring client commitment varies from client to client. For some it might mean a simple verbal agreement to stay with the counseling for a specified period of time until the client has an adequate taste of the process and can make a knowledgeable evaluation of whether or not to continue. For others, particularly those with no track record of following through on easily made vows, it might mean locking in the verbalized intention, increasing the level of confidence by having a client leave a valuable personal item with the counselor as a good-faith security deposit. The opposite trade is also more binding than a simple verbal statement: The counselor gives the client a book related to the counseling, the audiotape of the first session, or some other tangible momento of value to the counselor which symbolizes faith in the client. A contract can even be drawn in writing, and for some clients this is effective.

Suffice it to say that after the counselor has explained the counseling process and indicated how it will involve client risk taking, pain, and unaccustomed effort, the counselor must elicit a commitment or expect to lose a client when in later counseling strain and hardship are partly present. The promise of counselor support during such projected times has little meaning to clients in early sessions, because it has not yet been experienced, and the commitment to stay with counseling is thus all the more important.

Working on Goal Setting

Setting client goals in counseling, delineating the behavioral steps through which these may be attained, monitoring progress, and evaluating and reinforcing goal achievement all seem to be a common sense, obvious part of the counseling process; yet too few counselors place an emphasis here or know how to be effective as goal setters.

First, there are counselor goals for every interview. This list of essential components could have as easily been labeled "first interview counselor goals." But the truly meaningful goal setting, the absence of which means an absence of counseling help, takes place with the client, and the first counseling session ought to contain in microcosm what will come later in abundance.

The effective counselor has the concept of goals everpresent in mind. All behaviors that clients exhibit that are diagnosed as self-defeating, and all those areas in clients' worlds where not-yet-learned personal skill and competency development could help them to be more effective agents in their own behalf, are identified by the counselor as target territory for goal setting.

The process of goal setting is not complex, yet it is seldom conducted skillfully by beginning counselors. Skillful goal setting includes: (a) clearly identifying specific current behavior which is unproductive, including the lack of behavior in any given dimension where client action is called for; (b) specifying the new behavior to be acquired; (c) obtaining client understanding of these two points, agreement that the new behavior is desired, and a commitment from the client to work hard at new behavior acquisition; (d) eliminating all vagueness and ambiguity in the statements of what the client will do and specifying the sequence of actual steps to be taken; (e) selecting only those goals which have real pertinence to a client in order that some portion of daily living can immediately improve; (f) selecting only those goals which are clearly attainable by this client who has only his or her own set of resources upon which to draw, different from the counselor's and all others'; and (g) determining criteria by which goal realization will later be judged.

Realistic goals are always operational. A male client states that he finds it difficult to study math, or to get along with his father, or to have a gratifying sexual experience. Immediately the counselor thinks: *goals*. What kinds of goals can I help this client to set for himself that will assure early successful experiences and have a high degree of specificity? How can I help this client to state his goals so that he does not leave here believing that I set them for him? Productive answers and specific counseling strategies ought to flow from these questions and should lead to an early emphasis on the client's working toward behavioral change between sessions. A counselor goal for the first interview is to have prepared a client to work at the achievement of at least one objective before the second counseling session.

Summarizing, Reviewing, and Evaluating

Summarization and evaluation is a vital component of the counseling process which is too seldom used and which can take place at any time the counseling appears to bog down or lack meaningful focus. In the initial interview, a review and assesment of the counseling is crucial. Prior to the closing of the session, the effective counselor reviews events that have transpired up to the present moment. This includes an explanation of the structure of the interview, an explanation of the nature of and reasons for the questions asked, interpretations of behavior, a review of the goals the client has set, and a process analysis of what has gone on in the interview supported by a rationale for each segment. This summary assists the client in formulating a capsulized picture of the counseling process which can be mentally retained. It allows a client to see first-hand precisely what counseling is and why the counselor acts in particular ways. Moreover, the counselor demonstrates expertise by showing alertness, how each client datum and instance of manifested behavior has been registered and stored in the counselor's mind. Good summaries are fully packed with concisely and briefly stated interview highlights.

But summaries unaccompanied by evaluation lack thoroughness, and an evaluation by the counselor alone constitutes a misplacement of emphasis. At the very start of counseling, a client ought to be taught to assess critically the effectiveness of the counseling for himself, and this process is begun by the counselor asking his client to focus on what has happened to him in the previous hour. Following this the counselor can provide his own evaluation of what has taken place and hypothesize on the prognosis for future client growth within the context of the counseling. In every case, such counselor evaluation ought not to be an extrapolation beyond what the data warrant, and a thorough evaluation includes an honest assessment of the client's willingness to be counseled, his defenses against the process, and a labeling of what he has learned in this initial session.

Using Psychological Homework

The real significance of counseling cannot be measured by what occurs in the interview itself, but rather by what changes take place in client functioning in the client's world, the test for all counseling impact. It is crucial, therefore, that a client leave the initial interview having one or more extra-counseling behavioral assignments to work on. Effective counseling requires that a client leave *all* interviews with firm notions about what he is going to *do* differently to become a more fully functioning person. This process is begun during the first session to establish emphatically the connections between what is focused on in the counseling and what takes place in the client's life away from the counselor.

In contracting for the first psychological homework assignments, effectiveness rests in eliciting them from clients, not in counselor imposition. In mutually working out the behavioral assignment, clear specificity and high success probability are prime ingredients. If the client is to try out new behaviors in a classroom, or with a co-worker, or whatever, what the client will do is so specified as to eliminate all possibility of later excuse-making through feigning misunderstanding because it was couched in vacuous terminology.

For example, an assignment to initiate and be more involved in the classroom lacks concreteness; but for the client to state that he will, at precisely 2:15 P.M., raise his hand in his mathematics class and ask for clarification or recapitulation of a particular mathematical operation, regardless of what else was going on, has the kind of pinpointedness which can be checked on and examined later. Perhaps the client is going to make a list of the behaviors he would like to work on after the first interview. If so, then he ought to know how long the list is to be, when he is going to work on it, and what he will do with the list.

Client responsibility for behavior outside the counseling, learning to take charge of his actions, begins in the first interview with the assignment of psychological homework. The second interview, then, begins with a report and analysis of what happened in the interim.

Closing the Interview

Just as effective counseling begins on a business-like basis, so too does interview closure reflect a serious counselor posture. Effective closing salutations are those selected to reinforce counseling productivity, and inane, unprofessional remarks are those which retard it. To say, "Well, you certainly are an interesting person," or "I enjoyed meeting you," or "I enjoyed talking to you," all imply that the counselor got something for himself out of the interview, when his only reason for being in his role and position is to deliver a service. Effective closing statements keep the counseling on the track: "I'll see you next Tuesday at twelve o'clock. I expect that you will have begun working on your stated concerns, and I'll be looking for your report. Do you have any final questions that need answers?"

Final Thoughts

These fifteen essential components are not seen as exhaustive of all a beginning counseling session might contain. Nor are they intended to be restricted to the first interview: All later interviews contain more or less of this or that component, and in early sessions in particular, the same ground must be gone over a number of times, the extent of which is determined by client learning capacity. What has been presented here represents a specific checklist of behaviors and strategies that any counselor can incorporate and follow. By so doing he can eliminate the nonproductive, meaningless, misdirected, or intuitive groping and searching which characterizes so many initial counseling encounters.

3

Counseling and Addiction: A Problem of Internal Versus External Thinking

Taken altogether, workers in the helping professions have been relatively impotent in making differences in the lives of the many individuals who are either chronically dependent drug users or in some other way addicted to a foreign substance deleterious to physical and psychological health. Drugs are everywhere in our society. Being exposed to them initially or obtaining them regularly requires little ingenuity. From the entering junior high school student to the middle teen looking for a high to the adult seeking something different, drugs in multitudinous variety are a ubiquitous unsanctioned lure.

But for too many people drugs are more than an experience tried and rejected at a given developmental stage or a peccadillo to be overlooked as a thrill-seeker's privilege. The uses and abuses of drugs have become self-destructive and disproportionately central in the lives of many. Drug-taking and associated social and cultural life styles have the attention of the nation. It is understood that America has a severe drug problem, certainly one in which the counseling profession is inescapably involved. Funds for fighting drug abuse are becoming readily available from all levels of government and from many private sources; task forces are being convened to study and develop methods and programs for drug abuse alleviation and prevention.

Counselors in almost all institutional settings, bewildered by their ineffectiveness in counseling drug users, seek greater expertise as the incidence of addiction or pre-addiction in their case loads increases. But it is not the drug user alone who confounds the counselor: alcoholics, compulsive smokers, the severely obese, almost all clients who are overly dependent on some form of oral or other bodily intake are immune to the fine intentions of otherwise effective counselors. Counselors' lack of success in working with the addictive personality can be attributed to (a) a fundamental inability to understand the "external" predisposition of the drug-dependent person and (b) the

45

absence of skill in making effective interventions appropriately aimed to modify an addicted client's neurotic, ill-formed personality schemata. Drug users and others who are dependent on outside agents achieve what passes for positive emotional states through external means. Because negative emotions are intolerable and positive emotions make life tolerable or even pleasurable for the time they last, and because the addict seeks to expunge the former and embrace the latter by reaching outside of himself to change his state, the counselor cannot begin to be effective until he fully comprehends the nature of emotions and sensations and the concepts of externality and internality.

Emotions

Emotions are mentally caused physical reactions. When we *feel* bad, we are speaking of what is happening to us physically, whether it be a temperature change, an increased heartbeat, sweating, raw nerves or nervous afflictions, changed speech or physical movement, tears, adrenalin secretion, flushing, sluggishness, breathing difficulties, or a thousand other similar symptoms which occur in us singly or in combination. The fact that ugly or depressing thoughts accompany such physical reactions to earlier thoughts does not change the nature of what feelings are; rather, the ugly and depressing thoughts serve only to perpetuate the physical reactions and heighten their intensity.

Nor does it make a difference how the emotional state came about, whether through the processing in the mind of an external stimulus (because my senses have told my mind of the onrushing car in my path and my mind has instantaneously evaluated this as a threat to my existence, I experience fear in my body in the form of adrenalin release and its charge to my physical system) or through the processing of a thought or series of thoughts internally induced (I lie in bed and think unemotionally of things, and the thought chain draws up links from my subconscious which remind me of how lonely I am, and I cry). Thoughts cause emotions and they are experienced in the body.

For the counselor, the significance of the cause-effect relationship is that if he can successfully assist the client in reordering thoughts or substituting new thoughts for old, he can help his client to have different emotional states. And, correspondingly, if he can correctly read the physiological data which constitute the negative emotionality of his client, the counselor can begin to help his client make the connections to the illogical or neurotic thinking which result in somatic arousal, to have insight and understanding of the psychological maintenance system which causes the thinking and the reactive states to persist (helping the client to understand what he gets out of it), to critically examine and harshly evaluate such thinking, and to arrive at a commitment to work on changing his mental behavior.

With some clients, however, the helping process is complicated by the failure of both counselor and client to distinguish between emotions and sensations. External agents, such as drugs and alcohol, which are introduced into the body and which have the potency to "tumble" the mind, distort the directness of the cause/effect ratio of thoughts and feelings.

Sensations

Our five senses collect data to present to our minds so that our minds can work to steer our total beings in whatever reality we find ourselves. It is unnecessary here to introduce the complex schemata of sophisticated theorists relating to the make-up and functioning of mind and brain or the much debated chemistry of how thoughts are generated. Suffice it to say that the senses collect reality data and instantaneously ship it to the organ we call the mind and that any given sense datum can be called a sensation.

Aside from any symbolic meaning we might have attached to sensations, they can be pleasurable or distasteful. Thus, some sounds are naturally pleasant and are felt as so in the body, and some are grating, raspy, and unpleasant. The sensation of a cool breeze felt by the body on a hot day is pleasant. It is the same with all the senses. But when thought is directed to sensations, when they are acknowledged by the mind, they can be perceived incongruently. Thus, the cool breeze is experienced negatively when it messes a person's hair at a time when a photo is being snapped: The physical pleasure is denied. It is the mind that decides when an itching or tickling is pleasurable and when it is irritating.

Since sensations are all physically experienced, as are emotions, it is important to differentiate between them. Given a neutral mindset, most sensations could be grouped under pleasure and pain headings, and they are the result of external stimuli, not the result of the impact of thought on the body. Many of them are experienced in the body, however, in the same way as emotional reactions.

The sense of touch, physical feelings, comprises a special category of sensations in that we feel within our bodies. Activity in digestive and excretory organs, heart beating, and certain internal physical pains and pleasures are among the countless feels which can occur in us which, while experienced in the body akin to emotional states, are caused by externals. The class of externals we introduce into our systems that physically affect the brain and impair its ability to function normally (any mind-affecting drug) are the most troublesome for counselors to help clients with. While nicotine is *felt* in the lungs and bloodstream, usually pleasurably by the smoker, it has little impact on the brain; but the affect of alcohol on the brain is almost immediate, and the sensations experienced include those which are induced by the mind after brain functioning has been impaired, or at least altered, by the external agent. So it is with most of the drugs we have in mind when we say "drug abuse." Knowledge of the impact on the brain and its altered functioning which certain drugs can cause is important to counselors attempting to help drug users. But it does not provide the key to successful counselor interventions and strategies for eliminating self-defeating behaviors in clients and helping them to begin behaving in changed, self-enhancing ways.

Internality Versus Externality

The concepts of internality and externality are pertinent to understanding characteristic ways in which clients think and especially the mental-emotional make-up of the addicted personality. Figure 1 presents a paradigm of two distinct personality types and how each tends to assign responsibility for shifting emotional states within themselves. While neither type might be found in pure form, since everyone is externally oriented in some ways and internally oriented in others, one or the other tends to predominate. In some individuals the predominance is gross; they typically think, feel, and behave in largely internal or external ways.

When looking at any given individual's emotional state, it is productive for the counselor to ask himself, "Were the origins of my client's current feelings associated with this problem area lodged in external or internal causality?" The answer to such a question can aid the counselor in providing insight for his clients and will help in determining future counseling strategies.

The Externally Oriented Individual

People who are described as "external" are those who tend to place responsibility for their own feeling on someone or something outside themselves. Those mental formulations listed on the left in Figure 1 are representative of external thinking. Statements such as "He hurt my feelings," "I can't help it," "It wasn't my fault," "I

FIGURE 1

Emotional States and the Dimensions of Internal and External Control

←——— Positive Emotions ———→

←——— Negative Emotions ———→

Emotional Neutrality—Emotional Neutrality

Internal Causes of Emotional Shifts

C

1. I worked hard at being happy
2. I made things work for me.
3. I am telling myself the right things.
4. I'm learning new skills to avoid unhappiness.
5. I'm in charge of me, and this is where I choose to be.

D

1. I tell myself the wrong things.
2. I put too much emphasis on what others say.
3. I worry about what someone else thinks.
4. I'm not strong enough now to avoid being unhappy.
5. I don't have the skills to keep me from being miserable.

Beauty appreciation
Attraction
Oceanic feelings
Joy
Excitement
Love
Happiness
Ecstasy
Exhiliration
Self Fulfillment
Satisfaction
Pleasure
Elation

Death-wishing
Irritation
Nervousness
Guilt
Distress
Worry
Sorrow
Resentment
Frustration
Depression
Repulsion
Anxiety
Hate
Anger
Sadness

External Causes of Emotional Shifts

A

1. My parents were good to me.
2. My friends treat me nice.
3. Things are going well for me.
4. Nobody is bugging me.
5. The world is treating me well.

B

1. My parents mistreat me.
2. My friends don't like me.
3. Everything goes against me.
4. Other people think I'm no good.
5. The world is a lousy place

←——— Positive Emotions ———→

←——— Negative Emotions ———→

have bad luck," "I'm not to blame," and an endless array of similar thoughts are typical external ways of mentally processing data about self.

External thinking is a way of life in our culture; from the time a child learns to talk and on through his adult life, reinforcers of externality are ubiquitous. Schools, governments, families, churches, business institutions, the advertising industry, and the mass media all teach the individual to rely on someone or something outside of himself for making approved judgments, thinking appropriately, behaving in accepted ways, and feeling good or bad. From how to dress as a child to how to talk, read, and write in school to what to say and how to act in life as an adult, there is an infinite chain of undifferentiated outside stimuli which encourage an external orientation in us all. The determinists and fatalists fall into the external category as do the strict behavior modifiers who bypass the individual in making external decisions for him.

In counseling, hearing clients belabor all of the external causes for their misfortunes is more than just common; it is perpetual. Externality pervades the thinking of all clients at most junctures and predominates in the assignment of causality for emotional states. The phrase "I feel this way because . . ." is rarely ever followed by "I have made myself feel this way." The left side of Figure 1 illustrates typical external thinking about the causes of both positive (top left) and negative (bottom left) emotional states.

The Internally Oriented Individual

The completely internal person is so rare as to be almost mythological in our culture. Internally oriented people assign total responsibility for what they are and how they feel to the choices they have made for themselves. Such a person is independent of the good opinion or approval of others and uses self-references when examining his feelings at any given moment. In Figure 1 all of the mental formulations on the right are indicative of internal thinking. Assignments of causality for a given emotional fix are prefaced with "I."

The internally configured individual is giant steps ahead of his externally oriented counterpart, because causality for emotional states is anchored in the self. That is, he does not have to depend on someone else, nor does he have to wait for events to become more salubrious. If he is going to be at emotional neutrality or above, it is his own thinking that will place him there. Psychological independence from external factors is perhaps the single most desirable characteristic of fully functioning, mentally healthy people.

The internally oriented person also believes that his negative emotional states are a result of his own imperfect thinking and behaving. He does not blame, fault, complain, wish, hope, or ascribe incorrect intent or motivation to others. He thinks in the ways depicted in Section D of the figure. Because he assumes responsibility for his own thoughts and resultant emotionality, working at changing them becomes his rather than someone else's charge.

Internal orientation is seldom a personality configuration which came naturally to those in whom it predominates. Because our culture mitigates against it in a thousand ways, it is difficult to come by; it is learned and developed over time, often after persistent and painful struggle. Blaming others or anything outside the self for one's own shortcomings and for whatever happens in one's life in order to deny the painful admittance that feelings and the negative internalizing of one's circumstances are self-inflicted is a neat way to avoid changing and to remain fixed in a thoroughly mastered (and, therefore, comfortable, however neurotic or self-defeating) pattern of behaving. In counseling, helping is virtually impossible until the counselor has aided his client in seeing, understanding, and believing that self-improvement is inextricably linked to self-responsibility for all that one is and can be.

Before considering counseling strategies to be used with the chronic drug user, it is necessary that the counselor have an accurate picture of internal/external characteristic make-up and functioning in individuals. Because an addicted drug user relies on externals for his "highs" or positive emotional states, he must, by all sources of logic and definition, be classified as external in this behavior.

Understanding the Chronic Drug User

Many potentially effective professional helpers become handcuffed right at the outset because they fail to understand the external orientation of the chronic drug users they are attempting to counsel. When interviewing anyone who can be classified as addictive or actively involved in drug taking, it is essential to learn the individual's self-perceptions about the causes of his "down moments" or "bummers" (actually the emotional states below emotional neutrality, as depicted in Figure 1).

Perceptions of why he gets depressed, for example, are most often predictably expressed in external terms by the chronic drug user: "My parents bug me," "The system gets me down," "School is out of it," "No one understands or cares about me," "Getting high lets you escape reality," and on through an interminable chronicle of external reasons for going down or getting depressed. This is not surprising, and it is observable in virtually all hard-core drug addicts as a support system for beginning and continuing their habits.

Drug addicts are externally oriented about why they become depressed or frustrated or experience any of ·the negative emotions detailed in Figure 1. Knowing this about a chronic drug user is not enough; it is only half of the "understanding" dilemma. Because the chronic drug user has relied on a melange of external reasons to explain the cause of his depressions and distressing feelings, he also relies on something equally external to bring himself above the emotional neutrality line: drugs. The pattern becomes clear: Here is a chronic drug user blaming others, or events, or even bad luck for his negative feelings and then using something equally outside of himself to rescue himself without ever having to assume any personal responsibility for what is happening to him emotionally. "I go up and down, but it really isn't me at all. *They* make me go down, and *it* makes me go up." It is almost as if a person were not even involved in the process.

Counselors who work with drug users ought to be aware of this external thinking system as it is manifested in their clients. A drug entered into the physical system which provides its user with pleasurable sensations, mind distortion, euphoria, and emotional states which are a combination of sensations and emotions induced by distorted thought carries this powerful externality message to the individual: "You can't handle this one, but the drug can." But those who rely regularly on external stimulants to avoid "downers" or any negative emotional state are saying to themselves that the "I" is gone and that the "they," previously used only to explain problem areas, has now completely taken over. Thus, the notion of an internally oriented chronic drug user is not only absurd but impossible by definition.

Counseling the Chronic Drug User

Perhaps the single most common error in counseling with chronic drug users is asking the question "Why do you use drugs?" This is a universally ineffective way of helping the drug user to gain insight into his own behavior, and it certainly will not lead to cessation of drug use. "Why" a person chooses to use the drugs is insignificant only because the answer to such a question will be contrived. It is akin to asking the obese person why he eats or the nymphomaniac why she has sex, and the answer is patently obvious to the addict: "I eat because it gives me pleasure," "I copulate because I enjoy it," and

"I take drugs because they make me feel good." Such a question is absurd to the client, because he "knows" why he does what he does. It communicates to the client that the counselor must be pretty stupid if he doesn't know the answer to that one. In addition, asking the drug user about drugs puts the focus on the *external* rather than the person and simultaneously reinforces the self-defeating notion that the drug is more important than the client.

This is something that the chronic drug user has done repeatedly in his own life. He is externally oriented in his thinking about how he gets to positive emotional states, and any discussion of or allusion to drugs by the counselor helps to encourage rather than discourage this external self-destructive thinking. Furthermore, the chronic drug user does not understand the external nature of his thinking. He believes the things he tells himself about his world. So he will invariably parrot back such externally motivated reasons, and any chances for growth through self-understanding are effectively crunched before the counseling can even get started.

Counselors who have had positive experiences with chronic drug users recognize that (a) clients tend to repeatedly blame others for their misfortunes; (b) thinking about self is done in an external framework; and (c) taking drugs is not an escape at all, but rather a natural inclination for someone who has an external personality orientation, logically reaching for something outside of himself to bring himself out of a "down" he believes to be externally caused. Armed with these understandings, the effective drug counselor knows the folly and ultimate failure of focusing on the "why" of drug use and chooses instead to stress and probe the question "What precisely occurs in your world and in your thinking about it which causes you to create this down in you?" When the counseling process gets lodged initially in this area, it is ultimately possible to teach the chronic drug user that he has labeled others or events external to himself as responsible for his negative emotional states. The goal of the counseling is to have the client arrive at the kinds of insights enumerated in Section D of Figure 1 when he finds himself in a negative emotional condition.

The counselor knows that the reason for being "down" or in some other negative emotional state is to gain attention from others or self-pity, even though these reasons are often thoroughly disguised and unknown to the client. The "down" allows the individual to feel sorry for himself (to give himself what others do not), to wallow in the sympathy or attention of others, and to avoid doing and working on the important areas of his life. Clients do not readily admit to such reasoning. The effective counselor is one who persistently challenges the logic system for externally caused emotions and operationally demonstrates that friends, parents, unfortunate events, and the rest can never create a "down" unless the client internalizes external happenings and tells himself something bad or paints disaster pictures in his brain. The responsibility for "down" times then becomes lodged in the client himself rather than anything external. When such logic becomes a part of the chronic drug user's thought patterns, it is not a difficult shift to his seeing that he also reaches out beyond his self for getting above the emotional neutrality line. He will also recognize that when he is experiencing positive emotions he has always, up until this time, used the self-sentences in Section A of Figure 1 as the reasons rather than himself, as illustrated in Section C of Figure 1.

The counselor's interventions must come at the beginning, and they must challenge the self-defeating thinking that assigns responsibility for "bummers" to external factors. When this understanding has been incorporated into the marrow of the client's bones, then it is a short step to having new insights about "why I take drugs." The typical reasons for explaining drug use become impossible when the client recognizes his externality and gains insight into why he has chosen to be so. The entire focus of effective counseling is on teaching the client the following 10-point lesson about himself, in the order presented:

1. You alone create your "bummers" and "downers," usually for attention, sympathy, or self-pity.
2. Assigning responsibility for your "downers" to others is an evasion.
3. Self-insight into your "bummers" will make *blame* a nonexistent explanation for what happens to you in your life.
4. Working on yourself to avoid being "down" is the only sure-fire way to avoid depression, because relying on others is foolish and almost always "they" are unreliable.
5. Mastering not going "down" just because something outside of yourself isn't going well will teach you that you are regaining control of yourself.
6. Once self-insight and self-understanding on the "down" are gained and incorporated, the same logic and procedures for going "up" will also apply.
7. Reaching for something outside of self to go "up" is just as foolish as blaming others for being "down." It is equally as debilitating to rely on an external for an "up" as it is for a "down."
8. Mastering going "up" by yourself without drugs or anyone else is an inescapable result of becoming more internal in your self-thinking about your total emotionality.
9. Chronic drug use can only disappear permanently when the shift

from external to internal thinking and behaving becomes totally incorporated in personally troublesome areas.

10. Anytime you rely on someone or something outside of yourself for explaining *any* emotional state, that person or thing has control over you. Mastery of your environment means that you, not "it" or "they," are in charge of you.

This discussion makes a strong case for emphasizing counseling interventions which lead to self-insight in all addicted people of every description in prelude to internally oriented thinking. It is in no way implied that self-insight will make physical dependency on a drug go away. However, if the freedom from drug dependency is to become permanent, the insight and reordered pattern of thinking are absolutely essential. Too frequently the well-intentioned, over-zealous counselor bypasses the crucial client insights elaborated herein and moves to understand and help the drug user by asking "Why do you use them?" Additionally, the inexperienced drug counselor seeks to eradicate the difficulty by working on the drug user to stop taking drugs, or to remove the temptation, and thus treats for symptom removal rather than tackling the enculturated, externalized, self-defeating thinking that is the cause of drug dependency.

Any drug-dependent client may be in a state of entrenchment which requires the kinds of help that a counselor is unable to provide. Dependency on drugs, alcohol, or any external agent can have advanced to the point where a readiness to respond to the most effective counseling is impossible. It can come to where addiction is a disease and a person's control of his personal resources, including his mind, is lost. Given such, physical treatment and environmental manipulation, the creation of restraining therapeutic conditions, may be a necessary precursor to the introduction of counseling. The point here is that whenever counseling is introduced, it can only be as effective as the inroads it can make into reversing externally oriented thinking.

Although research is urgently needed to determine the most effective strategies for working with addicts of every kind, certainly a reordering of counseling emphasis is due, especially when we look carefully at the counseling profession's record in helping to rehabilitate people who have become victims of one of the greatest plagues in our culture, external thinking and behavior.

55

4

Using a Log to
Increase Counselor Skills

In counselor training the trainees have an insatiable desire for all
the communication and expert reaction it is possible for them to
receive under the natural limitations of time and energy scheduling.
They cannot get too much of a good thing, and this is true even
though they dislike exposing their inadequacies and resist doing the
kind of behavior changing necessary to becoming more effective. It is
especially true in that part of their training that includes counseling
actual clients under supervision. There never seems to be enough
time to analyze their own performances, to get at what it is that is
happening in their interviews, to ponder over and make sense out of
the client data being elicited, or to plan strategies for helping a client
in the upcoming sessions.

Log keeping increases the opportunities for supervisor interaction
with trainees which can be offered in a training program where both
trainer and trainee must be physically present for any communication
exchange to occur. But it goes far beyond enlarging the opportunity
for fuller interaction between trainer and trainee. Supervisors who
make effective use of the tape recorder communicate with their
trainees by making taped comments: (1) evaluation at the end of tapes
of counseling sessions to which they have listened; (2) by making a
tape of a tape (see Chapter 6); and (3) by direct audio commentary,
message sending, audio letter writing. Log keeping has benefits which
exceed face-to-face or audio communication exchanges in the realm
of individual counselor growth that has little to do with the supervision process.

As Sir Francis Bacon noted over three and one half centuries ago in
his essay "On Studies," there are differential developmental rewards
accruing to the doer who engages in the processes of conferring,
reading, and writing: "Reading maketh a full man, conference a ready
man, and writing an exact man." It is the precision in thinking, the
exactness, the efficiency that is being pursued by the counselor
desiring higher performance levels. Exercises in writing, whether they
be log keeping or case reporting or self-evaluations or whatever, aid
the burgeoning counselor in tightening his thoughts. But also, log

keeping provides a record of what her or his thoughts are. Counselors who are unwilling to be self-analytic seldom show much growth. Those who can systematically look at their own behaviors in counseling and self-world social interaction, with both significant others and those who count less, can do so most profitably by keeping a record. Professional development thus becomes reinforced through rereadings. Such counselors learn to know exactly what it is that they think.

Of all the mental activities in which counselors might indulge, writing is the most difficult, for some the most tedious, and therefore the one most avoided and resisted by the great majority of counselors in training and by counseling practitioners. Knowing this, effective supervisors who require that log keeping be a part of a trainee's practicum experience expend considerable effort in evaluation of early trainee log-keeping performance with the achievable goal in mind of enabling each tyro to produce personally meaningful notations.

What follows in this chapter are some specific training aids productive for counselor skill development which involve writing. First, specific guidelines, instructions to counselor trainees, for log keeping are presented. Second, the log of a counselor in training is reproduced along with supervisory commentary. From it the reader can draw a picture of what the practicum experience meant to one trainee as she lived through it. It is a sensitive portrayal of a neophyte counseling student's initiation into the profession. In addition her log contains her description of and reactions to case reporting. Third, this chapter contains specific guidelines for case summary reports, including a model report. Finally, guidelines for self-evaluation are included.*

Instructions for Keeping a Log

1. Keeping a log is a required part of your practicum experience.

2. *Purposes:* The log serves several purposes. First, it becomes another way for you to communicate with your supervisor. There are so many aspects to learning to counsel that it is difficult to keep track of them all. Many times questions will occur to you when you do not have the opportunity to discuss them; noting them in your log keeps them from being forgotten, and it gives your supervisor a chance to

---

*Counselor educators or others wishing to reproduce any of the guidelines included in this book for training purposes need not request special permission from the authors or publisher in order to do so, as long as they properly cite the source, but permission to reproduce the guidelines or any other part of this book in another publication *is* required. Such requests must be made in writing to the publisher.

respond. Reactions to what takes place in the practicum group or to interactions with classmates or supervisor can be noted in the log. Many times you will find reason to be in opposition to what you hear and see, and the log is an appropriate place to voice your position, if the opportunity to do so orally does not present itself.

Second, it is a depository for your learnings about the skill and art of counseling. Put your notes in it, whether they come from the class experience, your own thinking, or from your readings.

Third, it should contain your ongoing evaluations of your own development as a counselor. Discuss yourself, your counseling behavior, your feelings, the personal problems you encounter as you try to develop counseling skills, your interpersonal behavior, your achievements.

Fourth, it should contain your thinking about your own goals: learning goals, client-related goals, professional goals.

Fifth, it is a place for you to ruminate about your client or clients. The diagnostic process is one of continual re-analysis, and your log is a good place to think through whatever evidence is presented in counseling.

3. *Some guidelines:* Write in your log for your own sake. If it is well done, it will become of lasting value to you after the course is over. It is your personal record of all that has gone on in the course. Do not write to impress your supervisor as he will remain steadfastly unimpressed. Bulk is worthless. The log is not seen as busy work. What goes in it should be of worth to you: Question the meaning of your entries.

4. *Format:* The log is not seen as polished prose. It is basically a journal, a notebook. Therefore, rewriting is unnecessary. Write legibly. Use only one side of binder-sized sheets of paper. Leave wide margins for supervisor comments. Be neat. Use ink or typewriter.

5. *How much?* There is no limit on amount. Make at least one entry a week and write all you can think of at that time. React to each class meeting. Date your entries and keep up to date. It is a good practice to set aside a time or times when you can work on your log undisturbed. If you make entries during the class time or at some other time which is uncustomary (e.g., while listening to a counseling-related presentation in a group setting), note the date and the occasion. Leave large spaces between entries.

MY BEGINNINGS AS
A COUNSELOR[1]

Bonnie Giffin[2]

Supervisor's
Comments

Log Entries

October 5, 19—

Today was our first day of counseling and we were all pretty apprehensive. One of the women confided to me that she had the "shakes" so bad that her period started! The funny part of it was that her counselee did not show up and there she was, stuck with an early period. My partner had a bad time with his counselee. She was very hostile and uncommunicative, and I felt he made a few mistakes in the beginning which got him off to a poor start. He gave up after about fifteen minutes.

When you are aware of this kind of behavior, reflect it to the client; also reflect the opposite; help him to understand his own behavior; teach him to notice it in counseling, and he'll be able to seek feedback from others and to become aware of his own behavior outside of counseling.

My first counselee was a 19-year-old male named Claude. I noticed he appeared nervous: he averted his eyes and spoke very rapidly. He talked mostly about his academic record, and seemed concerned, maybe anxious, about his inability to make career and college plans. I felt his anxiety and nervousness and wanted to communicate to him that I would not be judgmental and could understand. Dr. Vriend thought I overdid it to the point of being "motherly." I have a feeling that most male counselors criticize women for being "motherly" and "too sentimental." I can't be a 30-year-old

[1]Reproduced with permission from three issues of the *Michigan Personnel and Guidance Journal:* Fall, 1970; Spring, 1971; Fall, 1971.
[2]Bonnie Giffin is a counselor at Kimball High School, Royal Oak School District, Royal Oak, Michigan. All names used in this chapter are fictitious, except those of the authors and Ms. Giffin.

The question, when evaluating your performance in any given area, should be: Was it effective? What did it accomplish? Are there other ways of doing it? Did my behavior in any way serve my needs, rather than the client's?

male, which I have been told (by a male instructor) most students prefer, so that's that. I was a little amused that two of the students had requested a woman counselor because the men "try to tell you what to do."

After listening to the tape, perhaps I did come on too strong with the friendliness bit, but I do feel a counselor should be approachable without fear of being threatening. I feel this is a very hostile world to kids and there are not too many adults who are willing to listen to them. I really tried to listen to him and I encouraged him to talk, and he talked . . . and talked. My weakness is that I did not get him to focus on some important details and problems that are blocking him from taking steps toward decision. The interview did seem to go in all directions. I do think, on the positive side, that we did have the beginning of a counseling relationship. It is my impression that he is dependent on his family and finds independence difficult to face. It is my belief that the father is the authority figure and he is unaccustomed to making his own decisions. He mentions several times how he agrees with "my father." He is not competitive: did not participate in extracurricular activities or sports in high school. I would like to focus on this in the next interview, plus his needs in a job. Is he familiar with occupational info? Perhaps we can make more progress in the next session.

October 12, 19—

Claude Fez came in today for session 2. He was not as garrulous and he did not appear to be as nervous. At the beginning of the session I asked him if he wanted to talk about anything in particular and he said he could not think of anything.

The suggestions that Dr. V. made on the tape seemed to have merit, so I tried to test them out: How familiar is he with occupational information? with college programs? I found out that he is very vague, has done no reading on occupations, training, etc.; in short, he is only familiar with occupations which he has come in contact with, i.e., mostly skilled blue-collar workers. He talks of a transfer to another university but has done little investigation. He wants to transfer from his community college in another semester. I spent half the session getting this information and telling him where he could find occupational books and college catalogues. Before next week I asked him to look into the *Occupational Outlook Handbook*. It should help him broaden his knowledge about the many occupations available. It is my feeling that he is not really interested in business administration but is going into it because it is something he thinks he can pass. He has no idea what jobs are available in this field. He stated that this was part of his problem; he has been thinking in terms of generalities, beating around the bush, and not getting anywhere. He was going to look into this *O.O.H.*, "even if he had to drive back down here to get it." He also indicated that this is one of the things he hoped to get out of the session.

He was also indefinite about what he hoped to get out of work: not be a garbage man, but not be a millionaire. He wants it to be imaginative. I tried to bring out that he may change jobs several times before he finds one that is "right" for him. I don't think he bought that.

The other half of the session was more affective than cognitive. I worked at getting to the relationship with his father which I feel is significant. These statements came out:

"My father always says, 'Go to school.' If I didn't go to school, I feel I'd be failing myself."

With this kind of statement you can do a lot by saying, "What does Claude say? Who's in charge of Claude?" Help him to realize that he must be the captain of his own fate and soul. Reinforce this by various references to it whenever appropriate.

Response: "Of course you will, because you don't want to take control of Claude. You're afraid to stand on your own two legs."

"I'm the kind of guy who'll go along with my father even if I have to go against what I really want to do, to tell the truth. That's kind of tough to admit, but it's true. I may fuss and fume, but when it comes to brass tacks, I'll do what he says."

Response: "But you let him."

"He always tries to give me advice. Sometimes it's better if he doesn't."

Re: "And you like that."

"He wants to protect me."

Re: "And that's what really concerns you."

"If I didn't finish four years of college, it would be a crushing blow to him."

Re: "As long as you keep telling yourself that, then it will affect your behavior. What do you owe him?"

"I'm going to make my own decision, but I feel I owe him something."

Re: "Scared of what?"

"I'm scared I might get into something that I can't get out of."

At the end I asked him if he was getting anything out of these sessions, and he said that he had gained the insight that he had been speaking in generalities as far as occupations go and had not gotten to specifics. He was going to see if he could find out what jobs are available. He did not admit insight into any feelings of dependency.

You didn't help him to have any.

Les (the doctoral student-assistant) listened to the tape and made his comments. I feel that the same instructor should listen to the same students and follow through or be aware of the other instructor's comments. This way there would be continuity of thought. Les rapped the whole vocational bit and did not feel this was his main reason for coming down to the counseling center. Les said that Claude is in a developmental stage of career development, with which I agree; but all boys have that, so why would that make him come? He underestimates the

But then you'd only have one viewpoint. Would that make you feel safer?

father-son relationship, in my opinion. Some of the other comments indicate that he had not heard last week's tape. He was correct that I did talk too much today. I felt I had to explain about the information, but perhaps I overdid it.

What did you do about it? What choices did you have?

The seminar today was exasperating! Two people in the class objected to taping the session. The "discussion" on this dragged on for almost two hours, until even they lost interest in it. Most of the comments were without value and so incoherent that I kept getting lost. I think the whole thing was because all of us feel so insecure in what we are doing, and we are afraid that Dr. V. will leave us "naked" in front of the whole group. There it will be, on tape; I guess that's the reasoning behind it. Dr. V. is right; we could learn from the tapes of the seminar just as we learn from the counseling sessions. I have an idea that the seminar is really a group therapy session.

Scratch "therapy" and substitute "learning," although that's as therapeutic as all get-out!

I was a little startled to learn in our first seminar that Dr. Vriend's seems to differ from the counseling approach which is generally adhered to at Wayne. The best I can tell, he leans toward the rational-emotive approach or the behavioral, a little. It's hard to figure, but it has caused so much confusion and frustration to me. I agree that counseling should not be psychotherapy but how much of a catalyst can I comfortably handle? I bought Dr. Albert Ellis' book, *A Guide to Rational Living,* and am trying to understand this viewpoint. I tried unsuccessfully to use some of these ideas in my first interview, but I felt uncomfortable with it and only succeeded in asking too many questions. I guess I am tainted by Dr. X's opinion of Dr. Ellis' approach to counseling.

Why try to categorize? Do you feel that if you give "it" a label, you can then dispense with it? How do you like the label "pragmatic"? If this or that doesn't work, what is it doing in a counseling interview?

My second interview turned out to be a "plant." A study is being made to study the counselor's prejudice in regard to occupational opportunities for women. She was an attractive, very capable, intelligent girl. I'm pretty sure I don't have any prejudices in that area. As long as a girl has the ability and desire, why shouldn't she be what she wants to be?

Frankly, I thought it was pretty amusing. I was wondering throughout the interview how I was going to keep this girl coming for nine weeks because she just didn't seem to need that much counseling. On the other hand, I thought, "Maybe she does have a deep-seated problem which I would have to 'psychoanalyze' before she could come to a decision?" That will teach me to take myself too seriously. How many counselors probe and muddy the waters when the problem is not that complicated and the client does not need anything even approaching psychotherapy?

Which, of course, makes a difference when it gets in the way of counseling. Do you know how it affects others —your clients? Can you help them to examine attitudes and the effects of attitudes, beliefs, opinions? Do you know why people have them? How an attitude or prejudice helps a person? Why he hangs on to an unpopular one, or how to help him replace it with a more functionally effective one?

Race prejudice came up in the seminar. I do not think I am prejudiced, but if I were challenged every day as the men say they are, I might become resentful.

October 19, 19—

I came out of my counseling session with Claude very dissatisfied with myself and the way it had gone. I was really worried before I went in today because I was going to try to get him to see himself as I thought he was: dependent on his father to the point that it was making it difficult to make decisions. I felt this was a delicate point and it might hurt him or make him mad. I guess this is something counselors have to overcome. Les had also told me to ask him flat out why he's coming here. Even though I had asked him

Why afraid of hurt or anger? If something is going to be helpful, why deny a client the right to it? People aren't so brittle that they fall apart at the first sign of difficulty.

before and was pretty sure I knew why, I vowed I would do it. The suggestion had also been made to go over the decision-making procedure with him. So, armed with these predecided subjects, I went into the session.

I feel that I committed one of the worst counseling sins: it was a counselor-centered session. When it didn't go the way I thought it should, I grew very impatient and it showed on the tape. I really hated it, but the worst part was that I disliked myself for trying to be something that I don't think I am. I swore that after today's fiasco I will not try to take all the suggestions that are made to me: I will not disregard all my instincts in dealing with counselees, and will try to rely on my own judgments when I feel I am right. Maybe if I do this I will become more relaxed and can be a better counselor. I really want to help these kids. I give a lot of time to reading and thinking about them during the week. This also has some drawbacks because I sometimes "make a speech" to get my point across. This is bad. Not many kids want to be preached to. Most will turn you off. Rightly so.

All in all, as dissatisfied with myself as I am, I think Claude is getting something out of the sessions. I think we do have a counselor-counselee relationship, and perhaps that helped get me over today. He did say that I was helping him to open his eyes to some things and that is what he wanted to get out of it. He thought the exercise in the *Occupa. Outl. Hdbk.* was beneficial to him. He had discarded some jobs outright, but he had looked into others and had written for an additional booklet. He had also said the discussion about his study habits was probably helpful because now that he thought about it, he guessed that maybe they weren't too good.

The overall practicum is not going too well. About 50% of the counselees who enrolled did not ever show up and some more have missed some sessions. Two girls came up but would not stay for the session because it was not "fun." So far my counselee has not missed. If I can get him to feel that I have an investment in him, he should keep coming. I feel I do have an investment in him.

The question came up in the seminar about how far the counselor should go to get the student to come back. It's a sticky question about how far and how deeply involved the counselor should get with the counselee. I'm sure the counselors feel defeated if the counselees did not return. (I know I would.) However, I am not sure the counselor should personally call him on the phone. If a real relationship had been established, it might be acceptable and desirable, but after only one or two sessions in which the counselees have been "forced" to come in the first place, I think the counselor may be in for some more hostility. The counselee may think the counselor "ratted" on him. Perhaps this could be handled in another channel.

I have been so torn by trying to follow what appear to me to be conflicting suggestions that I asked if it would have merit for the instructor and assistant to be aware of the other's comments. There needs to be a continuity of thought. What one thinks is important turns out to be "not necessary" to the other. This is one reason why I think it is necessary to rely on my own instincts more. Boy, I hope I live through this without losing my own mental health.

How dull if everyone thought alike—Dr. X, Vriend, Les Jones. How unproductive, unstimulating, and short-sighted. In counseling, distrust a "party line."

In the seminar we had another one of those penetrating discussions about our feelings toward Rudy's leaving early without forewarning to go to a wedding. This is the second class he has cut, but that's his business. As far as I am concerned, you get out of all these education classes just what you put into them. If he chooses to be elsewhere, that's his problem. Since beginning this program in guidance and counseling, I have seen so many people do just what is required

66

I think you're making good use of your log. Realize, too, that it's another communication avenue, and "log" questions and concerns to which you desire a response.

Bonnie: a brief reaction to the last paragraph on this page: perhaps you should examine the first sentence. Are you impatient with *your* slovenliness? Or others'? If *yours*, then you must be telling yourself that you must be perfect and then pounding on yourself whenever you aren't. If others', then you must be saying to yourself that they have to act the way *I want them to,* or else I will work myself up and get mad. But *why* should anybody do what you want him to?

and no more and even what they can get by with. I am here because I want to learn to counsel people and help them in the most efficient and knowledgeable way I know how.

I get impatient with slovenliness. I guess I was still feeling out of sorts from the counseling session, so after this discussion about Rudy had dragged on for almost the remaining part of the seminar, I just about blew up. I might as well have left when he did because we did not even get to the important part of our session: our counselees and how we can help them more effectively. I feel the time could be spent more profitably discussing, observing, and conferring concerning our performance and how we can improve. Dr. Vriend suggested I come in during the week for a private conference and I think this is good advice. Maybe I won't be so impatient with the slow pace on Saturday.

October 26, 19—

I felt today went much better in every way. After I had come to the realization that I must counsel in the way that I can live with, I was much more at ease in the counseling session with Claude Fez. I had no preconceived ideas that I was going to press to prove, only one goal: to try to learn more about how he functions. It paid off. He started off very easily by telling me he was doing better at school and then told me of an incident in his art class which had made quite an impression on him. He, and evidently some of the other students, consider the teacher incompetent and one of the boys was laughing at the teacher. The teacher reprimanded the boy, who got up, walked out dramatically, and slammed the door behind him. Although Claude said he did not think the boy should have walked out, I believe he really admired him for doing something he did not have the nerve to do.

You seem to be using your diagnostic ability to a fruitful degree and are seeing the value of listening for recurring themes and patterns of customary behavior.

I asked him how his radio club was going (the only extra-curricular activity he has ever belonged to) and he said he liked his part as disc jockey for the club, but "couldn't stand the people." This is a recurring theme. When I asked him about the records he played, he became very excited and talked about the 2,050 rock and roll records he has recorded, filed, and cross-filed. He knows the words of every song. He is extremely methodical. He said his father thinks he is wasting his time on this activity.

He mentioned his girl friend today for the first time. I have been hoping he would bring her up. When I asked him to tell me about her, he began by telling me about the difficult transition he had when he transferred from parochial to public school in high school. He had not dated until he was a senior because "I missed driver's training in my junior year," etc., etc. This is an area of some conflict, I believe, because this girl is pressing for some commitment on his part. "I'm only nineteen"—another recurring theme—"and I don't want to get married until I'm 23 or 24 at least, but I don't want to hurt her." . . . "It's better to go see her on Saturday nights than staying around home."

Dr. Vriend watched the session this morning and came back afterward and gave me some very good suggestions. He had seen Claude's previous counselor that week and Dr. V. suggested that Claude has had much counseling at Macomb C.C. He pointed out statements Claude made in our session which suggest that he is afraid he is not "normal" or manly.

Which, again, can be expressed as, what works? What evidence supports counselor action?

I found the two consultations with Dr. V. this week to be helpful and fruitful. At times like this it seems that his philosophy of counseling is not too different from my own. I realize that when he uses the "hit 'em between the eyes" illustrations, we can do it in the manner most suitable to our own personalities. It is the forcing-the-client-to-look-at-himself-realistically that we are after. He uses this blunt approach with us in the practicum, and at times it strikes me as being a bit crude, and at times, inaccurate. It is effective in that it makes us examine ourselves, but it does produce some hostility. The men have become angry at times, and Rudy, at the present time, is extremely cool to all of us. This is resulting from the discussion involving his leaving last week. He was given the tape and some of the remarks were quite cutting so I can understand his being hurt. I was uncomfortable throughout that discussion because I had the feeling we were talking about him behind his back even though I knew the tape was being made. A good deal of hostility was revealed especially from his partner. This is bound to affect their relationship unless they can get this ironed out. They did not seem to have much of a relationship anyway before this happened.

Of all the people in the practicum, Rudy and Alice seem the most insecure. Alice constantly fishes for praise: "Look at me this morning. I have on a new sweater. Don't I look nice?" . . . "Did you see me this morning? Didn't I do all right?" . . . etc., etc.

Seeking to understand the "other," not only fellow practicum members, but those in the world around you, is an important phase of counselor development.

Rudy constantly brags about how good he is at bridge and how many tournaments he has played in, how much liquor he can hold without passing out, how important he is at school. Much bravado, I believe, but why should they have to prove anything to anyone in the group? I found myself resenting Rudy's attitude at first. He seemed to have the attitude that only the black man is dedicated enough or capable enough to counsel a black kid from the inner city. This is a dangerous generalization and a wrong assumption. There are dedicated teachers and counselors of all races who have a profound desire to help kids with problems. Am I naive to believe that children will respond to an understanding, accepting person who may not know, but will try to help him with his problem? I may not be able to help some of these kids, but it will be from my own incompetency, not because I did not want to help.

I'd agree with your rationale here and have empirical data to support the position.

The other two men in the class seem to be fairly uncomplicated guys who will probably turn out to be pretty good counselors or administrators as the case may be. Gregory is easy to talk to and interested in his client. Horace, my partner, is not as smooth, but is making good progress. He has given me some good suggestions with my client. Horace has some real problems with his clients, but he is interested in them and is making an effort to help them.

The other woman, Helen, is a young girl who makes no real contribution to the class. She goes home for lunch to be with her husband so we don't get to know her too well. However, she is sweet and agreeable.

I feel I have misjudged Les in some respects. It took me three sessions to realize that Claude's real reason for coming here was not career problems—that it went much deeper. Les grasped this much quicker and suggested this to me, but I resisted the idea. Now I have come to realize that when most of these young people come in for career guidance, they are just picking a "safe" subject and most of them know that is not all they are hoping to get out of counseling. I feel as if I have made a big discovery. I feel that I am beginning to make some progress.

"Career problems" *are* deep. Leaving the nest and establishing one's self as an autonomous being who is responsible for all self action and reaction presents many problems and complications. In our society—as in all others—it is a crucial developmental stage.

November 2, 19—

Things are beginning to pick up in the practicum. I really had a busy morning. I had three counselees, one right after the other, and right now they run together in my mind. In addition to Claude Fez, I had two junior high girls. The girls are about the same age, but are completely different in personality. Maria is more vivacious and outgoing and Tamara is uncommunicative and insecure. Tamara is being brought here by her mother and is showing her hostility by not talking. I think she will, though. A few times she seemed ready to spill it out, but didn't. I could see indecision in her face. Maria is enjoying her trip down here with her friends. Five of them are coming to be counseled and they come on the bus, do a little shopping

You needn't have asked this question; even the slightest amount of thinking on your part would have given you the answer. We learn by experiencing, by stretching the limits that are set for us, by going beyond them. Just coping with the campus geography and dealing with the official strangers one encounters is a positive learning experience for our clients. You might have reinforced the learnings in the counseling and even helped to open up additional possibilities.

True for all clients, even those who are extremely limited in verbal ability. The counseling profession, almost by definition, requires *thinking* practitioners, if counseling is to be effective.

afterward, and eat at the White Castle. I asked her if this was kind of a little outing for them and she said, "Yeah, kind of." I guess the counseling is the pain they have to take with the pleasure.

She said that the other girls had talked about the counseling and they were mad because they had a man counselor. They were afraid of a man, but everything was going to be OK because they were supposed to get a woman. Dr. Vriend nixed this right away so the girls had their regular counselors. The men said afterward that the girls were very uncommunicative. I heard Horace's tape of his counselee and she was hostile as all get out. Both of his counselees, Gordon Phelps and Mabel Merk, seemed not only to resent him, but to have no respect for him. Both of them questioned his credentials, and he makes too big a deal out of how long he has been a teacher and how he knows kids. This loses them and turns them off. Gordon Phelps has dropped, and I doubt if he is going to get anywhere with Mabel. He can't seem to relate to them or to generate any warmth that they can feel. Horace is a very sensitive man, but when he thinks things are not going well, either in counseling or seminar, he gets uptight and gets splitting headaches. He doesn't have the aura, if that is the word, of a capable understanding counselor yet.

I think I generate the feeling of warmth and understanding, but I'm not sure of the capable part. I can tell in the session if I'm being helpful or if I'm responding correctly. This is most important. Many times I know the counselee is saying something significant, but often my responses are not what they should be or not soon enough. This is my trouble with Claude Fez. He speaks so rapidly that I have to be quick on my feet or he has moved away from a sensitive area. This is defensive on his part. Dr. Vriend was most helpful in giving me possible actual responses to use because I feel this is my weakness so far.

I brought up the idea of "brown-bagging" it instead of going out for lunch. I am always pretty excited about the morning's sessions and am ready to discuss them. There are so many things I need to know about improving my technique and ways to help these counselees. Only one person wanted to do it with any enthusiasm, so I guess the idea is dropped. I think I shall still stay in at lunch and listen to tapes or something if no one will stay with me. Two people feel they have to get away so they can breathe and relax. Unfortunately one of these is my partner.

November 7, 19—

I spent most of the day listening to tapes. I listened to Claude's tape three times, Maria's twice, and one of Gregory Howell's once. I am always a little appalled at my ineptitude in some of these sessions. I wish I were not so slow to react. Claude presents a special kind of problem. He is so garrulous that he doesn't give me time to gather my thoughts. The conversation goes so fast that I have to be quick . . . quick. I must learn to sharpen my senses. Still I think he is making some progress and today he realized an important fact: he "bends over backwards" in order for people to think he is a "nice kid" and he denies himself in order not to hurt others. He has not been a take-charge guy and as a result he has been frustrated and hurt, many times, in his dealings with people.

I thought I did pretty well with Maria's session. She has opened up far more than any of her friends who have been here. I have a pretty good insight into her fun life, and I was beginning to get into her problems when the knock on the counseling room door announcing the end of the session interrupted us. I wish these sessions were longer than forty-five minutes. Maria's a cute kid, precocious, and there's something very appealing about her. She's very feminine, and I imagine she uses that to advantage.

November 9, 19—

Today was a really good day. I had the feeling that all three of the counseling sessions went pretty well, and for the first time I believe I was being helpful. Up until now too many of the sessions have been full of interesting facts about the client, but how was the counseling helpful? How valuable is it to bring out events that happened in childhood and try to determine if they were instrumental in making him the kind of person he is today? I don't feel qualified to interpret those kinds of data and a wrong assumption can be damaging. It also takes a lot of time which is not always available in the school setting. If I spend all my time on ten kids while I delve into their past, what will the other three hundred do?

These data tend to come out, if they are important to the client. Clients often use past events and circumstances in their lives to explain and defend present behavior.

I am wondering if it would not be more practical and more in the realm of my competency to sublimate the past and start with the client as he is right now and ask him if he wants to stay that way. If not, what can we do about it, and proceed from there. This is pretty much what we did in today's session with Claude. He had pretty much "psychoanalyzed" himself before he began counseling. He thought maybe he was not "normal." He feels his father has made him so shy around girls. "He has made a woman-hater out of me." He wants to broaden his experiences with people and girls. "Maybe it's too late." He has convinced himself that he is too shy and if he drops his steady girlfriend whom he doesn't love (but who is pressuring him into marriage) he can never get another girl to go out with him for a "hundred years." This kind of thinking is self-defeating, and we talked about what he could do about it. This session was productive and we talked about things he was interested in.

Which is a "normal" way to feel.

As you discuss your last three clients (Tam, Betty, and Maria), a general question

The second counselee, Tamara, is an 8th-grade girl who has been referred by her mother who said she was underachieving at school and has no interest at home. We tried

and attitude seems to appear: How do you counsel people who have no apparent need of counseling? You seem to have an impatience to get with it, to start working on a problem area. The assumption seems to be that counseling is only for "deviants," not for the normal-functioning. To take such a stance is to give up on a client, almost. It's as though the client is not cooperating, not being a "good" client. My reaction to this kind of client is different: I question my own effectiveness, analyze my own behavior. Have I helped the client to understand the counseling process, what is possible in counseling? Have I helped the client to understand what value there is in self-examination, in analysis of behavior and life situations? Have I learned what the client's world is really like? What are this client's goals? How does this client deal with the stimuli which impinge upon her? These kinds of questions lead me to operate differently, if I have not been of previous help. The assumption underlying such an approach is that all clients can benefit from counseling. They can be helped to be more effective, to cope better, to replace self-defeating behavior or indifferent behavior with self-enhancing or mastery behavior. And as clients, they are never at fault. They are what they are.

to talk about incidents that happened at school, but she was very resistant to any alternatives in behavior that she might have made or could make to make things better. She said she might need to change, but wasn't going to. At home it was the same. She said she was very happy at home; everything was fine; and she didn't need to change. When I said she was a perfect girl in a perfect home and she was the first one I had ever met, she laughed and covered her face. She admitted she wasn't perfect, but she didn't need to change anything. From outward appearances it wasn't productive for her, but if she thinks of it during the week, who knows?

The third counselee was an eleven-year-old girl who is in the 5th grade at a Catholic school. She said her teacher asked her if she would like to come down, but Betty Kozol didn't know why. She seems to be a pretty bright little girl who makes average grades: C's, some B's, a D, and U. She has two sisters, one older and the other a baby with whom she shares a room "because I want to." She also has two younger brothers, one of whom is a "brat." There are minor quarrels, the dad is not much home, and the mother is tired a lot of the time.

The teacher at school seems to be strict, but her biggest complaint about Betty Kozol is that she begins her work without reading directions carefully, recopying her work because it was sloppy and wasting paper. We talked about what she might do differently, if she wanted to improve.

I really couldn't find anything that a counselor would be needed for, nothing that the teacher couldn't handle. There must be more to this. Betty said the teacher had sent "five or six others" down here to see a counselor. Her mother seemed quite anxious. "Do you think you can help her?"

Depends on what you have in mind. What hypotheses would you be testing? What would your rationale be? Your goals? Incidentally, have you ever run into any person at any age who does not tell "things out of context" or who is able to give completely error-free pictures of the actual situation?

While you're certainly not alone in this, Bonnie, I've felt all along that you were passing up an opportunity for growth by concentrating to such a great extent on your own affairs to the exclusion of others. Comparing ourselves to and really learning how others, peers and models, function helps to give us greater breadth of vision and provides reference points for our thinking.

Would it be desirable to work with the parents and the teacher too when it involves elementary school children? Many children this age seem to tell "things out of context" which gives a completely erroneous picture of the actual situation. Also, I wonder if they are perceptive enough to know where their trouble areas are.

My fourth counselee, Maria Blunk, did not keep her second appointment. It was my opinion that she was not very serious about counseling anyway. It was more of an outing with her friends. Today was not a good day for an outing. The weather was cold, rainy, miserable.

In seminar today we broke up into small groups and talked about specific trouble areas. Alice and I went with Dr. V. because we are both concerned about appropriate responses to counselees. I was glad we went together. I realize that I could have been pretty selfishly getting what I could out of this class and deliberately avoiding getting embroiled in other people's problems. However, this attitude has been bothering me, and I would like to be as helpful to Alice as I can. She is so insecure and she communicates this so much that the air is filled with it. Even so, I think she is sincere in wanting to help counselees, and she is frustrated at this point on how to go about doing it. I also suspect that she feels the rest of us are having an easier time in this practicum than she is. This has been a real struggle for me and very painful at times. Dr. Vriend has been very critical, and it has hurt, but I trust him enough to know that he can see things that stand in the way of my becoming an effective counselor, which I very much want to be.

Some of his early criticism seemed unjust and unfair to me, and I actively disliked him for it, but the more I thought about it, I realized he was doing me a favor. Then I could pick up my bruised ego and go ahead. If after a thorough examination, I find some of it to be unjust criticism, I can dismiss it. If not, I can do something about it. At any rate, I have become more aware of myself in all of these areas.

After listening to my tapes, I realize how heavy-handed and clumsy I am in so many instances. There has never been a session in which I have not blundered in some way. I am pretty sure I am not unique in this group.

November 16, 19—

I was really exuberant when I went into the practicum this morning. Last week's sessions had gone well and I was looking forward to today. For the first time I began to get the "feel" of what it is like to be a counselor. I had made arrangements earlier in the week for Helen to take over my eleven-year-old counselee because Helen is planning to be an elementary school counselor and had never had a young counselee.

Guard against "possessive" feelings in counseling. Why did you want to keep Betty to yourself? (Your text doesn't really answer the question.) And the answers to such questions increase self-awareness and improve counselor performance.

Actually, I was reluctant and a little disappointed to lose her because, despite the fact that I am in the secondary field, I felt I could still counsel her. I should think changing counselors would be a little unsettling for the child, but actually, if I am honest about it, I really wanted to keep her for myself. Betty Kozol is a pleasant child, sweet-faced, and with an innocence that seems to disappear in most of the counselees of high school age.

I was looking forward to Claude Fez this morning because last week we were headed in the right direction and had talked about things he was really concerned with. I was supposed to tell him about termination (since next week marks the end of this practicum for the clients), get him to evaluate our sessions, and hopefully he would have gained enough insight to recognize behavior which has been self-defeating and to change this. I was disappointed.

You should work on this in yourself. To live "through" clients is serving your own needs. Think of the analogy of the medical doctor. As patients, we don't feel that the

Claude obviously was not himself today. He sat quietly throughout the "termination talk" and in trying to evaluate what had been most helpful, he said that the sessions had all been helpful and there was not any-

doctor should "get something" out of the encounter, other than our payment "for services rendered." Nor do we expect him to be disappointed in any way. If we have neglected to follow his professional advice or take his prescription, we expect that he might engage in some mild censure, politely "bawling us out," but we hardly expect him to lose any sleep over it.

The "acne" data had a world of meaning in how much Claude had been "conditioned" by his affliction. It was visible; and had you in the early sessions gotten him to tell about it, tell you what meaning it had in his life, what he thought about his own looks and what this had to do with his relationship with girls, the counseling process probably would have been accelerated.

thing specific he could think of. He seemed unnaturally taciturn for him and, what I thought was an attempt to avert his eyes, kept glancing at the mike. When I mentioned last week's session, he laughed very nervously and said, "Oh, yeah, that really was a session, all right." He still seemed to want to be detached, so we did not delve into that too much. Instead we tried to think of ways in which he had changed in order to reach a goal, and I did some evaluating for him. "This is the way you have shown me to be now: concerned with college program, inability to make a vocational choice, fearful of making the wrong choice, shy, afraid of hurting people, letting others make decisions for you, needing to protect your image, limited contact with girls. Do you like the way you are? What can you do about it?"

I gave him an exercise which he indicated would be hard for him to do, but he would try. He is to walk up and talk to five strange girls this week. Some of them will probably tell him to "flake off," but the fifth girl he talks to may find him more confident and easy to talk with. I told him if he wants to talk about it next week, we can, and we can see where he bombed and where he succeeded.

I gave him a copy of Dr. Ellis' book, *A Guide to Rational Living*, and if any of it was pertinent to him, we could talk about it if he wanted to.

Claude did tell me he had been sick this week and had missed four days of school. He had had a reaction to a shot which he had taken for acne and his temperature had been 104 for two days. He could not study, but he said, "I did a lot of thinking about things and my life."

Did this account for his reserved behavior? When he stopped by the desk for next week's appointment, I saw Leo Capelli, our technician, sitting in the office. This was a moment I had dreaded ever since I learned that he was an acquaintance of Claude's from high school. However, Leo had assured us that he would not listen to any of

Claude's counseling sessions in the lab control room nor to any of the tapes and that he would keep himself out of sight when he was around in the event that Claude might not feel free to talk if he thought Leo might overhear. Neither Claude nor Leo looked up or spoke.

And whom did that help?

I really felt sick.

I do not know if Claude had seen Leo before or knew he worked here before today. Did Claude see Leo in the hall carrying mikes? I don't see how he could have missed it. Was that why Claude was so quiet in the session? My fears are that the incident will have an effect on the last counseling session. It is possible that I am over-reacting to this. This is one of my problems. As Dr. Vriend tersely put it: "You get so in love with your thesis, you won't let go!" Sometimes I seem to be overly empathic; that's another one of my problems. Still, I think the best course of action is to put it on the table and test this thesis, and drop it if it proves incorrect.

In spite of all the discomfort this aroused in you, it was an important, productive happening, not only for you, but for the others in the seminar. The full impact of the meaning of confidentiality was dramatically brought home.

Are you "mad" at her, therefore?

My second counselee, Tamara, the eighth-grade student, is very uncooperative. Open-ended questions are met with silence and direct questions with "No." She did admit that she was pretty mad at being made to come by her parents and had decided "not to talk." The other little bit of information was that she tries but is not very successful in pleasing people. I'd sure like to make the last session fruitful for her, so I'll do some hard thinking this week.

Because of what other reasons might she have missed? Why do you choose this one to believe?

My third counselee, Maria, the party goer, missed her second appointment. Guess she thought it wasn't much fun.

November 23, 19—

The whole business of closure is delicate, isn't it? In this case you have no choice since the practicum is ending; but in another instance you and your clients would agree that

Today was the last day to see our counselees. I had done a lot of thinking about this during the week, on how we could make it as fruitful for them as possible. I wanted to give them a feeling of closure from me, though not necessarily from counseling.

78

counseling ought to be terminated. You are right, here, in your intent to help your clients have a sense of severance from you as a person, though not from counseling as a beneficial process.

The important thing, of course, in effecting closure that is not abrupt or damaging to the therapeutic interactions which have gone on is the preparation of the client for the inevitable event, something an effective counselor does in gradual stages. But we've discussed this enough in our seminar.

You're learning to think like a counselor, I see.

Hypothesis testing is one of the most fruitful counselor behaviors you can make a habit of.

I had really let that business about Claude and Leo upset me throughout the week. I had determined that if it seemed appropriate we should talk about his attitudes on this subject. I must have rehearsed in my mind a dozen ways in which I could approach it naturally.

Claude began the counseling session by telling me how much he like the Ellis book, *A Guide to Rational Living*. He was sincerely enthusiastic about it. "I'm going to get a copy for myself. A lot of these books contain so much mumbo-jumbo that only a psychologist can understand them, but this book was really good. I think you should copy some of these paragraphs and give them to some of your other counseling students." The chapters on the fear of failure, overcoming the influences of the past, and controlling his own destiny seemed especially meaningful to him.

As I sat and listened to him, I could sense a change from last week. He seemed more at ease, more confident, more secure that at any time since he had been coming. What accounts for this behavior? I thought of several things while I listened to him talk: (1) I had made too much of last week's incident and had overacted within myself; (2) he had been "thrown" by the incident at the time, but during the week he had garnered the strength for it not to matter; or (3) he was putting up a smoke screen in case Leo was listening in the control room. I decided to test the last hypothesis. I asked him to tell me about the other "assignment" in which he had agreed to speak to five strange girls. This is an area of great anxiety for him, but he did not seem nervous of the mike. He was not effusive on this subject, but he said, "I did it. It was the hardest thing I ever did in my life. I wasn't very good at it and I realize this is an area I have to work on. And I intend to because I owe it to myself to know more girls before I get married. Still I can't do everything at once; I have to change a little bit at a time, but I'm aware of it. I'm going to stay with my girl until after Christmas because she's counting on it."

I asked him if our exchanges about her had made a difference in their relationship. He said, "Oh, yes. She's noticed it, too. I seem restless and don't go over all the time. I'm really wanting out."

After all the pre-programming that went on in your mind, it was a letdown for you not to get into the matter, wasn't it?

After this, I decided not to bring up Leo unless he wanted to. It just didn't seem to matter that much any more.

After the morning was over, I had mixed feelings concerning my two clients. I had a feeling of accomplishment in regard to Claude Fez: Claude had come to counseling because he wanted help, and I felt I had been helpful. It is my feeling that he is less fearful, more confident, and has more insight into his behavior than he had before he came. He said, "It has made me more aware about myself and how I function. Once you are aware, then you can make up your mind what you want for yourself." This, I think, is my goal in counseling, and to have him say this—well, it was pretty rewarding. We talked about his immediate plans, and he said there were areas that he realized he needed to work on, but they were difficult areas, and "I just have to change a little at a time." He said he realized he was the way he was because he had learned from the experiences he had had. "If I learned them, well, I can unlearn them." The interview was mostly to give him—and me, too—this feeling of closure. This was accomplished for both of us, so by the time the signal came, we had really completed our time together. This was significant for both of us because at the beginning of the practicum, he was overly dependent, and Dr. Vriend thought I was motherly: a combination that would not be beneficial to either of us. The fact that we both "let go" easily and naturally represented growth in both of us. The interview did not degenerate into a reluctant fond farewell.

It also represented a job well done of preparing the client for the event.

I had quite a different feeling about Tamara. She was as resistant as ever, up to a point. I

Why? It seems to me that here, and in the text which follows, you didn't share this with Tamara.

We need to help clients "to be prepared" for a number of events: for the counseling to come, for termination of a session or a series of sessions or a relationship, for referrals, for interventions of all sorts. Clients need to know why this or that is to happen, to agree with it, to want it for their own good, to be committed to a course of action, and since they feel unsafe, often, the counseling can focus on the nature of the impending event and their role in it. Tamara could have helped you to understand how you might have func-

told her that I would not send a report to her school because her family referred her to the counseling center, but I felt that I should give her father a brief report and a chance for him to ask some questions. She was very quick to say that she did not want me to talk to him. She did not say why, but I think she thought I would tell on her resistant behavior in the counseling sessions. She wants very much for them to think she is doing better in her school work and behavior, so she did begin to "open up" a little more. I was in a dilemma: I felt I should explain that counseling will be available after Christmas and give her father some idea of why he was bringing his daughter down here and what we were doing. I knew her parents must be concerned. Still I didn't want her to think I was taking sides against her. We went over what I was going to say, and she relaxed somewhat. Mr. Jordan was worried and concerned about Tamara. He felt he had had no communication with school until he learned she was failing and had been "unruly." Then he felt "it was almost too late" for him to do anything to help her. (Tamara had told me earlier that he whipped her with a belt when he received this report.) Tamara sat with her head down when her dad was in the room. I felt dissatisfied with this interview. I have some questions: Should I have talked with him privately? Should I have told him that Tamara had been resistant? (She told me she had made up her mind not to talk.)

What if I had threatened (I hate that word) earlier to tell her father there was no need to bring her because she would not cooperate? Would it have made her open up?

Should I have allowed her mother to talk to me as the "referral agent" as she wanted to do at the time of the first interview? It might have explained some things?

The question of parent involvement is not clear to me. I know they want more communication. Mr. Jordan said, "We want to help her. We're interested. We are more interested in her than anything. Without her, there's nothing."

tioned with her father, had you been able to get her to take charge. Your first obligation is to your client's welfare.

In this situation, it seems to me that ground rules were not established. If you had, at the beginning, had a joint session with Tamara and her mother (or father) where you elicited counseling expectations, corrected distortions, and explained the limits (e.g., "What goes on in here belongs to Tamara, and if she chooses to share it with you, that's her privilege. On the other hand, if she doesn't, then I will feel obliged to respect her wishes. This ought to be understood before we begin."), this would not have been the problem which it ultimately became for you.

The whole area of family—or multiple—counseling, and parent-client conferences, which you raise in conjunction with Tamara's case, has so many aspects to it, that these marginal notes can hardly do justice to it. But it shouldn't be lightly dismissed. I suggest that you do some in-depth reading in the area, carve out some operating principles for yourself, and define your ethics, your responsibilities to clients and "significant others" in your clients' lives.

I did not "rat" on her, but I felt a certain sympathy for Mr. Jordan, and I felt I was evasive, an action that is never satisfactory and makes me feel dishonest. What could I have done?

December 7, 19—

Today we were back in seminar after a week lay-off because of the Thanksgiving vacation. I rather missed not seeing counselees today because we had ended that before

Thanksgiving. Our case summary reports and agency referral reports were due today. That was a big job, but it is a necessary part of counseling. In order to make the report concise and valuable to the next professional person, long hours are spent in looking for patterns and themes, changes and developments, attitudes and significant behaviors. I imagine many counselors neglect to do this because it is time-consuming and demands us to sort and think. Still, if it was important to the client to be discussed, it should not be lost by not keeping a record of it. I hope that what I wrote will be beneficial to my former client whenever he sees the next counselor. I see this log in the same light. It requires a lot of time and work to sort out my feelings and thoughts in order to put them in an organized, usable instrument. Doing this is painful and I found myself procrastinating and setting up all kinds of "busy work" so I would not have to sit down and begin. However, I found that this is one of the most meaningful assignments I have ever had. I wish I had been "forced" to do it when I began graduate school, but because I did not, many of those feelings of anxiety and happiness, the fears and frustrations and joys, are forgotten now and lost to me because I find them difficult to recall.

In your log you've expressed yourself clearly and pointedly, a practice which all counselors benefit from as long as they function as counselors. We cannot get enough of it. Our communication skills are our primary tools. (I often think that a course in the "mechanics of communication and effective thinking" ought to be a required part of every counselor's graduate training program. Few would be exempt if proficiency tests were administered.)

It has also helped me to put down on paper so many feelings I have which are just floating around and around in a nameless, formless fashion in my mind. When I have it before me in a concrete manner, I can look at it, deal with it, and forget it. It doesn't have to remain in the back of my mind because it is in front of me in the log. This has helped me in my relationships with the other people in the practicum. If I am frustrated with some of the others, I have to organize my frustrations on paper, or else I look foolish and petty to myself. After writing them out, I am in a position to go to work on the "blocking" feelings, or at least to examine myself as to why I am frustrated. It has also helped me to raise some questions

You have used your log wisely and effectively, and, as you say, the process of logging your reactions and other kinds of mental formulations has had intrinsic value for you. The only thing I would remind you of is that the process is not uniquely valuable to you or me: it is very often effective for clients, too. Having certain kinds of clients (those who are willing and able) keep a log of their mental life, making notes between sessions to be used in the counseling, often accelerates the counseling process.

to my supervisor which I couldn't conceptualize at the time of the related happenings. Today in the seminar we talked about our feelings toward many things. This is a difficult thing for most of us to do. As Les said, "It is a profound thing to talk about." It forces us to think about our feelings. It also forces us to trust each other with these same feelings. If we are so reticent to share them with other counselors, is it any wonder that counselees are so reticent to share their feelings with us?

I admire the people who have been open and shared their feelings and then have been vulnerable to all kinds of scrutiny and criticism. My greatest fear is that I will become judgmental of them and perhaps say something about them that is erroneous because my perception of them is wrong. I want to become sensitive and observant without being judgmental.

December 14, 19—

Today was the last day of the practicum. The seminar assignment for the day was to write and tape record an evaluation of our development as a counselor and play it before the group. We were to focus upon our strengths and weaknesses, but most of us were very much aware of our areas of ineffectiveness, so we concentrated on that. After each report was heard, the group was asked to react. Each of us was understandably apprehensive because the tone of the seminar has been to make us aware of our weaknesses which may be a hindrance in the counseling process; any strengths we may have were rarely mentioned. The reasoning behind this, I suppose, is that it isn't helpful to our development to emphasize what we are doing right: it's the wrong things which we need to be aware of. I don't agree with this theory completely because it causes us to have an unbalanced picture of our worth as a counselor. Among some of the members of the group, this has produced an anxiety and insecurity which has affected all of us,

Your concern with "right" and "wrong" counselor practices belies your learning, Bonnie. What a counselor does is never "wrong"; it's only effective or ineffective. If it is effective, it is reinforced or supported by the results, by the evidence; if it is ineffective, the results show this, too. In the latter case, one looks for alternate ways to go. Since a counselor works alone, that is, without someone to take over for him or watch over his shoulder, it is important for him to develop a sense of autonomy, and to seek—not approval —consultative help when he needs it. If there has been a "theory" in the way Les and I have behaved in our supervisory role, this is it. I certainly don't see you as anyone who will buckle from critical evaluation; if it were so, I would rush to prop you up.

and it has made us more critical and less trusting of each other. Where there is such a wide discrepancy between the perception a person has of himself and his aspiration, I feel reinforcement or support is needed. I used this with Claude Fez and it gave him more confidence. However, throughout the seminar, rarely did anyone in the group try to support another member. At times, I felt a good deal of criticism—primarily directed at Alice and Rudy—was not offered in the spirit of love or helpfulness, but as a means of releasing frustrations and petty personal feelings. At these times, I felt compelled to come to the aid of the person who was the target of these attacks, thereby earning me the title of being the "mother" of the group by Rudy. This was an interesting observation to me that he should see a gesture of this kind in that term. Shouldn't the purpose of a practicum group be to understand, accept, empathize, and help the other members of the group? My evaluation of the group is that we were all to introspective to be aware of the needs of the others.

I guess my biggest disappointment centered around Les, our assistant supervisor. Les had been in a difficult position: he had not been included in our student group, nor had he indicated he wanted to be, and yet we did not look upon him as an instructor, either. I think we tested him in the early weeks, and it was my feeling that he was not as conscientious as he could have been in listening to our tapes, observing, and conferring with us after the counseling sessions. In fact, I resented his taking our practicum time to discuss with Dr. Vriend problems concerning graduate courses he was taking which were unrelated to the group.

Anyway, we consulted him less and less. However, we did ask for his reaction to our self-evaluation, and I was astounded at the emotions he had kept bottled up for ten weeks. I think he resented our attitude, and his comments supported this. It seems that he had labeled each one of us: "The

Well, Bonnie, we've come to the end of the string, *n'est-ce pas?* I am pleased with the way you have developed yourself during the short space of this quarter. I think you have a sturdy foundation on which to build an excellent beginning into a most trying, but rewarding, profession.

I hope not too much time passes between now and when you can enlarge on what you've gained in your training by actually practicing as a "paid" pro. Your critical remarks herein do not surprise me; most students, at the end of their program, are critical: it's almost a sign of health. (Don't all healthy human beings "bellyache" as soon as they get the opportunity?)

Now that the course has ended, I'd like to say that this was an outstanding log, the best I've seen in my short tenure as a counselor educator, a model of what a log can be. If you will give me permission to do so, I shall try to get it published for you at some future date. I think other student (and practicing!) counselors can profit from sharing your thoughts about your experiences.

Upper-Peninsula-Type," the frustrated "Man-Chasing-Type," "The Too-Professional-Type," "The Phony-Type." What frustrated him was that he could not typecast Rudy, the black man in the group. Was he an Uncle Tom, black militant, uninvolved middle class—what? Was he dedicated to a cause? If so, what is it? Les could not see Rudy as a man, but rather as a certain kind of black man.

I wonder if I'm being unfair to Les, or if this is an accurate interpretation? Was he doing this "on purpose"—for our benefit—or because he was showing his true feelings?

I regret this was the last meeting for the group. There were still too many defensive and anxious feelings, too many judgmental and critical comments. At times the group seemed to become unglued. We really should have had another meeting which would allow us to reestablish ourselves.

I am pleased with the practicum as a whole. It has been the most worthwhile, meaningful class I have had in this course of study. I feel I have learned how to be helpful to a client and not just friendly and understanding. I feel I have learned to recognize significant data and to establish patterns. Although there are many areas in which I need to develop, this practicum has provided me with some skills and a motivation to try to become a competent counselor.

Guidelines for Agency Reports and Final Case Reports

This instructional guide is to help you construct case summaries for each client you have counseled, *even though you may have seen the client only one time*. If the client was referred for counseling by a member of some agency (school, employment service, a vocational rehabilitation office, a clinic, etc.), one report must be constructed for that agency and addressed to the referral agent, if known. The agency report should be letter-perfect. Therefore, it must be submitted to the practicum supervisor for approval prior to final typing. When approved, three single-spaced copies should be made, the original to be sent to the agency, a copy for the client's on-campus permanent folder, and a copy for the counselor's (your) personal file. It should be no more than one page long and should contain no confidential information (unless approved by the practicum supervisor) and no references to the practicum counselor. A model for the agency report accompanies this guide. Some clients are self-referred or referred by friends or parents. For these clients no agency report is required.

For *every* client a final case report must be made. This report will become part of the client's permanent file in the counseling lab. It should be typed single-spaced and submitted to the practicum supervisor for approval prior to final typing. It is recommended that the practicum counselor retain a copy of the final report for his personal files. Confidential information of a nature relevant to continued counseling may be included. Again, references to the counselor should not be included.

Instructions

The potential importance of a counseling report cannot be overestimated, even though in many cases a competent worker finds little use for a report of previous contacts with a client. Reports serve many functions, not the least of which are (a) a permanent record helpful to the next counselor who will work with the client should the client desire to return for additional counseling; (b) a constructive intervention on the client's behalf which can influence the recipient to act in ways helpful to the client; and (c) a visible indication for the school or other agency of the fulfillment of the counselor's promised service. Therefore, careful preparation is desirable.

There is no "best" form of reporting, since each report should be tailor-made to meet the requirements of the particular situation. However, some general guidelines may be set down.

Critical thinking about the case is of utmost importance. The report writer might jot down the essentials of the case, the case aspects which are most fundamental, important, and relevant, before he or she does any writing. What is the client like? What personal difficulty areas did he or she have (and still has), big or small, internal or external? How did the counseling progress? What happened? What behaviors were recurrent in and out of the counseling? How does the client function? What did the counseling focus on? What goals (immediate, intermediate, and long range) does the client have? What repeated behaviors are self-defeating or ineffective for this client? How does the client perceive herself or himself, significant others, and reality? What recommendations do you have, both ideal and realistic?

Evidence in the form of client statements and tangible facts should be jotted down wherever possible to buttress your judgments and conclusions. What do you really know about the client? Separate the realities from the vague and uncertain notions. Putting your thinking into operational form is a good way to tighten up your judgments.

Organize your data into the most logical and functional sections you can devise, as determined by the client material available and relevant and the purposes of the report (e.g., the report sent to the school may include only that data which is relevant to the presenting problem, the referral basis). Some suggested sections for the final case report (for the on-campus file) are:

1. *Description and background information*: Includes physical description pertinent to counseling; health information; why referred; presenting problem(s); relevant historical and current material related to the client's life space circumstances.

2. *Counseling*: Includes the number of sessions (a must); dates; what happened, including sequence of major topics (focus areas of counseling); client responses in sessions and outside; contacts with family, school counselor, or other significant persons; client movement, if any.

3. *Personality and intellectual functioning*: Includes brief description of principal attitudes, values, self-defeating and self-enhancing philosophies, assessments, and limitations; functional intelligence evaluations, apparent aptitudes; vocational and other preferences; test data, if any.

4. *Summary and conclusions*

5. *Recommendations and action taken*: Includes recommendations to the counselor who may be seeing client in the future; understandings of the client at the time of termination concerning future action on his or her part; the degree of commitment to such action; counselor recommendations to client at termination; was the client helped to be aware that she or he could seek additional counseling at this agency or some other specified agency?

The briefer agency report might contain problems and behavior, appraisal, and recommendations, which may encompass more kinds of data than the headings suggest. These categories are by no means binding. Probably they are not appropriate for some client reports. The organization and content of the report should come out of the requirements of the particular case.

Brevity, clarity, simplicity, conciseness, and lack of technical jargon should be goals for the report writer. The report should be attractive and easily readable. Style should be objective, free of personal references (such as "Bill told me . . ."), and framed in operational and concrete language wherever possible.

Length: The agency report should not be longer than one page, single-spaced. The final case report may be two pages long. Longer reports will not be accepted unless there is a very good reason (discussed with your supervisor) for the length.

Format: The model of the agency report contains a heading which is appropriate. If the name of the referral agent is known, include it. If the report goes to an agency other than a school, use "agency" in place of "school." The final case report should include as part of the heading all which is part of the agency report plus the referral agency, if applicable, and the name and position title of the referral agent. As in the model, provisions for signatures and titles should appear on both reports.

Case Summary Report

Client: George Thompson
School: Benjamin Franklin High School
Livonia, Michigan
Home Address: 13642 E. Mackeral Dr.,
Livonia, Michigan 48074
Home Phone: 246-1970

Counselor: Thomas Gleet
Date of Initial Interview: 3/17/75
Date of Final Interview: 5/14/75
Date of this Report: 6/6/75

Problems and Behavior

The client, referred because he was "not working according to his ability," presented his problem as: "I want to find out about college—what I'm best suited for." In addition to these two, counseling disclosed the following problem areas which were focused on during the 10 interviews: (1) low initiative and activity level; (2) pattern of seeking immediate pleasure, lack of perseverance in the face of difficulty, avoidance behavior; (3) overdependence on others; (4) irrational ideas about why things occur to the client, reality distortion, unrealistic goals; (5) poor study habits; lack of organizing, integrating, and planning ability; (6) fear of success, reluctance to accept responsibility; (7) immature attitudes, lack of maturing experiences; (8) low self-esteem, approval-seeking behavior; and (9) inadequate knowledge of his school and social aptitudes and abilities.

Appraisal

During the course of counseling, the client moved from a position of indecision regarding his post-high school plans to one of decision: he now knows where he is, what his choices are, how he thinks about future schooling, a job or career, about the military service. He is aware of how he had failed to help himself in the past to be a more effective learner and why he has been unsuccessful in reaching his goals. He was administered two tests: Wechsler Adult Intelligence Scale and Strong Vocational Interest Blank for men. His WAIS scores show that with the proper motivation he would be able to get through college; the SVIB results were indecisive, although his range of interests suggest that he would not find occupations in the physical and biological categories congenial. As counseling progressed, the client became a stronger respondent, evidenced a more settled demeanor in contrast to his early nervousness and unassertiveness, reported that he was working at improving study skills and eliminating immediate pleasure behavior.

Recommendations

The client's post-high school plans are to enter the APEX program, for which he is a candidate, his first concern. In the event that he is not selected, he intends to seek work (U.S. Post Office or clerical position) and simultaneously attend adult secondary school on a part-time basis to make up college entry deficiencies. If he is chosen for APEX, it is recommended that he receive close supervision, tutorial help, and counseling support in the earlier stages of the program particularly. His present tendency is to give up, not to persevere. He has poor study habits; these need more modification if this client is to realize scholastic success in college. If this client is not selected for the APEX program, it is recommended that he be apprised of specific placement services provided by the school and community agencies, and employment opportunities, including those of the military services.

Thomas Gleet
Counselor
WSU Counseling and Guidance Center

John Vriend
Counselor-Training Supervisor
WSU Counseling and Guidance Center

Counselor Self-Evaluation Paper

Just as in the case reports you do not refer to yourself but focus instead entirely on the client, in this paper do not focus on anything other than yourself and do not make references to your client or clients. The purpose of the self-evaluation is to extend a process already begun in practicum, to encourage the habit of self-examination and analysis, and to give you explicit practice. When you become a counselor, self-awareness, self-examination, and evaluation is a constant process if development is going to continue.

Limit your evaluation to your own behavior as a counselor—how you have developed, areas of strength and areas of present ineffectiveness—to self-perception and to developmental goals. Do not evaluate your peers, the instructor, the course, your clients, the facilities, your textbooks, the procedures used in the practicum, or anything else outside of yourself. References to any of the foregoing should only be included as they pertain to your own development as a counselor, and they are better left out. The focus of this paper should be you and your counselor behaviors. There is no perfect or ideal counselor. All of us have a direction in which we would like to move, a better, more effective, more professional, more skilled, more competent counselor that it is possible for us, in our own unique ways, according to our own aspirations, to become. What areas should we work on? What steps should we take?

Counselors provide a service; they serve others, individual clients, groups, staff members with whom they work, every person in the professional setting. What kinds of personal characteristics, behaviors, attitudes, self-activity of all kinds can get in the way of such service? Resistance, counter-transference, projection, possession, identification—all are labels for the kinds of behavior often exhibited by counselors who are unaware or deliberately unconcerned about using a client to serve their own needs. A counselor who does not meet his own inadequacies head-on, who is not concerned about development and does not continually re-evaluate personal performance, very often structures (manipulates, uses) a situation to serve personal ends. The answer to inadequacy is not avoidance or "faking" it. The answer is competency. Most unethical practice in counseling is a direct function of a lack of competency.

One day you will be fully competent in ten times as many areas as you are today as a counselor; you will be a pro. Evaluate yourself with this in mind, within the time limits (agreed: very short) of the quarter. Do not use "others" as yardsticks, whether they be counselors you know or fellow practicum members. Read over your log, maybe listen to early tapes, and think honestly, critically, relevantly.

Don't moralize or apologize or make excuses which no one is interested in (not even you). Say it like it is.

Produce a carefully written, professional statement: a typed, double-spaced, three-to-five-page evaluation of your developmental experience in practicum. Fill it with the kind of meaningful data about yourself which, a year from now, or two or three, will tell you how far you have come.

5

Counseling
the Reluctant Client*

Most professional helpers agree that the establishment of an appropriate relationship is crucial to success, particularly in individual counseling. In his early work, Rogers (1942) saw the client's wish for help as an important factor in successful therapy. While Carkhuff (1969) provided a much needed breakdown of the components of helping relationships and systematically detailed the stages that counselors must pass through on the way to problem solving, he carefully prefaced his approach to "helping technology" with "The person with a problem seeks help [p. 35]."

Similarly, Combs, Avila, and Purkey (1971), in discussing the formation of helping relationships, specifically mention voluntary interaction and dialogue with the helper as a critical component in the helping process. The behavioral counseling model has an implicit assumption that the client is willing to enter into an agreement for promoting adaptive behavior (Krumboltz & Thoresen 1969). Indeed, each of the basic counseling approaches and theoretical positions include a degree of counselee volition as a postulate of effectiveness. Yet a gross number of clients continue to find themselves in counseling encounters in which they have no desire to be cooperative.

The Reluctant Client

In the writings on psychotherapy and in much of those on counseling are many discussions of resistance to professional assistance as an elusive but pervading element that resides deep in the psyche of almost everyone. Certainly, writers say, resistance is manifest in cases where some behavioral or emotional pathology exists. Redl (1966), for example, sees it as an omnipresent phenomenon: "Resistance is an unavoidable process in every effective treatment, for that part of the personality that has an interest in the survival of the

*Reprinted with permission from *The Journal of Counseling Psychology,* May 1973, Volume 20, Number 2, pp. 240-246.

pathology actively protests each time therapy comes close to inducing a successful change [p. 216]."

Counselors ought to be able to recognize the forms that resistance takes and should have an appreciation of its primacy in many of the counseling relationships into which they enter, although it comprises only one part of a description of the reluctant client. Reluctance, as herein understood, refers to involuntariness—to the prospective client's not wanting to be a client in the first place. Reluctance to receive counseling is not seen as an indicator of resistance nor of pathology. Indeed, often it may be the most reasonable and realistic approach for a client to take, a sign of social and psychological health.

In this discussion Beier's (1952) definition of the reluctant client is, by broadening it, acceptable: "An individual in whom resistance toward giving up symptoms and substitute gratifications is greater than his desire for help [p. 332]." Also included under the rubric of reluctant client herein is any individual who, if given a choice, would avoid having contact with a counselor, let alone the imminent counseling, and any individual who, for whatever reason, cannot admit that he desires counseling nor even that he secretly believes such an experience would be of value.

A large proportion of students who visit school counseling offices come under this umbrella of reluctance: (a) students referred for "academic counseling" or for transfer to another class; (b) discipline cases of every description who are "sent" to their counselor; (c) students who have been isolated by the counseling staff for special assistance by displaying such behaviors as poor attendance, grade failure, possible drug use, and adjustment difficulties; (d) those with signs of being potential school dropouts; and (e) those who underachieve. From clients in each of these global categories the counselor will encounter an observable flare of reluctance when he offers his services. In fact, the concept of the self-referred client in an overwhelming number of school settings is almost mythological. The norm more likely is typified by the school counselor who spends most of his or her time dealing with students who demonstrate some measure of reluctance to the counseling process, even when that process takes the form of a one-shot, quick session that focuses on a specific problem resolution.

But the involuntary client syndrome extends well beyond the school setting. Prisoners who have "counseling" prescribed as a necessary part of their sentence or whose parole consideration is contingent on counseling are examples of reluctant clients. Marriage counseling practice is a fertile arena for viewing the reluctant client. Marriage partners required by the court to attend counseling sessions as a condition for obtaining a divorce often are prime examples of reluctance. Similarly, counselors in community agencies spend a considerable amount of time in working with court-referred clients or children who have been sent for help by well-meaning parents. Many counselors in employment agencies work with clients who are interested in getting a job but who have a record of unemployability and who only reluctantly subject themselves to the well-intentioned efforts of the counselor. Most clients who agree to participate in counseling to please a third party are generally merely tolerant of the activity at best, and their commitment to the process seldom is earned. These are but some of the kinds of reluctant clients. His is a common species.

Forms of Reluctance

The dimension of reluctance pervades the entire spectrum of services in the counseling profession, and it may take many forms. Silence—absolutely refusing to speak—or simply nodding and shrugging as a form of minimal communication is an ordinary expression of reluctance in counseling. Hostility toward the counseling process (or the counselor) is another guise reluctance wears. Such comments as ''I wouldn't be here if I didn't have to be,'' ''I didn't ask to come,'' or ''I didn't want to see you'' are typical of the overtly hostile client.

Yet Redl (1966) reminds us that resistance doesn't have to be expressed as open anger or determined silence to be strong: ''Remember the patients who plague you, not by their outspoken hostility, doubt, and disbelief, but by overcompliance, over-expectation, and semi-phony hero worship [p. 96].''

An additional form of reluctance is manifested by the overly sophisticated client who reveals only what is expected and can anticipate counselor responses. This type of reluctant counselee is faking his way through the process, and his conditioning as a client leads him to attempt ''put-on'' games. Similarly, both the overly solicitous and the excessively agreeable client often represent a serious kind of unwillingness to cooperate; these client approaches to counseling are frequently symptomatic of resistance to looking honestly at one's self or one's behavior.

A client may have a number of concerns but is reluctant to parade any except those of low priority, cleverly hiding the most important. His reluctance takes the form of diversionary excursions, trips down numerous byways of great insignificance. Reluctance can take the form of defensiveness, of taking the focus off the self, of avoidance, of an out-and-out refusal to accept the notion of need for any kind of counseling in the first place.

Clearly, resistance to counseling may take many shapes. Although open hostility, noncooperative silence, strained civility, defensiveness, avoidance, even silliness are among the most obvious examples of reluctance, the counselor should not be fooled by seemingly positive behaviors (agreeableness, compliance, or the eager advice seeking evidenced by some) that may indicate a more difficult, because more creative or subtle, kind of counseling resistance.

Why Are Clients Reluctant?

While an understanding of the sources of uncooperative behavior in clients does not automatically suggest the means for overcoming reluctance, it behooves every counselor to be aware of them. Clients are reluctant for many reasons that are singular, even guardedly personal, but broad causal categories crop up repeatedly.

An involuntary client, for example, faced with the probes of a well-meaning counselor, must make some decisions about himself. In most counselors' offices in order to be a client he must admit to some weakness, the price he pays for counseling. "What is your problem?" many counselors begin. He is forced to admit to another person and to himself, which is often harder, that he is less than acceptable in a given area of his life. Acquiescing to the counseling enterprise can become symbolic of failure by his having to internalize the notion, "I'm inadequate." Reluctance becomes a shield against this kind of assault on one's sense of well-being.

The involuntary client commonly has been referred by a third party, and a cooperative demeanor is an open admission that this party knows more about the client than he himself does. Hence, a mind-set of reluctance will disprove the notion that the person responsible for the client being in a counseling setting was, in fact, correct. This is another example where counselee obstructionism is a defense (often fully warranted) against surrendering to the implications of a diagnosis or value judgment of a referral agent, be that person a teacher, parent, psychologist, or government official.

Some reluctant clients have negative attitudes toward counseling because they are waging a constant skirmish with the "system." Many referred clients are almost professional system disrupters who discharge a major bulk of their psychic energy in such activity. Being a rebel is a way of life and not a particularly unproductive one. Rebels often arrive in front of counselors because they may threaten the status quo of those persons who identify with the system in its present form and who seek not so much to help an individual but rather to protect their own position in the hierarchy. Thus, boat rockers are perceived as unhealthy and need counseling. The counselor, thus confronted, remains the institutional representative of the system, the eminently distrustful authority figure by virtue of his very role, the one who is paid to straighten out conscientious objectors. For most rebels, whether full flowered or just budding, cooperation in counseling implies yielding to a value system that is anathema to their own.

In searching out the causes of reluctance, we should remember that the act of being nonconformist or uncooperative is an avenue for acceptance in certain circles. The acting-out student gains peer attention and, frequently, approval. Similarly, the aggressive student adopts recalcitrant behavioral strategies and militant tactics of one kind or another as a means of gaining dominance, awe, acceptance, or a higher place in the pecking order. The presence of the same behavioral characteristics may quite naturally and unremarkably carry over into the counseling interview. What are ordinary adaptive and functional behaviors in the client's world frequently are perceived by counselors as maladaptive and dysfunctional resistance to the helping process.

Failure with Reluctant Clients

Any experienced counselor trainer has learned that reluctance, when overtly displayed, constitutes a general source of panic for counselors in the beginning stages of professional development. When confronted by reluctant clients, beginning counselors almost always are ineffective in establishing a productive relationship and in setting and achieving counseling goals. Such ineptitude has many causes but a predominant one is that counselors often are inclined to project the client's reluctance onto themselves personally and thereby feel rejected. Apparent hostility, silence, or other manifestations of unwillingness immediately are interpreted as devaluation of the counselor as an individual. The counselor's thinking follows this peculiar form of internal logic: "My client is not cooperating. He's rejecting me. He doesn't like me. There must be something wrong with me. I'm doing everything I can to establish rapport and be warm and accepting, but he's not buying it. He can't relate to me. I'm probably not the right kind of person."

Such errors in thinking stem from the inability of the counselor to accept his client as he presents himself, thereby allowing his client to be reluctant. This involves having a set of expectations for clients that when not fulfilled represent disappointment. To the extent that the counselor is unable or unwilling to accept a reluctant client and contracounseling behaviors as belonging to him without declaring either the client or himself persona non grata, the counselor probably will experience frustration and failure in his helping efforts.

Many counselors harried by time and the pressures of an institutional existence display obvious impatience with uncooperative clients. The impatience often signifies an unwillingness to accept the client or an inability to understand him in his present involuntary status. Many counselors ignore the immediacy of the reluctance, becoming in turn reluctant themselves to identify what is happening in the relationship, avoiding mentioning the resistance or pretending it doesn't exist. The impatient counselor commonly becomes irritated at his clients, and such slightly veiled anger is communicated through body language and other clues when the client won't agree to do what the counselor insists is necessary in order to get straightened out.

Perhaps counselors see overt reluctance in their clients as causing role conflict. Being warm and accepting (wrongly construed as liking and making overtures of friendliness) to many counselors means they cannot be forthright and focus on here-and-now behaviors. Unfortunately, the counselor who experiences this role conflict is saddled with frustration and tends to hope that the resistance will disappear without having it mentioned. When trying hard to be likeable and the efforts to care a lot don't work, the most common result is that the counselor gives up on the reluctant client in favor of working with those who are more "cooperative"—more responsive to his efforts.

Many counselors fail with reluctant clients because, just as most people in our society, they are not good at handling negative feelings, their own or those that surface in others. The usual counselor response to the negativism that so many clients bring to counseling is placation, throwing oil on troubled waters, an effort to return the client to an unthreatening state of neutrality or to induce positive feelings. Rather than deal with negative feelings, the counselor tries to change them, avoiding or redirecting rather than working through the emotional reality of his client.

Probably the saddest reason for counselor inability to be effective with reluctant clients is that few training opportunities exist where the counselor can acquire the skills and competencies needed to deal with counselee reluctance. Specialized training designs for role working the various symptoms of reluctance in counseling sessions combined with practicum and internship experiences of working through client resistance are absent from most counselor training and inservice training programs (Dyer & Vriend 1973).

Strategies for Counseling Reluctant Clients

After noting resistance, the effective counselor automatically looks first to himself for his own reactions and consciously strives to avoid

99

feeling as though he is the target of the reluctance by virtue of his own projection. Internalizing the reluctance through a process of self-reproachment is a self-defeating counselor behavior that follows a neurotic line of reasoning such as, "My client must approve of me, cooperate with me, and live up to my expectations or I will not like myself as much. If I don't get this client to move in the direction I think he should, then I am failing at my work. Why does he obstruct me?"

The effective counselor questions the source of the reluctance. What rewards does this client receive from his obvious resistance? Is this behavior typical for this person? Despite his overt rejection of my helping efforts, can I allow him this behavior and continue to accept him as a person of worth who can be taught to benefit from counseling? Is the resistance due to my being a symbol of authority? Would he see cooperation as an admission of his own weakness? Does resistance protect him from having to admit it? These questions help the counselor to avoid the trap of projecting the client's reluctance onto himself, thus creating strong possibilities for ultimately giving up on the client.

An effective counselor also develops techniques for reflecting the feelings of reluctance, thereby directly confronting and focusing on the barrier to productive counseling movement. Dealing with the reluctant behavior as it is manifested, rather than ignoring it, communicates to the client that (a) his feelings are acknowledged and understood, (b) counseling is not a process that pretends that feelings do not exist, (c) counseling does not avoid feelings, (d) the counselor has an integrated personality and is strong enough to handle resistance in any form without being personally threatened, (e) by looking at the client and his behavior openly and directly the counselor is full of attention and respect for the importance of what is going on in him and his world, and (f) the counselor is capable of avoiding moralization by showing the client that he is entitled to his behavior, even when it is antisocial, ineffective, and does not have the impact it was generated to produce.

Effective counselors also use the technique of interpreting reluctance, particularly in stages following the identification of such behavior. Reliable interpretations of silence, hostility, or excessive acquiescence tend to (a) provide the client with greater self-understanding, (b) demonstrate counselor competency and capacity as a resource for further help, (c) help the client learn the nature and causes of his own resisting behavior, (d) teach the client that counseling is not a one-sided effort in which one party does all the work, and (e) show the client that counseling does not skirt behavior just because it makes most people feel uncomfortable.

100

Solid interpretation reveals that the counselor is not intimidated by outward signs of resistance. Productive interpretations, of course, flow from particularized behavioral data that arise in a specific context, but it is possible to cite a few models here:

- Your reluctance to get involved in this self-help program may be your way of saying I'm afraid of being all I can be.
- Perhaps this very kind of hang-back behavior hurts you most in those areas you would like to improve.
- Perhaps your silence helps you to stay as you are and avoid taking the risks that will result in change?
- Not talking about it may be your way of protesting the whole system.

If counseling is viewed as developing through successive stages, then the exploratory stage, almost by definition, ought to help reduce client resistance, providing the exploration takes the form of a mutual investigation into the client's circumstances related to the possible counseling services that can be rendered and not as an inquisition—an interrogation suggestive of third-degree tactics. By attempting to gain a window on the client's world through pertinent questions and responses related to selected background information and initial interview data associated with the client's reasons for being there in the first place, the counselor assists the client in expressing himself. Self-expression serves as a catalyst in reducing reluctance while simultaneously moving the client toward self-understanding and eventual action. The notion that involvement in the counseling process will help to assuage reluctant feelings toward being helped is basic to an understanding of the dynamics of resistance.

The counselor who sees the helping process as goal-oriented is better equipped to combat client reluctance. The counseling process, how it works, and the behavior that the two parties will engage in is a mystery to most clients. Every client has a right to understand what counseling is all about and client resistance can take the form of demanding that right. Why should the client surrender himself to what he has been conditioned to see as manipulation of himself for the sake of someone else? Explanation and demonstration of the counseling process is therefore a necessary part of effective helping. Expectant outcomes need to be detailed, mutual goals need to be arrived at (even such short-ranged goals as keeping an appointment for the second interview), and the behaviors and attitudes that impede becoming a more effective, take-charge kind of person need to be targeted early. The client who encounters the accepting goal-centered counselor, committed to helping and willing to go right to work at eliminating barriers to the mutual task, can hardly maintain his pose for long. Resistance is seriously challenged when a client is asked, "Are you ready for us to do some things together to make your current life a happier one?" Or, "Can we agree to meet for three sessions and set up a goal for the end of that time?" Or, "Can we establish as a goal that you tell all you can about yourself in relation to this kind of difficulty?"

Similarly, mutually agreed on behavior contracts are effective in contesting resistance. Even simple contracts to stay for 30 minutes, return one time, or write down feelings are steps that involve the client in the helping process and allay inchoate or conditioned resistance.

An absent client can hardly be counseled, so until the counseling process begins to make a positive difference, the counselor needs to be resourceful. A productive assumption in converting involuntariness into a commitment to be counseled is that any client's chief interest is himself. The counselor's repertoire for providing clients with self-data is extensive; psychometric devices can produce comparative information about the client's interests, attitudes, aptitudes, scholastic achievement; audio- and videotape feedback are potent reinforcers for continuance in counseling; multiple and peer counseling arrangements often succeed better as ice breakers than does a steady dose of dyad counseling; even programming a client for a pleasurable noncounseling-related experience in exchange for more counseling can be effective with certain clients. The effective counselor strives to "get a handle" on the reluctant client. Until he achieves the goal, more advanced efforts are usually futile.

The case of the reluctant client, both on the job and in their training, is for a majority of counselors a painful enigma. Many a practicum student has spent the night prior to a first interview asking for divine intervention in the granting of a cooperative, talkative client only to encounter the more common client who is testy, overly restrained, feeling abused, or outright hostile. The fledgling counselor seldom forgets the sinking feelings of impotence that were engendered by his beginning struggles to be effective.

Effectively dealing with reluctant clients might be the most important overall competency that counselors can develop. Involuntary clients may well account for the majority of counselor caseloads throughout the land, and most counselors might sense success only with the submissive minority of those they are being paid to serve. In contrast to helping only the willing, self-referred client, the mandate to develop the professional skills necessary to help the alienated client is clear. Abraham Lincoln could just as easily have been talking about the reluctant client when he said that God must have loved the common people because he made so many of them.

References

Beier, E.G. Client-centered therapy and the involuntary client. *Journal of Consulting Psychology,* 1952, *16,* 332–337.

Carkhuff, R.R. *Helping and human relations.* Vol. 2. *Practice and research.* New York: Holt, Rinehart & Winston, 1969.

Combs, A.W.; Avila, D.L.; & Purkey, W.W. *Helping relationships: Basic concepts for the helping professions.* Boston: Allyn & Bacon, 1971.

Dyer, W.W., & Vriend, J. Role-working in group counseling. *Educational Technology,* 1973, *13,* 32–36.

Krumboltz, J.D., & Thoresen, C.E. *Behavioral counseling: Cases and techniques.* New York: Holt, Rinehart & Winston, 1969.

Redl, F. *When we deal with children.* New York: Free Press, 1966.

Rogers, C.R. *Counseling and psychotherapy.* Boston: Houghton Mifflin, 1942.

6

Analyzing a Counseling Interview: The Tape-of-a-Tape Continuous Feedback Approach to Trainee Supervision

The ideal feedback from a supervisor to a counselor in training about his or her performance in an actual counseling session would be provided to the latter at the moment when the counselor behavior was manifested. Given the nature of most counselor training experiences, such on-the-spot, continuous feedback is seldom provided. Feedback from expert to novice is generally accomplished by the supervisor consulting with the trainee after observing an interview.

Postinterview feedback can be provided in many forms: (a) the trainer can discuss with the trainee in a conference the notes the trainer has made while observing the interview; (b) the trainer can listen to a tape recording of the interview and comment directly onto the same tape at the close of the interview; (c) the trainer and trainee can jointly listen to the recorded interview, react to the session content, and zero in on specific counselor behavior; (d) the tape of a session can be played in a group of trainees with the trainer and other trainees all participating in the postinterview analysis; or (e) the trainee could produce a typescript of the counseling session, and the trainer could then respond with appropriate written commentary. All of these procedures (and others) serve to advance counselor learnings, and each has special advantages which might determine a given selection by a supervisor. But none of them affords the kind of instantaneous feedback from which a learner could most profit: reinforcement or distortion correction at the time of performance. Videotaping procedures introduce important nonverbal variables and heighten the learning experience for the counselor in training up to a point, but they, too, lack the dimension of present moment feedback.

The concept of instantaneous feedback is a well-understood essential component of training programs requiring the development of physical skills. It is difficult to imagine pilot training, driver training, or the training of typists, to name but a few areas, as being effective without trainer-trainee interaction during the learning process. The use of modeling, simulations, films or similar audiovisual aids, or programmed learning are effective precursors to actual performance delivery, but they all lack present moment feedback capabilities, which must be introduced at some juncture if the training is to result in mastery performance.

Counseling is a highly complicated human activity, perhaps the most challenging and difficult that any person could set out to learn. Becoming an expert in counseling, mastering all of the endless skills and strategies, learning the infinitude of ways in which human beings have incorporated and manifest self-defeating behaviors and how these can be traded for self-enhancing alternatives through effective counselor interventions—this is a lifetime professional development undertaking, one which only *begins* in a training practicum. Having an effective practicum training experience, however, is therefore all the more important, for it provides the fundament upon which later experience is added, against which it is tested. Any training procedure which solidifies, broadens, or increases the value and summation of learnings of the practicum base within the time, staff, and facility limitations, any which is more efficient, more productive, more direct and telling, ought not to be ignored by counseling practicum designers.

The deficiency of a lack of present moment feedback to counselors in the act of counseling is currently being circumvented by the use of a technological aid, a "bug-in-the-ear device" which allows a supervisor to cue a counselor. It consists of a transistor radio which is set on a particular FM band, an earplug which is worn by the counselor and attached to the radio in the counseling cubicle, and a wireless microphone set to the same band which is used by the supervisor as he observes the interview behind the one-way mirror. The system allows for a host of interventions on the part of the observer. The creative possibilities are endless. This technological innovation promises to revolutionize the training of counselors in much the same way as interview recordings did in the early 1940s and as one-way mirrors and audio- or videotapes continued to do in the decades following. It has already been thoroughly researched and systematized into an effective training procedure by Wilbert J. McClure (1973), whose doctoral dissertation details all aspects of the system and specifies a number of creative ways the device can be used.

McClure's findings are amazing. Virtually no resistance to the employment of the absentee-cuing system was found to exist in either the counselors or their clients, and in every case the procedure accelerated counselor skill development more than any other training practicum component. The "bug" has also been used experimentally in the training of group counselors (Cohn 1973; Vriend 1973). It would appear that this device and the training systems which incorporate its use will become regular practice in counseling practicums, for the problem of how to provide present moment feedback to counselors while they are actually counseling is thus effectively resolved.

Tape-of-a-Tape Use in Counselor Training

The foregoing discussion has been presented in order to place in context a training method which achieves penetrating feedback goals. In the absence of wireless microphones and implanted ear receivers, counselor trainers can still provide far more useful feedback to student counselors than has been accomplished by them in traditional postinterview evaluation sessions in the form of written or oral data about recently completed counseling interviews.

Recognizing that postinterview critiques were often fruitless in effectively changing inappropriate trainee behaviors, we implemented the tape-of-a-tape method in order to provide a continuously running critical commentary of particular trainee counseling sessions. Two tape recorders are needed for the production of such a tape: one to play the taped student counselor interview and the other for the creation of the new tape which includes the running commentary of the training supervisor.

On tape recorder A the student counselor's interview is played. Tape recorder B is set on "Record" with a blank tape, and both tapes are begun simultaneously. Tape recorder B is played continuously for the remainder of the procedure with the microphone close enough to tape recorder A to pick up all sounds and produce a high fidelity recording. Recorder A is then stopped after selected counselor and client responses, and the supervisor talks to the trainee about his or her specific counseling behaviors. Tape recorder B records the trainee and client dialogue along with the supervisor's running commentary.

This interrupting and recording procedure may be used to provide positive reinforcement of effective counselor behaviors, to demonstrate why the client reacted as he or she did, to reshape trainee responses immediately after they appear on the tape, and to give diagnostic insights as the supervisor picks up clues missed by the beginning counselor. The trainer can point directly to the clues as they occur in the interview and show how the trainee's responses were either facilitative or otherwise. Furthermore, tape A can be stopped immediately after a client's statement to tell the trainee how the trainer would have responded. The trainer can then play the trainee's response and demonstrate within the counseling session how alternate responses might be generated from the same client data. This allows the trainee to indulge in comparative analysis and evaluation.

When the procedure is completed, the supervisor gives tape B to the trainee. The student counselor now has a complete interview interspersed with a running critical analysis of his or her counseling ability along with supervisory recommendations at key points in the interview. The trainee is then required to make a complete transcript of tape B, listing client/counselor dialogue on the left side of the transcript and the supervisory commentary on the right (see example beginning on page 109).

Although the assignment to transcribe the "tape-of-a-tape" is laborious and often meets with more than a modicum of resistance, it is perhaps the most significant and useful ingredient of this entire process. Transcribing the tape serves to (a) totally involve the trainee in his own counseling; (b) create a listening environment in which the trainee must carefully consider and record all supervisory criticism of his counseling ability; (c) create a learning atmosphere in which effective counseling behaviors are positively reinforced and ineffective trainee responses are extinguished, both on an intermittent reinforcement schedule; and (d) provide the trainee with a permanent, readable record of his counseling and the corresponding feedback from a knowledgeable supervisor.

Student Reactions to the Tape-of-a-Tape Process

The following comments are verbatim evaluations of the tape-of-a-tape supervisory feedback method from counseling practicum students who experienced it:

• Excellent technique! I really learned a lot about myself, my counseling, and my client. After digesting the tape, I really began to work on counseling in my counseling sessions. You were right. Listening to it, writing it, and typing it really forced me to internalize the feedback.

• I think this is the best type of feedback you made available to us from the standpoint of a total evaluation. I learned more about myself in that tape-of-a-tape than anything else. Great technique; need more of it.

• From the "tape-of-a-tape" the most important thing I got was that it is absolutely essential to listen and understand what the counselee is saying and feeling before trying to suggest alternate behaviors or even set goals. Typing it up was a pain, but when I was through, I had digested the whole picture, and I was determined to work on myself in the next session.

• The best thing about the practicum. A really great idea. Especially hearing you respond, after my "screwed up" efforts, with a genuine helping response. Thanks for taking the time to make one of these for me. I know it must have taken a lot of your own time.

Of fourteen students who received the "tape-of-a-tape" feedback in this practicum, all felt that the technique was exceedingly useful. Certainly, it provides a bridge across the enormous gap between the uninformed student counselor's present level of knowledge and performance and the experienced counselor trainer's acumen and repertoire of competencies in the teaching of effective counseling skills.

What follows is an actual "tape-of-a-tape" transcript produced by a counselor in training. The instructions were to record all counselor/client dialogue in the left column and *everything* that the supervisor said in the right column directly across from the counseling dialogue.

Transcript of a Tape-of-a-Tape

Counselor (Co.) and Client (Cl.)   Supervisor (Sup.)

Co: Oh, you did your homework.
Cl: Yeah, but it was a lot harder than I thought it would be.
Co: Really?
Cl: And I got more than, well, I think I got more than three.
Co: Good!
Cl: I started doing them Tuesday when I got home and I just continually thought about them. I just redid them this morning.
Co: Great! That's the purpose of something like that.
Cl: Yeah. I don't know if it's exactly what you wanted.

Sup: Okay. The first thing he says to you is that he doesn't know if it's what *you* wanted, so you probably gave the assignment in such a way that it reflected your imposing it on him rather than him coming up with it or having initially agreed upon it jointly. So that's a clue for you, to think in terms of it's not what *you* want here. "You're not doing it for me. You're doing it for yourself." You don't have to actually say that. You have to give the homework assignment in such a way or have the assignment work in such a way that it becomes a natural thing, an outgrowth of the counseling.

Cl: A lot of what I wrote down there were just notes to myself that I thought I might bring up. It crossed my mind and I wrote it down.
Co: Ha! These are great!

Sup: That's inane. It is unnecessary to label them as "great" or "wonderful" or to be giving all the superlatives. Really, I know it's a part of what you do in your teaching, but it isn't really necessary in counseling. Counseling is a businesslike relationship, and he had an assignment and he did it and that was expected. He

109

doesn't need any strokes for it. It's something that's in you, that you do regularly, and it's nice in noncounseling settings, but in counseling settings it can really get in the way, being the soft, sugary person who constantly tells people how wonderful they are. I'm not putting you down for that at all. I just don't feel that that kind of reinforcement is necessary every time somebody does something that you expect them to do anyway. Positive reinforcement is most appropriate in counseling, but your "just greats" are condescending and out of place with this adult client.

Co: Just before we hit on any of them, explain "give a shit" attitude, which you have written about here. I don't quite . . .

Cl: A lot of times, I just, I don't care what happens. I mean, I kind of like, uh . . . well, generally, I do believe what happens will happen and, uh, that I'm just not gonna do anything about it to change it or to help change it. It's almost as though I have no control over it.

Co: Kind of like . . .

Sup: All right, I would respond—I haven't heard your response yet—I would respond, "There are times in your life that you act like you don't care what happens, and what you're saying to me is that you don't care anything about doing anything about it. You've also indicated that you didn't think you have any control over it. That is, whatever will happen, will happen. Is that accurate for you and is that a way you like to live?" Now let's see what you said in response to that.

Co: Lack of motivation.

Cl: Yeah, I've, uh . . .

Sup: What you did, Claudia, was take it on to the next item on the list rather than deal specifically with the first one.

Cl: I've always had trouble motivating myself, when it comes . . . par-

110

ticularly when it comes to school-
work.

Co: You've *always* had trouble. Do
you think you will always have trouble?

Cl: Well, I don't know.

Sup: I know what you're gétting at,
but you're not doing it well. A better
way to go about that is, "You're
saying that that's something that's
always been a part of you and would
you like it to continue to be that way,
or would you like to work on it?"
You're getting a little more emotion
into your voice, or not emotion but a
little more non-monotony, more reaction into it. But to say it the way you
said it is sort of a putdown, and
you're not really interested in either
stroking or putting people down. You
really just want to label his behavior
for what it is, and you're diagnosti-
cally thinking in your head, "All
right, this is an 'I'm': he's always
been this way and I'm gonna get him
to recognize that and that he's using
that description to keep himself continuing to be that way." That's what
you're thinking, and you want him to
have that insight. The way to get him
to have that insight is to label it:
"You've always been that way.
Would you like to continue to be that
way?" Or "What do you get out of
being like that?" Or "Because
you've always done things in a certain way, you are suggesting that
there's nothing you can do about
changing that?"

Cl: I . . . it's almost as . . . well,
I've never—I shouldn't say "I never
had a goal that I've wanted to work
towards," but I guess there's a history to it. When I was in high school,
we used to get all this stuff about
what we wanted to do for a career
and everybody said, "Don't worry
about it. You don't have to decide
until you're a junior in college." I
used to think, "Wow! That's really

too bad. I'm a junior in college and I know what I want to do!''

Co: (laughs)

Cl: And I had that in mind and I went off to college and I transferred colleges after my first year and then things kind of fell apart. I just didn't study for a while, and I found myself on probation and, uh, I got off probation after a few years. I went into the School of Business. I applied and I was accepted.

Sup: You're laughing. I don't know if that was deliberate or what. But it doesn't seem like the appropriate time to be laughing. I thought maybe the first one wasn't a laugh, but sort of like a giggle. Wonder what the purpose of that is and whether or not it's planned and if it's not, what are you getting out of doing that yourself, Claudia?

Cl: I pulled some grades to stay in, and I just kind of stopped studying. I just was concerned about having a good time. That's always been my primary concern. And, uh, then I found myself having problems with the draft and all sorts of things. Then I wound up in the School of Education.

Co: Wound up?

Cl: Well I . . . I flunked out of the School of Business, but I had transferred before—that's a technicality—but I transferred before I was officially told not to re-register.

But teaching wasn't my initial thing. I didn't enter college thinking "teaching." I also knew I had to get a degree, and at the time the only way I could get a degree with the draft on my back was education, a lot like many single guys my age. But I just haven't had a goal that I've wanted to work towards.

Co: Um hum.

Cl: My main goal at that time was staying out of the army.

112

Co: Before all this started happening, did you, uh, kind of think you knew what you wanted?

Sup: You're not reacting to him. You're reacting to the content of what he said, and that's not appropriate. What you want to practice doing, Claudia, is listening to him so intently that you can respond back with "you" rather than thinking up another question to elicit more information. Although you're still in the exploratory stage here, it seems to me that you're exploring unnecessarily. Let me take them one point at a time. When he came into the interview, he said things about not being motivated and not having any goals for himself and feeling that the world could just do whatever it wanted to do—he didn't have any control over it. All of which seem to be perfectly appropriate counseling areas. Then he went off into a slight history of himself and status with the draft and so on, and that's all perfectly appropriate. Then, when he laid that on you, you should have responded by saying, "So, you've been a man, a person who's been without a goal or without motivation for a long time, and this is something you'd like to begin working on now." Or "You're feeling a lack of purpose in your life and you're not satisfied with yourself at this time." Such would be like a summary facilitative response with an action orientation, the action orientation being "You're not satisfied with yourself and you'd like to move in some kind of direction." That's what counseling is all about. Instead, you're data-gathering, using gleaning as your counseling strategy, indicating that all of the things that he just said in the last 15 or 20 feet of tape don't have too much meaning. "I'm gonna ask you another question and try to get some more information out of you" is your strategy. And even if you are looking for more information, the appropriate way to get it, the effective way to get it and get the person to talk about himself, is to respond with what he just said and then toss an action lead onto it like I suggested.

Cl: When I started college, I wanted to be an accountant and I was going to be a CPA making $25,000 by the time I was 40, and then I flunked out of the School of Business, but then I don't blame them. I just kind of think that that goal became less meaningful to me. If it had kept its same meaning, I would have applied myself to attain that goal.

Co: Maybe you've been unmotivated because you've never really had anything that you weren't either forced into by circumstances or you've never had anything you really wanted to do, to accomplish.

Sup: Well, the response is all right, except you shouldn't preface it with "maybe." That means you're suggesting that you don't know what you're saying, and, also, you're putting the emphasis on circumstances and things outside of himself rather than on him. That is, you would say, "You seem to be projecting the causes of this flunking out behavior in life onto other things. Here's what I'm doing when I respond to you the way I just did. I'm saying maybe the circumstances weren't right, maybe somebody else didn't push you into doing it, putting the emphasis on things and somebody rather than on you. You behaved in the following kinds of ways, you got the following kinds of things out of it, this is what the consequences of your behavior were, and maybe now you want to reorient those behaviors so you'll have different kinds of consequences."

Cl: Basically, that's what I'm trying to say. I don't know. I guess I've always given the impression I'm carefree, have a good time, and I'll worry about tomorrow tomorrow. I still do have that attitude to a degree, but as I said before, I don't think I want to stay in the classroom, so I've got to do something where I can get out if I want to.

Sup: All right, now a response to that from me would be, "You label yourself as a carefree person, as a person who lives for today and who enjoys today and doesn't worry about tomorrow. Yet, the fact that you bring it up as a problem in counseling indicates that you're not satisfied with that and that you'd like to work on it."

Cl: Because of my past history of my lack of studying, my lack of study habits, I was freaked by some of the requirements that I have to do for my classes. To give you an example, we had a sociodrama that we had to do today, and the whole class was broken down into groups and each group had two situations to present role-playing episodes. I originally just wanted to sit back and watch the people in my group give their role-playing. I was just going to observe. There were seven in the group, so four would be taking part and three wouldn't be, and I was more than happy to be one of the three not taking part. But we drew straws, and two people would be playing the role of the counselor and one do the role of the counselee. Well, I drew the counselee's role and then I traded for the observer's role and then I volunteered for the counselor's role for a specific situation and it kinda overwhelmed me. I kinda let it get the better of me. And I was thinking about it yesterday and this morning and I kept saying, "It's not a really big thing. I should be able to handle it." And we did it and it turned out pretty good, but that's the point I think I'm trying to make, how freaked I was just by doing it.

Co: But you did it.

Sup: Nope. Inappropriate. You know that he did it and you don't respond to that. You respond to the affect of what he said, i.e., "You are a person who worries a lot about things that are going to happen and kind of put yourself down like you don't have the skills or it won't come off well and then find out that when it comes time for the pay-off, you can deliver the services. You can be effective. Yet the thing you don't like most is the anxiety that it creates in you or the worry that accompanies having to do anything." All right, that's a comment. Now, what's behind the thinking of that is "Now, if I can get him to recognize this and deal with this and talk to me about the worry, maybe he'll have some insight into his own behavior because this is one of the very things that keeps him on this level that he doesn't enjoy being on. He talks about being carefree, not doing things and being happy-go-lucky and easy-going, but he doesn't like this about himself. But he doesn't work at changing it, and the reason he doesn't work at changing is because it's so damn anxiety provoking to have to take a risk and do something in front of other people. And this involved other people not liking him or feeling a need for them to care about him, or maybe he's neurotically telling himself that he had to do it well and it has to be perfect." Whatever the cause may be, you can use this anecdote very effectively, but you don't say to him just "You did it and you should feel proud of yourself." You *label* it, as I just told you.

Cl: Yeah.

Co: You did it and that's the important thing.

Sup: That's not the important thing

116

in counseling. What you've just done, when you said, "You did it and that's the important thing," is that you've denied all of the feelings that he just told you about having and how they debilitate him from being effective and how they'll continue to do that. He was forced to do this in one way, but how much initiative is he going to take when he thinks about the anxiety about having to worry whether it's going to go well or whether other people are going to like it or not. And if you reinforce the idea that just because he did it once he can do it again and not deal with the things that are operating on him that keep him from doing it, you really have denied all of his feelings about what he just told you.

Cl: Got quite good at it, too.

Co: Did you enjoy it?

Sup: Doesn't make any difference. It has no relation to whether or not he enjoyed it. The point you want to get on is the debilitating feelings in him or the self-defeating behavior that's in him. You don't want to reinforce all the good things that he did; you want to label the behavior that was ineffective for him so that you can begin working on that in your counseling.

Co: Now, you were doing it before . . .

Cl: I, uh . . .

Sup: He just told you that he enjoyed it while he was doing it and got something out of it, so it's a redundant question, one designed to make him feel good rather than to make him grow.

Cl: I could have enjoyed it more. I was thinking too much of how the other people were reacting while I was doing it. I could have enjoyed it more, if I could have blocked out everything . . .

Sup: There's a clue for you. He was thinking about others and worried about what they would think. That's an indication of one of his difficulties, that he does put too much emphasis and concentration on others.

117

Cl: . . . and was thinking about how much better I would be doing if I was alone with the counselee.

Co: Yeah, that's an impression that I got last time we talked and you bring it out again. You really seem to care an awful lot about what the other person is thinking about you.

Cl: Yeah, I do. I didn't used to, or I didn't used to admit that I do.

Cl: And it bothers me because I shouldn't be that concerned about what other people think. If I'm good at what I do, no matter what it is, it doesn't matter what other people think. And I think that basically, as a teacher in social studies, I have no qualms whatever. I'm confident that I can do a good job and that I will do a good job, but other than that, I don't know.

Co: What about last week: you said that you feel that you treat . . .

Co: . . . the kids in school fairly and that you don't get the same kind of treatment back, or they don't pick

It's a hypothesis that you have in your head, and you find that he just reinforced it.

Sup: Okay, you've got him on the thing that you want to get him to deal with now. How does that work against him? He's given you one example of where it might have worked against him, but didn't. He didn't let it, because someone else told him not to—the instructor in the class. You should look at the things that happened and how he brought it about, rather than how you brought it about. In introducing it, you said, "I get the impression," and that's a wasted kind of thing. You just label what it is: "You spend a lot of time being concerned about what other people think."

Sup: You didn't respond to what he just said. You went on to something else, establishing a connection from the past. He just gave you some important information about himself, and you're ignoring it and going on to something else.

.

that up in you, so they don't give it back.

Cl: Too many of them. Yeah, that's it generally. That's one of my complaints about teaching and I think that I can probably . . .

Co: Um hum. That's a hard situation to try to work on, caring about what other people think, because you have to realize that you're teaching for the benefit of the kids, so you really have to be concerned with how you're coming across, because that's why you're there.

Sup: You're giving him a lecture that's absolutely not necessary, and you're defending him against his own neurotic thinking. He's not even talking about himself as a teacher. He's really talking about himself as a person, and he can't get out of the bag about being concerned about what other people think about him. And you're telling him "Well, it's hard to do, especially when you're a teacher because you have children and you have to be concerned about them and you want them to be concerned about you." And all that does is reinforce the idea that he can continue to behave that way in all areas of his life, and you tell him "It's difficult and that's okay. You're a good boy anyway." That just doesn't work. It isn't hard to work on that at all. You can give him specific kinds of thinking and behavioral assignments that will change that right away.

Co: They think of you as a person, or what they're getting from you as a teacher? And that is what you're concerned about as a teacher? How you're coming across as a teacher in your content, in your explicitness, but not what they think of you as a person, because you're not concerned with that?

Sup: But he is, and you're denying that. And this lecture about separating him out from his "teacherness" and his personhood is really very

Cl: I don't care what the kids think of me as a person, or I didn't use to, and if I do, I'm trying not to. I'm aware of that feeling.

Co: How are you trying not to?

Cl: Just the way that I teach.

Co: Like?

Cl: Well, in my social studies class last semester I didn't worry about that at all, what they thought of me personally.

Co: And were you satisfied with how you were?

Cl: Yes, but in the English classes, I was concerned . . .

Cl: . . . about survival. So if they liked me personally, it was the only way that they as a class and me as a person could survive together in the classroom. Since I felt so uncomfortable and so incompetent as an English teacher, I couldn't expect them to like or respect me as a teacher because I was almost nonexistent in that role. So to survive, they had to like me personally.

Co: Do you think that's right, now that it's over?

Co: Do you think that was the right way to handle the situation?

Cl: Uh . . .

Cl: Yeah, I think so. I think that if they didn't like me personally it probably would have been a disas-

foolish. A person *is,* and all the things that he does just contribute to what he is, so while he's a teacher and he's a husband, or whatever it may be, it doesn't make any difference.

Sup: Instead of saying, "How are you trying not to?" a more effective way to go would have been: "You're trying not to in specific kinds of ways. Can you give me some examples?"

Sup: Your intervention turns out to be inappropriate.

Sup: What has rightness got to do with anything, Claudia? Right or wrong is irrelevant. Is it effective for him? Does it work for him? Does he get anything out of it? These are more important kinds of things to be thinking.

Sup: Substitute "effective" for "right."

trous classroom situation, because I couldn't handle it and there would have been no classroom control.

Co: You approve of how you handled it. Okay, but can you think of another way that may have given you the same results?

Cl: Uh, yeah. I could have prepared myself better for teaching the course.

Co: Okay. How about the first day you walked in there? What could you have done?

Cl: I don't know. But the first day I walked into class . . .

Sup: I don't think you've identified what it is that he's done inappropriately or ineffectively. He said he's satisfied with it, and you're talking about having him do something differently. Are you trying to get at not having him worry whether these kids like or don't like him as a person? Because he's saying that's part of his teaching strategy and that's something that's necessary for him. That is, "In dealing with the kind of kids that I deal with, relating to them and having them see me as a total person is more important than having them see me as knowledgeable about English." So, I'm not sure what you're trying to get him into changing. How much more appropriate it would be to look at the inconsistencies between the things he says now and what he said earlier. The business about being a teacher in a school: He talks about not caring and not being concerned about whether the kids like him as a person or not. Then he says, "But I didn't use to, anyway. I do now." So there's an inconsistency there. And then the business about the sociodrama that he acted out in class, being so concerned about what the people were thinking about him at that time. There are inconsistencies there that you can point to.

Cl: . . . did pretty much what I do for any class: go through my stand-

121

ard classroom procedures, setting the classroom rules, what I expect from them, and what they can expect from me.

Co: Do you think you gave off an air of confidence?

Cl: The first day? I don't know, I don't know.

Sup: Okay, I'm gonna stop it at this point; we've almost got 300 feet. What I think you've got to really label for him is the things that you notice about him and whether or not he likes that about himself. He talks real low. It's very hard to understand him. He talks very slow and slurry. He has a lackadaisical kind of appearance to him. He looks lots of times like he's half high and is into not caring much about anything. And he's even reflecting some of these things, which you might be observing, and the behavioral kinds of things in his life. He hasn't really done much. He's flunked out in one instance. He has kind of a "don't give a shit" attitude about almost everything, and that's reflected in all areas of his life. And now he's saying to you—he's trying to say to you—that he doesn't like that about himself. He'd like to work on presenting a little more confident image, a little more motivated image, and you are not taking him down the path toward understanding. First of all, exploring, then understanding, then developing alternatives and changing. He came in at the very first minute with homework assignments that he had done, and you didn't deal with them at all. What kinds of things happened to him as a result of the homework, and is he going to reinforce it and continue it? You kind of ignored it and let him take it down a teacher path, really an almost nonproductive path. I think if I'm going to give you specific counseling feedback about yourself, it would be to get you to listen better and, instead of trying to think up another question, to design a response that gets at the affect of what the person has just said and communicates it back to him in an action dimension. That would be one. And two, it would be to not be so agreeable. You think up questions in order to be kindly to your client, rather than "How can I effectively intervene in this person's life to help him to go someplace?" Goal orientation is very important when you get a client like this who's just kind of rambly. Not to give him accurate feedback about what's going on is to abuse him. Another thing: rather than your laying on insights for him, have strategies for helping him come to the insights. That is, you don't tell him that he's into approval-seeking and worrying and being concerned about how others feel about him: you design interventions which get him to see that. "Approval, other people worrying about you, being concerned about you. Now, how can I get you to have that understanding? Well, in the group sociodrama thing that you were required to do in one of your classes, you lived with a whole lot of anxiety. That anxiety is a part of you and something you'd like to get rid of. Do you have any idea what you get out of that? Where that takes you and what the cause of that might be? I have some hypotheses, but I wonder if you could share what you get out of that, why you do that, and what's maintained that in you all these years?" and you help him to see that "Hey, maybe it's I'm just so concerned about whether these people are gonna like me or not like me. Maybe even his whole appearance and lackadaisical and easygoing, cool kind of attitude might be an attention-getter for him, might be a way of getting other people to pay him some regard. He might be very deliberately doing that. And you know in your own diagnostic heart that any behavior which is designed to get other people to pay attention to you and care about you all the time is neurotic or is certainly unhealthy, even if it's nonconforming behavior. The self-actualized person's nonconforming behavior is natural for him, behavior that he doesn't think will draw him attention, whereas the neurotic's behavior of deliberately seeking out people's attention, either by gauche behavior or really boring behavior or trying to be just the opposite, still has the same unhealthy goal in the end. That is, to get other people to notice me and give me attention. So think about these things and lay them on. I don't think it's a bad interview, Claudia; I think it's much better than the first or second interview that you did. I think you're getting rid of some of your second-grade teacher behavior, but there's still a lot of it overlapping with your positive reinforcers all the time and how wonderful and how happy you are that somebody's doing something. Remember, you're delivering a service and you're not there to feel good or get happy or any of those things. You're there to provide help for this person.

References

Cohn, B. Absentee-cuing: A technical innovation for training group counselors. In J. Vriend and W.W. Dyer (Eds.), *Counseling effectively in groups*. Englewood Cliffs, N.J.: Educational Technology Publications, 1973. Pp. 276-280.

McClure, W.J. The absentee-cuing of counselors: An evaluation of extended and abbreviated cues and various effects of the system upon clients, counselors, and trainers. Unpublished doctoral dissertation, Wayne State University, 1973.

Vriend, J. A fully equipped computer-assisted group counseling research and training lab. In J. Vriend and W.W. Dyer (Eds.), *Counseling effectively in groups*. Englewood Cliffs, N.J.: Educational Technology Publications, 1973. Pp. 265-275.

7

A Matter of Choice*

At the core of counseling is decision making. A client making up his mind (meaning he decides to choose a course of action) is what counseling is all about. The counselor helps the client to consider the alternatives and then choose and cling to the best. Perhaps, in more thorough counseling instances, he even helps the client to apply tests of the goodness of fit of a particular choice before finally accepting a given alternative.

Ah, how we prize that goal: helping the client to make wise decisions! In our young and arcane profession it is certainly one of the cleanest, neatest, and most defensible descriptions about what it is we do. It juts out of the mysterious water like the slick top of an iceberg and it gleams in the sun.

Like the iceberg, however, the greatest part of its bulk lies beneath the surface. Wise or unwise, decisions are never made in a vacuum; they are neither isolated nor unrelated. And when we agree to recognize that fact, we have gotten into an adventure where we must, like frogmen, descend, grope around, and try to fathom the size of this gelid underwater giant.

There is even some pressure upon us to do so. Are we living easily with our thoughts about our relationship to the decisions made at My Lai or at the trial of Lieutenant Calley? Or our relationship to the authorities' (our?) decisions made at Kent State University, Jackson State College, or New York's Attica State Prison (where the lives of nine hostages and 28 prisoners quickly became a new layer on the stockpile of vile carnage which we carry around in our collective consciousness)?

More and more, we who are concerned with the making of wise decisions (if anyone) surely must explore and struggle to understand the looming immensity beneath the sharp silhouette of the iceberg's peak. To do less is to be underwhelmed; and to do as much is to look again at the spare center of ideas in existential philosophy.

*Reprinted with permission from *Rehabilitation Counseling Bulletin,* June 1973, Volume 16, Number 4, pp. 239-243.

Existentialism Revisited

Existentialism, more than any other, is the philosophy of our time. It is strange, therefore, to discover that it is not a philosophy at all (in the sense that a philosophy is a rational system wherein imponderables are pondered upon conclusively, and conclusions are subordinated, classified, and so ordered that mystery is answered), but rather a heading under which are grouped the writings of many men who are, or have been, in opposition to the philosophies of philosophical systems of previous epochs (Kaufmann 1956). Existentialism is not so much a system as it is a frame of mind, an outlook for coping with the press of life. Indeed, in the fullest sense it may be conceived of as a way for the individual to be most intensely alive.

Historically, existentialism evolved from two philosophical statements: Dostoevsky's observation that in the absence of God anything is possible ("all is permitted"), and Nietzsche's proclamation that God is dead. Dostoevsky was a prophet: A paperhanger managed to hypnotize the world and foreswear the real death of six million Jewish human beings. And, if this were not enough of the "anything" that is possible, an atomic explosion at Hiroshima made the point more dramatically on the stage of the world. These occurrences were the acting out of man-made decisions—those of Adolf Hitler and Harry S. Truman, respectively, each of whom absolved himself with the palliative that he had the good of the many, or at least the most important, in mind and heart.

Were these two men responsible? Yes and no. Yes, they were indirectly the cause of the acts by their decisions to bring them into being, but the masses of men who sustained them in power, who endorsed and executed their decisions—this collection of backers without whom there could have been neither act—continued to reinforce, to reaffirm the decisions, to redecide, until all were implicated. Fate had not intervened; no divine hand had reached down; nothing in nature had precipitated either "anything." Man's decision had superseded God's and Satan's.

Such is the reasoning about life and death in the latter half of this century which gives to existentialism a heavy philosophical priority. Responsibility for his actions and their consequences lies with man, each man and all men, for men choose their destinies piece by piece. Neither Hiroshima nor the death of six million Jews were chance happenings, nor were the deaths in the American riots of the sixties, the My Lai massacre, the Kent and Jackson State shootings, or, most recently, the police invasion of Attica prison. For the godless secular world there must be a rational peace, if the world and its most highly evolved species are to endure.

Jean-Paul Sartre is the writer most responsible for the dissemination of the concept that existence (being) precedes essence (that which makes a thing what it is). Of course, the concept is not new; Plato believed in a reversal of the concept, while Aristotle did not agree. The idea of becoming, of potentiality, is at least as old as the classical Greeks. What is refreshing, and demanding, about Sartre's molding of the concept is his emphasis upon conscious choice—our essence, at any given time, is the sum of our previous choices. Indeed, the very notion of consciousness is defined by choice. A man who loses the power to choose loses consciousness. He loses self-control and can claim a loss of sanity. Even when we do not know *why* we choose, even when we have no specific end in mind, even when by any standard our choice is a bad or harmful one, we choose, nevertheless. And in choosing we create our essence.

Meaning for Counselors

For the counselor the implications of these existential precepts can be nothing if not disturbing. The entire role of choice, as it is manifested in himself as well as in his client, must be dealt with by the counselor. An understanding of all the facets of choice making must occur in the counselor. He must understand the consequences of choice, the infinite number of possible choices in almost any given situation, the internal feelings which tend to predetermine choice, the external stimuli acting upon choice, the character of any given choice, the qualitative difference between "this" choice and "that" choice. The counselor must also realize all the subtle little ways in which two human beings can interact to condition each other's choices; the temporal factor involved in many choices (should choice be deferred, suspended, made now, made conditionally, made irrevocably?); and even the extent to which not choosing is itself a choice.

Most assuredly this means that the counselor must involve himself in the painful process of self-examination, not only for an understanding of his essence to this point in time, but also in all forthcoming moments and especially those in which he is interacting with a counselee.

The counselor needs to be aware of relative considerations which are beyond, but which surround, the relationship he has with his counselee. The culture in which both he and his counselee are "choosing themselves" is founded on the idea of free will. Since men choose to act in this or that fashion, to perform this or that act, they are punishable under law. Their ability to choose makes them responsible. Though we say we "fall in love," for example, and marriages are "made in heaven" and "sanctioned by God," we cannot fall out of love and marriage without social and legal consequences. In our culture most choices are ethical, and the ways we act receive approval or disapproval from almost any witness to our actions. Whatever is chosen by either counselor or client is most definitely not chosen in a womb-like void.

That there is a subliminal factor in many choices needs conscious recognition by the counselor, too. Has he not been aware that he buys more than he needs or buys other than he needs in the times he has gone shopping for groceries on an empty stomach? Has he not driven his car too fast at times when he was in no actual rush to get to a destination, just because the plethora of passing images striking his senses, the physical vibrations radiating from the wheels on the pavement to his bones on the seat, and the sense of extended power so jazzed up his psyche? Has he not intended, on more than one social occasion, to say a thing and then uttered its precise opposite? Has he not often acted upon his choice to do a specific thing just because, at some forgotten time, he has told another he would do it?

Finally, in the matter of choosing, what is the role of vicariousness (or identification, transference, or empathy)? Can we live through the choices of another and thereby receive thrills, while absolving ourselves of consequences? Can we take on or absorb the choices of another? The related process, almost the reverse of vicariousness, is projection: Can we give away our choices?

An awareness of the ponderous bulk in the murky depths of decision making need not, indeed will not, make a Hamlet of the person who counsels. The problem is not "to be or not to be," to choose or not to choose. The problem is one of taking all contingencies into account; the problem is how to be most aware. This matter of choice, when properly considered, ought not disturb the counselor committed to examining the process of interaction. Rather, it ought to help make him hypersensitive. It can enlarge his concern, his care, and his respect for his client, for himself, and for his society. It can make him mindful of awareness as a growing part of his own essence.

If the aim of the counselor is to engage in helping relationships, it then appears that being an existentialist almost ceases to be, existentially speaking, a matter of choice.

Reference

Kaufmann, W. (Ed.) *Existentialism from Dostoevsky to Sartre*. New York: Meridian Books, 1956.

Part
II

8

What Effective
Group Counseling Is
and Twenty
Underlying Assumptions

Group counseling is a helping procedure that begins with the group members exploring their own worlds for the purpose of identifying thinking, feeling, and doing processes which are in any way self-defeating. Members determine and declare to the group what their counter-productive behaviors are and make decisions about which ones they can commit themselves to work on. The group counselor helps each member set individual goals related to the replacement of undesirable thinking and behavior with more positive thinking and behaving. The counselor helps the individual members to identify significant associations, relationships, situations, self-logic, and self-performance in their current lives in which thinking, feeling, and doing are evidently self-defeating. Then the counselor helps move each individual toward self-understanding by examining why such self-crippling behavior persists and what the psychological mainte-nance system for such behavior is. This means fully answering to each counselee's satisfaction a key question: what are the positive and negative results of perpetuating the behavior which chains the client to self-defeating conduct? The counselor (or any group member acting as a helper) then moves the individual to explore ways of breaking the chain and to seek possible alternatives to self-defeating thinking, feeling, or doing. The next step in the process involves setting goals which are specific and realistically attainable for the individual member or additional members who share a like concern. After goal-setting, the individual tests proposed alternate behaviors in the group where genuine helping interventions, structures, activities, or simulations are provided. Psychological homework assignments are then mutually initiated and the member tries the new behavior in his or her personal world, outside the group, where it truly counts. In subsequent sessions, the member reports on new thinking, new feel-ings engendered by the new thinking, new behaviors, and follow-up behavioral goals which are established as a result of analysis and evaluation in the group. Such reports go on throughout the life of the group. The individual then either incorporates the new thinking and behavior or rejects them or gets recycled back for additional exploration, self-understanding, and goal-setting. The total emphasis is on the acquisition and incorporation of productive new behaviors into the self-system.

This is the definition of group counseling. While it is a repetition of the definition of individual counseling in every essential regard (see Chapter 1), it differs in that the counseling occurs among several clients, each of whom is competing for counseling service and involved in the process of helping others. Group counseling means counseling in a group setting wherein the resources are increased by the number of members in the group. In the definition, the group as a group has been given no emphasis as a mighty or mystic entity which has restorative properties unique unto itself. Nor has any focus been given to the group as an enclave which goes through stages, as though it had an independent existence apart from the individuals who make it up.

As group counseling is defined above, a number of assumptions are implicit. The most significant among these are the following:

1. *Each individual is more important than the collective.* A counseling group is an amalgamation of human beings, individual people. There is nothing magic, sacred, or beautiful about a group, nor is there anything to the notion that the group, as an entity, has any significance of any sort. The parts have significance and there is no whole. One plus one plus one plus one never adds up to two or more. The concept of synergy does not apply. One is where the counseling is always centered, although the ones change. Group counseling continues to be counseling: helping individuals to understand themselves and to learn increasingly more effective behaviors for more in-charge functioning in their personal worlds. There is no goal of helping the group to function more effectively in its own world, simply because the group has no external world in which to function.

2. *The leader is not a member of the group.* Member status within the group is self-denied by the counselor from the outset. The paramount, all-embracing characteristic which separates group leaders from their groups is that they never use the group to serve their own needs or for self-gain. Counselors are paid professionals who deliver counseling services to individuals regardless of the methods, structures, or behaviors they might employ, including counseling in a group. Counselors do not use the group to promote their own self-development or to work on personal concerns. Nor do they become player/coaches, who "play" at being members because they feel that membership status brings about more facilitative action. Any self-

references leaders might make are designed to be of particular help to a given group member or to several members simultaneously. The role of leaders is to counsel, not to receive counseling.

3. *Group counseling is for everyone.* Anyone who can admit to being able to improve in some personal way can benefit from group counseling. Whereas admission to a psychotherapy group requires the acknowledgement of some pathology, membership in a counseling group requires only the admission that growth in a number of areas in personal life is possible. The counseling group is a place where members can practice and acquire new behaviors, a supercharged learning environment where members can learn to master themselves, a place where even the most self-actualized individuals can get more out of their personal endowments. Each member is seen as "normal," not sick, regardless of how "deviant" some of the members' behaviors might appear to be in a given life dimension. For each member, the overall personal goal is the acquisition of the greatest possible personal effectiveness. The counseling group is growth motivated rather than deficiency motivated.

4. *A counseling group has no group goals.* Basketball, football, and hockey teams have group goals. Committees have group goals. Juries have group goals. Counseling groups do not. Only the individual members have goals. A counseling group has no significant end unto itself. Each person in the group is seeking ends of particular self-enhancing thinking, feeling, and doing. Any emphasis which treats the group as an entity reinforces the self-diminishing notion that the collective is more important than the individuals. Emphasis on group cohesiveness, for example, is inappropriate.

5. *Counseling individuals in groups is not only permitted: it is necessary.* Just as individual goals are stressed in group counseling, so too is individual counseling within the group. Although interaction and feedback are important, the notion that somehow the "group counsels" is ludicrous. The counselor knows how to counsel, models the process in the group, teaches members how the process works, reinforces counseling behaviors that are manifested by members, and recognizes and helps to channel whatever counseling resources individual members have. While counseling individuals is the goal nonpareil in each group session, the group leader need not be the person from whom the counseling emanates (indeed, some members tend to be more responsive to effective counseling behaviors which come from a particular member peer); but it remains the counselor's responsibility to determine if the interaction is of a counseling nature and to orchestrate what goes on. Moreover, to assume that when one person receives counseling the others do not benefit is a hypothesis which breaks down under testing. Members witness effective counsel-

ing, make applications to themselves, and internalize learnings continually. A group does not counsel or receive counseling. Individual people do.

6. *Group interaction is not a goal unto itself.* Positively correlated to the above assumption, the amount of group interaction is not a measure of counseling effectiveness. Such is the criterion of the novice counselor, not the experienced one. Group interaction for its own sake, for the promotion of involvement, is not counseling. It is far better to have only two people interacting and one person receiving help directly (and specific others vicariously) than to have eight people talking and no one growing. As a counseling group gets moving, interaction increases. Frequently, groups having the most interaction and participation ironically offer the least amount of help to each individual member. Seldom does a protagonist grow from a barrage of personal viewpoints in a multiple advice-giving forum. Client growth in a group setting comes from a sequence of specific counseling steps.

7. *The counselor does not seek to heighten natural pressures inherent in a group.* Any member of a counseling group has the right to choose to participate or not. The group leader protects the right of a group member to make such a choice and intervenes when members coerce, cajole, or otherwise seek to increase group psychological pressure on a given member. The small group, wherein no set role or task for individuals exists other than each member working on the self in personal ways, is threatening to many who have experienced nothing similar in their lives and who lack operational skills for existence in such an environment. Partly because there is a *natural* pressure inherent in the structure of a counseling group, such counseling succeeds where one-to-one counseling does not.

While nonparticipating members tend to feel that the pressure on them to participate in the counseling process is mounting as the life of the group goes on, the effective group counselor is sensitive to any such member's fears and protects the right of the individual to choose the time of entry into involvement. Each member has a right to resist changing, even though others in the group, including the counselor, have a contrary perspective. If a given member does not feel ready, denies the existence of self-destructive behaviors, or sees no merit in acquiring new self-enhancing behaviors, the effective group counselor sees this as not simply tolerable but as understandable and acceptable.

8. *A counseling group is not a confessional.* When confession for its own sake is promoted, counseling effectiveness is diminished, however much some members may relish hearing about the juicy emotional life data another member brings forth. The focus of coun-

134

seling is on present-life circumstances and what help can be provided to any individual in altering these in positive directions. Data about past living which has no bearing on present and future living is extraneous to effective counseling in a group. "Letting it all hang out" as a strategy for counseling in a group is infrequently the productive tack to take. Very often "putting it away forever," because nothing can be done about it except to feel guilty or hopeless, is the direction in which lies ballooning mental health.

9. *Gripe sessions, focusing on outsiders, having conversations, and focusing on topics constitute inappropriate group counseling content.* A strong temptation exists on the part of many group members to gripe about the "system," the "establishment," or the "institution," particularly when all members are from the same institutional setting. If grumbling, complaining, finding fault with others, and blaming are reinforced by the counselor, the group may quickly adopt this mien as a way of life, finding as they will some neurotic value in it. A feeling on the part of each individual that "I'm right! It's a lousy, unfair world, and my peers agree with me" will soon develop. Unless such activity results in political action taken to modify the environment, it has no value beyond catharsis. But a political action group is not a counseling group. When members of a counseling group engage in large doses of such activity, they leave the group having had their "blaming" behavior reinforced, their environment unchanged, and their individual coping or mastery skills underdeveloped.

The same may be said for focusing on "others" outside the group. If the others are not part of the group, they can hardly be counseled. A husband or wife, a parent, a boss, or any other person cannot be helped to be different, though in every case a group member can be effectively counseled to think, feel, and behave differently in interaction with significant others. Nor are "topics" or "interesting conversations" of any value in counseling groups. While these make engaging social intercourse at parties or on other occasions, they are extraneous to the principal business of group counseling.

10. *What goes on in a counseling group is privileged communication.* Confidentiality is the watchword of group counseling. What happens in the group belongs to its members and no one else. To the extent that others are aware of what happens in the group, its activities are limited. The effective leader establishes the extent of how privileged the communication will be at the outset. Each member's safety depends on it. If the group is an unsafe place for a member to go to work on self-change, such change will hardly come about. Breaches of confidentiality, therefore, become front and center business in the group whenever they occur.

11. *Group members speak for themselves in a counseling group.*

Independent thinking and speaking are regarded as the most healthy behavior mode human beings can adopt. Each member of a counseling group is encouraged to talk for himself or herself and to have a personal point of view or outlook. While in every group there are variations in personality, talent, intelligence, and social skills, this does not mean that the offerings or perspectives of any given member have any more value than those of any other. When a more verbal member speaks for a less verbal one, or when a member speaks for the group as a whole, the effective counselor intervenes. Psychological independence is a goal to be fostered in everyone, and the effective counselor works at helping each member of the group to achieve the greatest degree of psychological independence possible.

12. *Feelings are not emphasized over thoughts in counseling groups.* It is quite possible for group members to confront each other on a variety of levels without feeling overly emotional or "gutsy." While feelings are not devalued as inappropriate in a counseling group, neither are they considered as having mystical significance, greater in some fashion than unemotional content areas. There is no goal of "getting down to feelings" in a counseling group. Many misguided group counselors assume that there is a clear distinction between feelings and thoughts and that somehow the latter are unpalatable while the former are to be drooled over. Not so. Feelings are quite impossible without thoughts; they are physical reactions to thoughts. To attempt to separate thoughts and feelings is to induce confusion, and to insist that group members express feelings as though they are separate entities to be called upon at will is psychological folly.

Inasmuch as the overall purpose of a counseling group is to help each member work at becoming more effective in self-chosen life areas, the role of feelings inevitably must be examined. Helping a group member to understand his or her feelings, to become unthreatened by them, and to learn how to control them is an essential part of the counseling process. Having an expression of feelings, however, without specific goals for improvement is not productive in a counseling group.

13. *Group cohesiveness is not a group counseling goal.* Every counseling group ultimately seeks its own dissolution, however long its tenure. Cohesiveness takes place as a function of time and being together. People stranded in a stalled elevator for twelve hours become cohesive. There is no goal in the group counseling process related to having a cohesive, together group. All goals are for the individuals in the group, and the group itself is but a tool to help members grow, a specially designed environment for more potent

individual learning. At the end of an allotted time the group dies, but the members go on to function in their own private worlds.

Group cohesiveness occurs whether or not it is fomented, and energy spent in trying to bring it about is wasted. Should divisiveness occur in a counseling group and therefore inhibit individual member goal achievement, then it may be necessary to spend time working through the roadblock. To say that cohesiveness is not a group counseling goal is not to say that it is undesirable or an impediment to effective counseling.

14. *Session-to-session follow-up is an integral part of group counseling.* Group counseling is not composed of ten or fifteen distinct experiences. Rather, it is one experience which has continuity and follow-up throughout. A member who has gotten counseling help, who has spent a prolonged time in the spotlight, is not then forgotten for the remainder of the life of the group. Each session has degrees of carry-over from former sessions, and a monitoring of client goal achievement goes on, just as it does in effective individual counseling. While it is taxing on the group counselor to recall all the psychological homework assignments, to remember all the declared goals and all the specifics each member is working on, the counselor has the resources of many others for so doing, a feature lacking in one-to-one counseling.

In the early sessions, the effective group counselor institutes a "reporting back to the group" procedure and continues it as long as the group lasts. Brief reports, continuous intermittent reinforcements, recasting of goals, transfer of training, and the movement up a ladder of more difficult and, therefore, more desirable self-gains for every member are the hallmarks of effectiveness in counseling groups. Successful reports from those who have already benefited from the counseling stimulate others who have not become involved to the same extent. Programming follow-up reports is vital. When this is not done, the process will appear to members to be "jerky," composed of singular, isolated, happenstance cases of random help. This destroys the benefits of long-term help. Members who are continuously held accountable for working at improving their own behavior grow the most in counseling groups.

15. *In every group counseling session, one or more members receive specific counseling help.* Although most group counseling sessions contain activity that by definition would not be labeled counseling, sessions wherein individual members are not receiving some counseling tend to be less productive. Individual members receiving counseling help toward the achievement of personally determined goals is where the heart of all group counseling lies, but a number of activities supplementarily occur in counseling groups most

appropriately. The point here is that while such activities abet the counseling process, they ought not to replace counseling per se. Analyzing the process, summarizing, reviewing, working through difficulties that members experience as a part of the process, exploring for the sake of determining new directions, establishing priorites, giving information, clarifying leader behaviors—the list of ancillary activities can go on and on. But to have these activities dominate the use of the group time to the exclusion of the delivery of individual counseling is to create a nonproductive group. The early sessions are particularly important; early delivery of counseling help to specific members establishes the prime group purpose and enables all members to witness what the payoffs of membership are and how they are attained.

16. *In group counseling there is no positive correlation between member comfort and effectiveness.* Statements made in a group which signify that everyone is relaxed and comfortable are often indicators of immobility rather than progress in a counseling sense. Varying degrees of discomfort, awkwardness, and frustration accompany change toward altered thinking and behaving. Self-satisfaction and comfort go hand in hand; when people experience discomfort, change is desired. Preoccupation with helping members to relax and be comfortable is the hallmark of the ineffective novice group counselor who is probably incompetent in dealing with negative emotions in others, as well as being unable to deal with the same in himself.

To say that comfort is not a sought-after state in counseling groups is not to say that discomfort is. Promoting anxiety for the sake of group member movement is seldom effective, but dealing with anxiety that arises in a group member who is trying to change is always a part of effective counseling. Reaching the mind of an overwrought person in a teaching or learning sense or reasoning with an understandably unreasonable person obviously makes no counseling sense. It is incumbent upon the counselor of groups to become increasingly knowledgeable and expert in dealing with the emotional states that arise in others.

17. *Negative emotions are neither bad nor avoided in group counseling.* The fact that self-restricting or negative emotions are not to be avoided in counseling groups naturally follows from the last assumption. While the expression of strong feelings of an anti-social nature has no inherent value, not permitting them to surface results in no growth for members in many vital self-world areas. A placating group that shuns any expression of fear, guilt, worry, anger, hostility, depression, hyper-anxiety, venomous prejudice, hate, or revulsion (the list is virtually inexhaustible) borders on being unreal. It will become another exercise in social game-playing where the object is to

not make waves, to fool each other into believing that all can live together harmoniously for as long as it takes to do so. Most people have trouble handling disquieting emotions. In counseling groups, all can learn to acquire more effective means for so doing, provided denigrating emotions are not denied or explained away. If emotions are debilitating or psychologically immobilizing in any way to any given member (and seldom, if ever, are they not), then working at their elimination is a prima facie goal in group counseling. Without their appearance, or even a recognition of their existence, such a goal is a fiction.

18. *There is no agenda in group counseling.* Structure in a counseling group is minimized. Group members are entitled to know why they are there, what will happen, what will or will not take place. This is basic. How the process works and what each member will do to get personal payoffs as a concomitant of membership in the group is essential to member participation. But no one can predict what will happen in a given session, nor is there a program to be followed. In any given session the extraordinary number of possible ways to go boggles the mind, as any half-alert group counselor knows. The counselor has guidelines and priorities related to serving each and every member, any one of whom is equally entitled to receive the benefits of the experience, but no session can be preordained in structure or outcomes.

This does not mean that the group counselor has not carefully considered where the group has been, what has previously happened, and where her or his efforts might best be applied in an upcoming session. Group counselors plan, but they do not fall in love with their plan. Flexibility and on-the-spot assessment of what is and what can be are necessary criteria for effective counselor interventions. The absence of a specific agenda is inherent in the very notion of a counseling group.

19. *All behavior in counseling groups is neutral; it is neither "good" nor "bad."* Members frequently make statements such as, "Oh, that's wrong, isn't it? I mustn't do that" or "Was that good? Did I do it right?" Just as in life less effective people will check out with others in an approval-seeking way how they ought to behave, so too will this crop up repeatedly in counseling groups. When the counselor believes members should act in this way or that and intervenes to make this known, reinforcement of behavior which is primarily a put-down of self occurs.

In group counseling, behavior is assessed as being caused and having effects. All behavior is owned by its initiator; that person is in control of it. All behavior is manifested at some level of effectiveness, and criteria can be established to judge performance levels. Individuals can be helped to understand how the behavior can be upgraded. The effective group counselor does not like or dislike this or that behavior or individual. There are no favorite group members. The counselor operates from a mindset of objectivity and neutrality.

20. *Effectiveness in group counseling is measured by what goes on outside the group.* If members of a counseling group are behaving in ways within the group which can be judged as productive, yet in their own lives outside the group nothing has changed, all continues to be status quo or gets worse and the group counseling experience has been an abuse of the time of everyone involved. While this seldom occurs, the point is that any degree of positive meaning which can be attached to the experience must come from differences which are measured in the lives of members in their own lives outside the group. No one cares, really, whether or not the experience was enjoyable, a "gas," a bore, or whatever. If the group members received no counseling, if they were not self-enhancingly different in their own lives outside the group after experiencing membership in the group, the entire process has been fruitless, something other than effective group counseling.

The assumptions which underlie the definition of group counseling and which were delineated above are only the most outstanding. There are many more. Out of our broad experiential base as therapeutic counseling helpers, we are poignantly aware of the fact that group counseling provides for some clients an environment for self-enlarging growth of such greater potency than does one-to-one counseling that it was a resisted temptation throughout the presentation of these assumptions not to focus on the kinds of individuals and individual concerns which might most productively invite amelioration in the group counseling setting. So be it. The mission herein for us was clear-cut: Say what group counseling most viably and vitally is. In so saying, we do not want to be judged by what we have not said.

In giving our definition and presenting underlying assumptions, for example, we have ignored or only infrequently acknowledged the existence of a vast literature on groups, particularly writers about groups who in one way or another claim individual member growth as the core of the group experience. This is a conscious, deliberate choice, not one based on ignorance of the literature. The fact of the matter is that most of the writing on group counseling is repetitious; the same concepts are endlessly repeated, and most have little to do with effective operationalizing. After picking everyone's brains, after trying out anything and everything we would possibly garner from the reports of others, we were still novices, strugglers, bunglers, well-meaning do-gooders striving hard to emulate our more experienced professional brethren. The result was stultification: little progress, much frustration. As we strove hard to discover our own way, as we analyzed the experiences we had, countless hours of co-leading close to a hundred different groups of every conceivable variety, we began to lose respect for what we earlier believed as a result of our ingestation of what we had read. Reality was elsewhere. Today we are convinced that there is no substitute for experience, that there is no substitute for expertise, that one cannot become an expert by reading, that group counseling is the most neglected of all therapeutic practices, that training for group counselor effectiveness is almost nonexistent in North America (or anywhere else), and that almost everyone knowing how to do effective group counseling does not know how to write about it or is unwilling to do so.

None of the above says that there is nothing in the literature about groups which lacks value. While we have ignored or de-emphasized certain truths, this does not mean that we devalue them. In the reported results and history of the study of human behavior in small groups, for example, are learnings of great import to any counselor seeking to be effective as a group leader. Group dynamics, a behavioral science subdivision of momentous importance, is either a neglected area for counselor trainees or one given perfunctory attention. Yet, the area yields important learnings. Every group counselor ought to know, for instance, that just sitting next to a timid or fearful member in a group gives that member support, or that openly hostile confrontation will more likely occur between members who are situated opposite each other. Any counseling professional bent on becoming more effective owes it to himself to become a devourer of the writings of all predecessors. This we have done. As we have stated earlier in this book, it is never enough. Life always supersedes reading and thinking about it, and our life, no part of it, is yours.

9

Learning Group Counseling
Leadership Skills:
Twenty Specific Behaviors
for Group Leader Mastery

If conducting a counseling group involves the application of scientific principles, what are these? What are the principles and practices that would comprise a technology of effective group counselor behaviors were such a technology to be collected into a manual of operation? In this chapter, we present twenty such counselor skills, which are crucial determinants of group counselor effectiveness, ready and waiting behaviors in the repertoire of experienced professionals who know what they can do in a group and have a rationale for any intervention they might make. Implicit herein is the contention that practitioners who "wing it" or who "do what comes naturally," because they have not taken the time or expended the effort required to master the component skills of their human development craft or for whatever reason, either are not engaged in group counseling or are operating at low levels of professionalism. Far too many practitioners seeking to be helpful in groups deny that there are specific leadership skills to be mastered other than a collection of unmeasurable virtues and traits such as kindness, warmth, authenticity, openness, cognitive flexibility, empathy, genuineness, good intentions, and love. While none of these are undesirable, their relationship to effective group counseling is questionable.

In the twenty specific group counselor skills listed below, no priorities of importance or temporal ordering are presumed. Each has its own importance and each its time for use.

The first three skills are essentially diagnostic and are alike in their manifestation but different in their objectives. The effective group counselor masters the ability to identify, clarify, label, and reflect personal data which come from the group members. The counselor is not simply aware of the veritable flood of data or an observer of it, but rather a sorter of it who puts it into three clusters: emotional data, behavioral data, or cognitive data. The *when* of identifying, clarifying,

142

labeling, and reflecting emotional, behavioral, and cognitive data is impossible to specifically pinpoint, since doing so is a constantly recurring group leader responsibility. The counselor is always on the alert for "fuzzy" areas, concerns that are unclear for the group members, behaviors that people exhibit that they don't understand, avoidance of obvious feelings, and so on. Whenever group members ignore, avoid, or systematically deny emotional, behavioral, or cognitive data which are important counseling focal areas, the effective group leader engages in an identifying, clarifying, labeling, and reflecting intervention, a specific and measurable leader behavior. This involves exposing and making clear for the group members, not just for the counselor, all problem-related material which group members themselves do not pick up and deal with. It is axiomatic that the more a counselor focuses on such happenings in the group, the more proficiency he or she will acquire. Moreover, as the counselor models the identification of feelings and cognitive and behavioral data, group members will see how vital such identification is and engage in so doing themselves, a practice which the effective group counselor then endorses and reinforces.

The *why* of identifying, clarifying, labeling, and reflecting feelings, thoughts, and behaviors pertinent to the movement of individual members in a direction of positive life changes has already been explained in the assumptions underlying group counseling practice (see Chapter 8). In common life groups, people seldom have their feelings and behaviors pinpointed by others, labeled, reflected, and clarified; the natural result is that they are neither skilled at so doing nor understanding of what it is they customarily do. Life groups require that participants be polite, that displays of emotion be avoided, that deference be given, that direct and honest personal reactions be squelched, that "if you can't say something nice, don't say anything at all," that flattery and compliments make up for or smooth over deficiencies in one's self or those which crop up in others, that others be made to "feel good." Our culture conditions us to avoid the touchy, to not make waves, to become skilled in being socially dishonest for the sake of lubricating the difficult business of living together even when doing so is detrimental to our own self-interests and to our healthy mental, emotional, and social development. When a counseling group is a replication of such life groups, it is programmed to assure further entrenchment of feelings, concepts, and behaviors which are normally self-defeating for the individuals who make up its membership. The group counselor who doesn't learn the skills of identifying, clarifying, labeling, and reflecting problem-related material, emotional data, and intellectual and attitudinal data that is not being picked up and dealt with by the group members teaches the group to gloss over meaningful counseling content material, and the members end up concentrating on that which is the most comforting and the least productive for effecting group member changes.

Identifying, clarifying, labeling, and reflecting feelings. Feelings are omnipresent; they are absent in no one, ever. They are reactions to thoughts and experienced in the body, and at any given moment they take on a given shape. Facial expressions, body posture and movement, voice tonal quality or delivery pace, eye activity: these are indicators of feeling states emanating from thought processes. The more subtle physiological manifestations, such as increased heartbeat, sweating, stomach tightening or growling, nerve activity, and many, many more, are less easily observed or inferred. People feel at all times. They are high, or low, or neutral. They are bored, indifferent, or involved. They feel fearful and ready to retreat, or they feel powerful and ready to approach. The experienced counselor never loses sight of this fundamental understanding of human nature.

In a counseling group, the leader chooses to identify and focus on feelings when he or she has a rationale for doing so. In the following example, the counselor has perceived that the group members are reluctant to talk about anything having emotional overtones and sets about clarifying and labeling with this intervention:

Each person in this group appears to be afraid to talk about things that are difficult to handle. For example, when Joe mentioned the very involved problem he has in getting along with his boss, and the deep nature of his agony became apparent as his face flushed, his hands trembled, and his voice started cracking, everyone fell silent, and Jeff, you then changed the focus to something else by bringing up your decision about going to college. Joe expressed frustration, fear of losing his job, and the living hell it has become for him just to go to work every day. By running away from these feelings, we are teaching Joe, and everyone here, that we can't help someone who has a serious, emotionally laden difficulty. Jeff, were you aware that you had difficulty in talking about touchy concerns? And Joe, perhaps you could tell us more in detail what feelings go on in you whenever you think about your relationship to your boss and your job situation—not only the feelings which arise in you here but on the job and at home.

This kind of leader use of identifying, clarifying, labeling, and reflecting feelings within the group brings focus to the main business of group counseling and helps Joe, and others in the group with similar difficulties and concerns, to explore, set goals, and ultimately to come up with alternate modes of thinking, feeling, and behaving in relationship to his boss or any other troublesome individual.

A typically *ineffective* use of this counseling behavior occurs when the group leader chews out the group or otherwise neglects to label and clarify feelings.

Joe, you mustn't be afraid of your own feelings. This is a place for you to examine your hurtful emotions and get rid of them. I want everyone in the group to remember that we aren't afraid of negative feelings here and that we are not going to avoid talking about them. Now, Joe, why did you get so darned upset when you got into the business about your boss?

Identifying, clarifying, labeling, and reflecting behavioral data. People behave one way or another continuously. At any given moment, any individual in the group is behaving proactively or reactively. The astute counselor knows and understands this and is a constant learner about what particular behavior *means* as it is manifested by any given individual. The same piece of behavior—smiling, for example—might occur in one group member at appropriate times but in another member smiling occurs in an anxious way, in an approval-seeking, please-like-me-because-I-can't-stand-it-if-you-don't way, and it crops up at times which leave no doubt about its meaning.

All behavior is caused and has meaning. Understanding the meaning of any behavior is the job of the group counselor, because he is always in the position of making choices about what interventions to exercise productively. Identifying, clarifying, labeling, and reflecting behavioral data is a skill which accompanies the effective counseling of any given individual in a group in a singular sense. But it also is a skill which is applied to the group process, to the interaction among group members in relationship to each other and the individual goals they hold in common.

In the example below, the counselor has diagnosed certain pieces of behavior and shares this with the group members.

What appears to be happening here is that almost everyone wants to protect everyone else and deny some things that seem obvious to an objective observer. For example, Bob mentioned how he skips school because it's boring, and Mary suggested that maybe he didn't have the skills to avoid being bored in his life, that the responsibility for not being bored was in Bob, not in the school. George moved closer and got very intense in his defense of Bob. Susy changed her position for the first time today and complained about the lousy teachers. Georgia laughed sarcastically at Mary's suggestion to Bob, and Leroy waved his hand in disgust and disapproval. Bob, are you aware of all this rushing to your defense? Can we take a harder look at this whole area and help you to work at eliminating boredom in your life?

Frequently, inattentive counselors ignore the kind of behavioral data clarified above. Use of the skill of identifying and labeling behavioral material in the group members requires that the counselor be aware of it, that the behavior is registered in the counselor's head and its meaning ascribed. Thus, the effective counselor is skillful at attending to everything that goes on in the group. An illustration of an ineffective use of the clarification of behavioral data isn't necessary, for a counselor who has low skills in this area either defaults, which is to say that the behavior is not picked up by the counselor, or the behavior is misinterpreted. In the latter case, where counselors ascribe inaccurate meaning to perceived behavior, group members can at least react, and the counselor learns how to improve such interventions as a result.

Identifying, clarifying, labeling, and reflecting cognitive data. Cognitive data refers to thought processes and products, logical and illogical formulations, to the structuring of meaning, to analyses, to the exposition of morals, motives, values, opinions, to the ways in which group members put their perceptions and understandings into language. The process of counseling, whether one-to-one or in a group, has as a primary objective the helping of individuals to alter their mental behavior so that they make more productive use of their minds, that they think more clearly and more rationally, and thus feel and behave in more self-promoting, in-charge ways. Modeling effective thinking and communicating this is an inescapable responsibility of the counselor.

Waxing intellectual is a common way of dealing with or, rather, failing to deal with reality, and group members commonly indulge in explaining away and theorizing rather than dealing directly with matters which beg for new handling, not explanations. In the following example, the counselor focuses on the tendency of the group members to indulge in explanations by labeling their actions.

We seem to have fallen into a habit of explaining each other's behavior, something that has been going on in every session. It's almost as though, because everyone in the group is or has been married, everyone is an authority on marriage and that entitles everyone to know everything about everyone else whenever any one of you brings up any matter related to marriage. We are explaining things for each other rather than helping each person to explain himself or herself more effectively. This became particularly noticeable twenty minutes ago when Conrad talked about how he's currently relating to his wife in his marriage. Betty Lou, Cindy, and Everett then not only explained Conrad's feelings and why he acts the way he does, but they wrapped up why his wife, Becky, feels the way she does as well. Cindy, especially, indicated that she understood what was happening better than Conrad himself did. Perhaps we can explore what it means to explain something for someone else rather than attempt to help that person see for himself. Conrad, has anything been helpful to you in these explanations?

By clarifying and reflecting cognitive data and returning the focus to Conrad, the counselor moves the group back to its main business, mainly, providing counseling help to individuals. If Conrad had found some help in the explanations, this gets specified and built upon. How Conrad views his own situation and mentally processes his own life-space data will determine whatever new possibilities there are for productive change in his relationship with Becky.

A typically ineffective application of identifying and clarifying cognitive data takes place when the counselor waxes authoritative and intellectual, too, and engages in the same kind of unproductive behavior as the group membes.

146

I'm sure you're not aware of it, so I'm going to have to stop the group here and explain just what it is that all of you are doing. You all tend to explain things for each other. Now, this comes from the group moving too quickly through the exploratory stage and bypassing the understanding, and, of course, getting trapped in the too-much-action-too-soon syndrome that typifies so many counseling groups. Explaining something for someone else is a violation of someone's right to be. Maslow discussed this very point in his treatise on self-actualized people. We must guard against becoming too dependent on each other and too facile in summing up each other. Then, too, we must be concerned with our mutual roles in here related to group syntality. So, let's limit our explaining and keep our eye upon the doughnut, not the hole. Now, Conrad, do you want to continue with what you were telling us?

The point is clear. The counselor whose leadership behavior is bogged down with intellectualizations and unnecessary theorizing confounds the group members and places obstructions in the way; some members want then to discuss group purposes and dynamics or to take issue with the counselor; others become avowed skeptics of the entire process and perhaps of the leader's sanity or competency to lead. Effective group counselors avoid being mysterious and carefully monitor their own communications in the group. In their use of any identifying, clarifying labeling, and reflecting of emotional, behavioral, or cognitive material, they stick with the data, state these clearly, share their rationale for doing so, and help move the group purposively in a given counseling direction.

Questioning, drawing out, and evoking material appropriate for counseling focus. Eliciting self-data from group members which is appropriate for counseling focus is an important skill. "Appropriate" here refers to a number of factors. While there is a mountain of self-data which any member of a group could emit, only a portion of it has counseling relevance: that which has personal pertinence to the member in his or her current life. Individual counselees decide what they are willing to work on in themselves, what they are willing to change, and what risks they are willing to take. Helping each individual to explore his or her own world in search of personal areas and relationships which can be altered in positive ways, in search of thinking, feeling, and behaving which can be upgraded, is an ongoing part of counseling in a group. But this search is not without ruddering principles. Many members enter group counseling with self-identified "problems" that they are eager to work on: Their lives, in part, are being lived unsatisfactorily by their own definitions. Others discover as a result of being in a group that they can productively go to work on concerns and difficulties which they would not have labeled as such at the time of group entry. The discovery occurs principally because members get honest feedback in a group about their thinking and behaving and acquire insight as to how they can alter their own living by witnessing others alter theirs. Any effective group counselor is attentive to the self-data and behaviors revealed and manifested by each member right in the group and has formulated hypotheses about how counseling focus on that member could be self-promoting for the member. But beyond what self-definitional and behavioral data are generated in the group, the counselor understands that help could be enriched and extended for any given member whose life-space conditions and concerns are further elaborated.

Beyond that, the counselor has an understanding of what constitutes personal mastery for people and what the characteristics and competencies of the in-charge person are, and he or she then explores in the group to make assessments of functioning levels of the participants in the component areas of personal mastery.* That is, the counselor looks for how well members structure their days; how well they handle guilt, worry, fear, boredom, and anxiety; how good they are at giving and getting love; the extent to which they live in the past or future instead of the present moment; how they deal with the unknown; whether they are inert in their living or progressing in meaningful directions; how effectively and self-enhancingly they communicate; whether or not they engage in blaming, fault-finding, or approval-seeking behavior—the catalogue of important counseling focal areas can be endlessly extended.

While effective questioning and drawing out is a vital group counselor skill, overdependency on its use can be stultifying in a group, particularly when little is done with the evoked self-data. The quantity of questions asked in no way is a criterion for effectiveness. Novice counselors tend to ask silly or irrelevant questions, or they act as though they were interrogators administering the "third degree," when they are "fishing," hoping something will crop up which seems important or particularly revealing. When counselors do not model effective drawing-out behaviors, group members tend to initiate low-level questioning performances because that is what they generally are accustomed to doing in their own lives whenever they encounter new individuals and make efforts to relate to them. Group members will ask a whole series of extraneous questions simply because they do not know what else to do. Typically unproductive counseling groups are those wherein rapid-fire questioning has gone rampant. Questions, questions, questions, without reflection, interpretation, encouragement,' or focusing, is threatening as well as inappropriate,

---

*The authors have defined and discussed these components in an audiotape series (eight one-hour tapes) and delineated how they may be diagnosed in counseling and how clients can be counseled to upgrade their behavior in all component areas. The series, "Counseling for Personal Mastery," published by the American Personnel and Guidance Association, is available from APGA Publication Sales, 1607 New Hampshire Avenue, N.W., Washington, D.C. 20009.

because the one being subjected to the barrage doesn't know where he or she is being led, what is wanted or expected.

Nor does the effective counselor ever ask a question of the group as a whole. Groups cannot answer questions, only individuals can, and any question directed to the collectivity is really not directed to anyone.

Effective questioning and drawing out derives from the counselor's knowledge of the counseling steps outlined in the definition of group counseling given in Chapter 8. These relate to helping individuals to explore and to work at self-understanding and ultimately to the development of action alternatives in specific life areas. While interrogative sentence forms are normally understood by the word "question," other forms are frequently even more effective. Thus, a sentence stem which an individual completes elicits pertinent data, or a hypothesis made about a member's self-data gets accepted or rejected and distortions thus get corrected. The significant point in effective delivery of the draw-out skill is that the counselor has a rationale for the data being sought and is able to exercise good judgement about the next steps in dealing with that data.

Below are a few examples of how effective questioning and drawing-out interventions are formulated.

Walter, have you ever considered what *you* get out of upsetting yourself when you don't come off looking as good as you would like in these performances you've been telling us about?

Alan, you went around all day complaining and feeling rotten because you told yourself . . .

Give us an example of what you mean, Jerry, when you say that no one understands you.

Your mother ought to act differently. She should be totally sane and rational and have your best interests in mind. Otherwise you are going to walk around smoldering and being angry all the time. Is that it, Mary?

Laurel, did you notice that Diana and Bonnie expressed concerns very similar to yours?

Some typically ineffective questioning leads are evidenced in the following examples.

Why are we all afraid of so many people?

Margaret, how many children are there in your family? Do you like being the youngest? Does your mother like you when you act like this? Your older brother doesn't act this way; how come you do?

Why do you just sit there when I ask you a question? Are the questions too hard for you?

Why don't you just stop taking drugs? Then your problems would all disappear.

Who handles the money in your marriage? Do you go out a lot? Do you do your share of making up? If you never approach your husband and give him the love he needs, how do you expect him to act any differently?

The examples can be endlessly multiplied. Questions which are irrelevant, rapid fire, directed at the entire group, advice-giving, or otherwise demeaning rather than motivated by a rationale for understanding and helping are of little consequence to effective counseling and could produce a question-and-answer environment more reminiscent of a police station, a job interview, or a classroom than a counseling group.

Confronting. Confronting is a skill which, when improperly exercised, many group members perceive as an "attack." Partially this happens because confrontations in our culture, when compared to the normal range of social behaviors which are commonly manifested, are proportionately rare. When they do occur, there is likely to be some strong emotionality in both the confronter, who is steeled to do battle, and the confrontee, because accusation calls for determined self-protection. Normal social confrontations arise because someone feels cheated or discriminated against in some way: The victim rises up against the victimizer, usually as a last resort.

There are no victims in counseling groups. The group leader who is confronted by one or more group members and engages in denial behavior has attached a victim label to himself or herself rather than appreciating what is being perceived by the group member and helping that member to arrive at an understanding. Similarly, when a member is feeling victimized by a confronter, the "victim" feelings will dissipate if the person who is the target of the confrontation can be helped to understand the motives behind the confrontation, presuming the motives *are* of a counseling nature. The essential ingredient is the use of reality data: no data, no effective confrontation.

The effective counselor is an accepting, nonjudgmental person. Confronters in our general society are seen as rude, unkind, disapproving, disliking, hostile, exploitative, self-aggrandizing, or, at the least, discourteous. The effective counselor is none of these. The difficult task of the group counselor is to confront while simultaneously conveying acceptance and approval of the member and indicating no personal interest in the action. That is, no member ought to feel that a counselor is being confrontative because he or she dislikes the way the member is or behaves or that somehow the counselor benefits if the member changes.

In order to be effective in helping individuals to change, a group counselor identifies discrepancies in how members think, feel, and act, which is what confronting is all about. Confronting means that the counselor is not just one more person who turns his or her head when a group member manifests obviously discrepant behavior. The counselor fearlessly labels the behavior which is self-defeating or inconsistent and demonstrates concern for the group member by such attention: Personal growth for each member thus confronted is always the counseling motive.

Discrepancies can take many forms. For each kind of discrepant behavior detailed below, one example of effective and one of ineffective leader confrontation are offered.

A discrepancy between what a member is saying now and what was earlier stated.

EFFECTIVE COUNSELOR CONFRONTATION

Larry, last week you indicated that you had no apprehension about making it in college and that if you didn't make it, you would simply join the Navy for one hitch. You just said that you were frightened about not being accepted at the State University and were not sure what you would do.

INEFFECTIVE COUNSELOR CONFRONTATION

Larry, you can really be inconsistent at times. I wish you would make up your mind. One week you say you're not worried about getting into college, and the next week you say you are. Did anyone else in the group pick up Larry's inconsistent thinking?

A discrepancy between what a member is saying and what a member is doing.

EFFECTIVE

Bruce, you've said that you are really capable and intelligent and can handle almost anything which comes your way, and yet you are having great difficulty in passing three of the four courses you're enrolled in. What you say you are and what you do seem so far apart.

INEFFECTIVE

You really are a bullcrap artist, Bruce. You say that you are smart, and yet you don't show any of your smarts, especially in the three classes that you're failing. How many here think that Bruce is as smart as he thinks he is?

A discrepancy between what a member says and what a member feels.

EFFECTIVE

Cindy, you keep telling us how your parents don't bug you, and that you're totally independent from their control. Yet you get welled up with emotion whenever you mention how they treat you.

INEFFECTIVE

Come on, Cindy. I can tell that they get to you by the teary-eyed look you get and the dry-mouthed way you start to talk whenever their names come up. They still control you, and you're trying to deny it. You may fool yourself, but you're not fooling me or the group.

A discrepancy between what a member is saying and what the counselor feels in reaction.

EFFECTIVE

Loretta, you have been saying that you use drugs because of the way they make you feel and that you really dig being high. Yet you also say that you don't have any true friends and that being liked by others is important. Is there any possible connection between your wanting to be liked and your taking drugs, rather than just the high you get from the drugs themselves?

INEFFECTIVE

Loretta, I just don't believe you when you say you like to get high and that's the reason you pop those pills. I think you are trying to be liked by others and because they think you should do it, you do it, rather than risk their disapproval.

Of course, there are more categories of discrepancies than those named above. Also, confrontation as a group counselor intervention may be used in other ways than to point out discrepancies. The counselor seeking to master this skill will concentrate on sticking with the data, using confrontation to advance the counseling, and defusing all such interventions of those loadings which turn a member into a victim. Effectiveness here means being an accepting confronter, and the counselor's body posture, gestures, facial expressions, and voice tonal quality convey member acceptance as well as do the structure and content of his utterances. Effective counselors check out their own discrepancies first.

Summarizing and reviewing important material. Summarizing and reviewing, like all other group counselor interventions, are done for a purpose. That purpose transcends what the same skill means to effective counseling in a dyadic relationship, since a group is composed of many minds, each of which has a perception and understanding of what has transpired in a part of a session, a whole session, or a series of sessions, and none of which are exactly alike. Effective summarizing and reviewing in a counseling group helps to correct distorted perceptions and to locate meaning accurately. Summarization techniques help to provide focus, to provide directionality and movement in pursuance of counseling essentials. They are of paramount importance in preclosure moments, both at the end of group sessions and when shifting from the concerns of one group member to those of another.

An effective summary will contain a drawing together of the large bulk of what group members have said for the purpose of focusing on goal setting and goal achievement. Solid summarizations succeed in curtailing tangentialism, the tendency of group members to radiate, to rummage around in their own brainbags according to their own hidden agendas, searching for stray thoughts and novel ideas which might be related to a given individual's dilemma.

The summary as a learning principle is modeled in most textbooks, where authors attempt to recapture for the reader what the meat was in the meal the reader has recently digested. So too are summaries important in counseling groups. Members tend to forget what has happened or to become unproductively repetitive or to miss the important meanings of group action because they have not been steadily attentive.

Group counselors can upgrade performance levels in the skill of summarizing by practicing them prior to a shifting of focus in a session or when a session is ending. This means yoking together the salient features of the group interaction according to a precisely understood purpose, a task that is difficult to accomplish if the counselor has not been mentally storing away all the passing phenomena which the group has generated. In the following example, the counselor makes an effective midsession summarization intervention in order to help a member settle on some specific goals with the thought in mind that further activity similar to that which has been ongoing will yield little advancement toward member.change.

> Maynard, everyone has been giving you feedback here in the group for the past half hour. Let me attempt to summarize what has taken place and help you to focus on setting some pertinent goals for yourself. Mary, Sally, and Mark have been trying to convince you of the folly of dropping out of school with only four months left until graduation. Mona feels that you have a right to do as you choose, even though her own biases were apparent in the advice she gave you. Sam and Donna have kept relatively quiet even though their intense interest was obvious from the way they attended to everything that was going on, and perhaps you would like to hear from them before you set your own goals. Almost everyone seems adamant that you should give more consideration to staying in school. And you, Maynard, still appear to be as confused as you were when you brought it up, even though you have been receiving a great deal of friendly support from everyone in the group. The group members are almost trying to persuade you to be like them and choose school for a short time longer, and some pressure has begun to surface which is making you somewhat anxious.

Ineffective leader summaries in groups frequently arise out of counselor frustration, anxiety over a perceived lack of progress in the group. A poor summary tends to ignore what has previously transpired and is summoned forth merely to close the lid on a given part of group life. In the example below, the counselor obviously feels that time has been wasted and chastises the group for not being more helpful.

> Well, Maynard, I think we've stayed with this topic long enough. It's obvious that everyone has a different opinion about what you should do and that we are getting nowhere by constantly barraging you with our own personal viewpoints. You can think about what's been said. Let's move on to someone else, now.

Interpreting. The process of giving the underlying meaning of a statement, a series of statements, or of an experience which includes nonverbal as well as verbal behaviors is called interpreting. Making effective interpretations is as important as any other ability a group counselor might develop. Any effective counselor knows that all behavior has meaning which is seldom apparent in the face value of the behavior itself. Indeed, the face value of most behavior usually contains the least important meaning. Thus, one group member says to another "Chris, you really worked hard yesterday, didn't you? You were under strain all day." The chief underlying meaning of this utterance could be any one of a number of possibilities, depending on what had previously gone on in the group: (a) Chris, you're finally admitting to dealing with pressure; (b) Chris, I'm stroking you because you've earned it; (c) Chris, I'm beginning to get the point; or (d)

Chris, I like you and identify with your scene. The meanings can be endlessly multiplied. What is vitally understood about interpretations is that there is no such thing as a *correct* interpretation of the meaning of any behavior. Interpretations are guesses, however "educated" they might be.

What the counselor infers from these or those data might sound believable and plausible to everyone in the group, but that does not necessarily *attach* truth to the interpretation. The counselor makes interpretations because, as the expert on counseling and the meaning of human behavior, doing so is a part of effective group leadership and interpretations help to move members toward goal setting and positive behavioral change. Interpretations amount to hypothesis tests. Alert counselors ask themselves why this or that behavior is going on and what meaning it has. Then they test out their own answers to these internalized questions by saying aloud what the underlying meaning seems to be; but this overt declaration is always done with a rationale. Assume, for example, twins who have grown up in an environment they have both shared, orphanages and foster homes: having become men, one twin is fearful and withdrawn, lacks self-confidence, is easily embarrassed and prone to look to others for support and approval; the other is confident, self-reliant, a leader, outgoing, psychologically independent. Using the same data, the counselor might ascribe causation inherent in a deprived childhood environment to the current attitudes and behaviors for each, even though they are diametrically opposed, helping the first grown twin to identify what it is he needs to work on and helping the second to build on what he already has achieved. The primary purpose of the effective interpreter is to provide some measure of self-understanding for group members which will lead to the changing of self-defeating behaviors.

Interpretations are necessary if members are to be helped in correcting their own distortions about why they customarily behave in the self-defeating ways they do. In the following example the counselor's aim is to give the group member a different way of looking at her own behavior.

Jean, you appear to be intimidated by the other members of this group. You have asserted that it is natural for you to be afraid of strong people because everyone is the same way. I'd suggest to you that you have learned to be afraid and that you use it to keep yourself from becoming different. As long as you hang back and act fearful and tell yourself it is because others are strong and might hurt you, then you never have to change because it really isn't your fault. In this way you assign the responsibility for your weakness to others. So being fearful is something that works for you. You conveniently use it whenever you are in groups like this to remain the way you are, to avoid taking risks, and to avoid developing your social skills.

This kind of interpretation gives Jean something to think about in relation to the way she programs herself to be controlled by others. The interpretation contradicts her own assertion that it is *natural* to feel embarrassed and afraid and that she has no control over this because everyone feels that way. The purpose of the interpretation is not to convince her, but to give her food for thought that will help her ultimately to go to work at eliminating her fearful behavior by assuming responsibility for it and determining that the payoffs are undesirable and that she has more self-enhancing choices.

Most ineffective interpretations are those wherein the interpreter is pedantic, obtuse, jargonistic, or generally unclear. Such interpretations are difficult, if not impossible, to follow up with further counseling steps leading to positive behavioral change, as in the following example.

Your fear of losing weight, Damon, is actually a manifestation of castration anxiety. Overweight people have repressed their sexuality and denied their own humanity. You, Damon, are living with the terrible fear that if you were normal in appearance, you would be unable to handle all the interpersonal responsibilities that go along with being average. So you, and millions of others like you, wallow around in your own excess baggage afraid of your own self. When you lose this fear, your fat will fall off with little effort.

Obviously, this kind of leader intervention creates a mistrustful mindset and does little more than alienate group members. Interpretations help to provide insight, when they are well done. When they are purposive but off the mark, they frequently help to establish where the "mark" actually is.

Restating. Restating is another key ability that effective group counselors master. It simply means that a group member's statements are recast by the counselor into different words so that the members of the group will find such statements more pointedly meaningful. Restating ought not to be confused with interpreting, which has been explained as ascribing meaning to statements not inherent in their content. But restatements are not simple repetitions. After carefully listening to what group members are saying to each other about themselves, the counselor restates a message in such a way as to assure clarity and pertinence.

Effective counselors practice restating in their own lives in order to increase their proficiency. Restating doesn't mean repeating or substituting synonyms. It involves focusing on the heart of messages, extracting their essence and delivering them in different words which eliminate all ambiguity. When a group member struggles to explain something and takes a long time and it is apparent that few others in the group are understanding his or her utterances, the effective counselor cuts through the oatmeal and restates in precise language whatever had significance in the member's statements.

In the following example, Rudy talks about himself and the counselor restates what Rudy had delivered.

Rudy: I guess I've always been this way. What I mean is, I'm not sure when it got started, but I know I've been concerned with what others think about me since I was just a little kid. My brother was my idol, and when I was little, I never called the signals when we played neighborhood football. I always waited for someone else to tell me what to do, so most of the time I ended up playing center or just blocking out because I wouldn't speak up. I was sure they would laugh at me if I said something, so I said nothing and never got a chance to catch passes or run with the ball. In school I was always afraid to have the teacher call on me because I was sure everyone would laugh at me if I gave the wrong answers. Even now, I won't ask a girl to go out with me because I'm sure she would turn me down and I wouldn't know how to cover my embarrassment. I hate this about myself, but I still keep doing it.

Counselor: You've always been fearful and anxious when you are around others who you feel might judge you in some unfavorable way. You'd like to change this, but you're not sure how to go about even starting.

The counselor restated in clear, succinct terms what Rudy has said and simultaneously added a dimension of self-responsibility for making some kind of change in his life. As Rudy becomes aware of where he is by his own data being returned to him with an action imperative tied to it, he now considers it in a new light. If he admits to wanting to change, it is more than likely that the other group members will chime in with helping efforts, and Rudy has gotten his start down a road to goal setting and becoming a less fearful activist in his own life.

Ineffective restatements usually involve repetition of what has been said without offering a new dimension of help. An ineffective treatment of Rudy's statements appears in the following example.

Rudy, you say you've always been that way, and that you've always been concerned about what others think of you. You told us about three incidents in your life when you waited for someone else to tell you what to do, and now you're afraid to ask for dates. You feel that no one would want to go out with you, anyway.

Such a restatement gives Rudy the comfort of being heard, but provides no potential for movement. In groups where the counselor continually engages in such playback exercises and goes no further, members only wonder why such mockingbird behavior is necessary. Is the counselor having trouble hearing and understanding? Does the counselor feel that it is important to correct the way members talk? Is the counselor simply showing that he or she is paying attention?

Establishing connections. When the counselor pieces together fragments of problem-related material which group members do not perceive as related, he or she is establishing connections. In order to do this effectively, the group counselor must attend to member data which has been given, see relationships between data pieces, and be able to recall data accurately. It is thus obvious that acute attending and listening skills are vital to effective counseling. This is admittedly a difficult part of group counseling, since the mountain of data continues to build as the life of the group goes on, and the responsible counselor is always crowding more and more into the data memory bank.

In establishing connections, the counselor's goal is to hold up a new way of looking at an individual's data for the purpose of providing insight and, ultimately, helping the individual to make a decision to go to work at changing behavior in a productive direction. In the example below, the counselor reclaims Joshua's self-data and points to a commonality.

Joshua, at one time or another in the past five weeks, you have mentioned your grandmother and how you can't get along with her. You have focused on both your mother and sister, your fights with each one. You told us about your run-ins with Mrs. Carlson, your neighbor. You have complained about the two staff women who try to get you to operate differently in your office. You even seem to get the most upset by Denise, here in the group. Denise, like these other figures in your life, is older than you. You give the impression that you are making it on all kinds of fronts with all kinds of people, except for older women. From grandmother and mother, to neighbors, your sister, your coworker, even to Denise, and perhaps others you have not yet told us about, you seem to resent any woman who is older telling you how to act in any way.

Similar connections can be established in correlating specific incidents group members have expressed in a number of life areas such as dealing with authority figures, fearing failure, running away from or handling love encounters in self-deprecating ways, seeking approval, displaying immobilizing guilt, anger, or worry, and on and on through a long list of behavioral areas. Seeing the interrelational thread which winds through member transmissions is the important insight for the connections-establisher. Naming the theme or pattern helps the group member to see how the behavior is self-defeating. If a pattern is clearly present, a member will acknowledge it and be willing to set goals aiming at pattern realignment.

Ineffective connection-establishment occurs when the counselor contrives to make one exist, usually based on some farfetched thesis, as in the following example.

Bill, last month you told us that you had dropped your night school class. Then, a couple of weeks later you mentioned how overly organized you are about everything. Now you're talking about being guilty because you didn't attend your aunt's funeral. You see how all these things tell something about you? You were afraid of failing your class, so you dropped out. Then your fear of failing was revealed in how you keep everything so orderly that no one can tell that you're hiding your fear. And your guilt about staying away from your aunt's funeral means that you were afraid of how you would act around all the family members, afraid that you would fail again and appear too emotional. Your fear of failure seems to dominate your life.

157

Information giving. Many counselors are imbued with the notion that lecturing and giving advice are taboo behaviors and so resist appearing knowledgeable and hold back on the delivery of information. There is occasional merit in such a stance, but when guarded retention of knowledge and information becomes a regular leader practice, individual member movement can be impaired. Not responding to member requests for information or squelching leader advice-giving and lecturing behavior is usually justified by such logic as the following: (1) Giving advice means telling people how to be, and no one is an authority on how another person ought to be; (2) when members dig out their own information, it has more meaning to them; (3) lecturing and giving advice put the focus on the leader, not the members; (4) leaders ought to be facilitators, not experts, and appearing to be the expert increases the psychological distance between the leader and the group members; (5) a group is not a classroom, and the leader needs to avoid whatever might appear to be teacher behavior.

With such an outlook a group leader might respond to a member request with a remark such as "My role does not allow me to lecture or give advice" or "Perhaps someone else can answer Trudy's question. I do not give out information. Rather, I'm here to help you find it out for yourself." Such leader statements get interpreted in many different ways, mostly negative, and the leader is seen as uncaring, detached, or evasive or as a deliberate withholder.

Information giving is necessary in counseling groups, and the counselor is inescapably the expert in the group. Giving information effectively is an important skill. Efficiently providing specific data —whether these are directions, explanations of procedural matters, the introduction of background knowledge related to the counseling process, or whatever—involves discernment on the part of the counselor: Is the information necessary or useful to this person or several persons? Is this the appropriate time to give it? The effective information deliverer checks up on how the information is understood by group members and whether it has been received accurately and its significance ingested.

Every counseling group has a beginning, and members are then apprised of procedural matters, what the counseling process is like, what can be expected, what the ground rules are, and how each member can make the most of the experience. A precise statement about such expectations and contingencies is the group counselor's most effective strategy, and he or she could even back up the statement with a written handout. Belaboring such information giving and turning the entire meeting into a discussion of mundane procedural concerns weakens the essential impact: Group members learn how all such knowledge is operationalized as the counseling process goes on, in the unfolding of the doing. Further information is provided as called for, as the group interaction proceeds, or reminders are provided when clarifications are needed, when distorted perceptions are manifested in members.

So that members can quickly learn how to use the group counseling experience most advantageously, the effective counselor issues occasional pointed verbal bulletins or lecturettes which relate to process analysis and operational dynamics within the group. Periodically members become concerned with the typicality or normalcy of what is happening in their group: "Do most groups have these kinds of problems?" "Is it unusual for us to be struggling with silence like this?" One way of handling these and similar inquiries is with a counselor mini-lecture, though the "mini" part ought to be stressed, as it is easy to succumb to the temptation to be worldly wise and engage in the construction and delivery of a treatise where the counselor, rather than the group members, becomes the focus. It is far better that the counselor respond to member questions and periodically talk about group processes than to avoid such leader behavior systematically. It is generally fruitful at the end of a session to have members give their perceptions of what has taken place in the group and for the counselor to give a diagnosis of the dynamics which have transpired. A short process analysis might go something like this:

As a group we have moved from everybody competing to get his or her opinion registered to a truly helping unit where the focus is on providing constructive attention to individuals who want to work on particular concerns. If you noticed, I intervened on three occasions to keep us from going into a simple discussion or gripe session, first by returning the focus to Tom, then later by getting Roger to acknowledge that the way we were dealing with him and his concerns was not productive for him, and the last time when Melody introduced the topic of how the agency ought to be run and several of you got seduced into the discussion. There was considerably more support-giving and confronting going on today than there has been and many of you are making effective interventions, such as yours, Maryann, when you interpreted Sam's complaining behavior, and yours, Tom, when you helped Cathy to see how she blames others for the problems she herself creates. Our silent periods are shorter and less frequent and they bring less discomfort than they did two weeks ago, and the obvious nervousness about being in the spotlight has almost totally subsided. The two members who have not participated before got in on the action today, which may say something about the deeper sense of commitment and trust they are now feeling.

An ineffective group leader lecturette would be one which deals with such content as customarily appears in group dynamics textbooks. While it may sound impressive, it has little value to the members of a particular group and does not go much beyond convincing some members that the counselor has read a book or two, as the following example illustrates.

We have now passed the challenging stage and moved to the involvement phase of group development. This is attributable to the higher degree of group cohesiveness and the fact that the norms of the group have become more firmly established. Several group members are assuming typically occurring group member roles. Sam has seemingly become the isolate, while both Maryann and Tom are stars, in group dynamics language. We have acquired what the theorists label a syntality of openness, and our communications channels are now intrinsically rather than extrinsically oriented.

Information giving is not something that the effective group counselor does automatically in a group. It may be that some information can best be delivered outside the group on an individual basis. When questions are asked about educational/occupational information, referral information, group procedures, scheduling, leader behaviors or credentials, regardless of the information sought, the effective counselor determines what purposes it will serve to respond immediately, more or less fully, inside or outside the group, or even if some other person in the group, including the information-seeker, is best suited to convey a particular particle of information.

Initiating. Initiating refers to the counselor's ability to take action at any given moment to bring about group participation, to introduce worthwhile focal material to the group. The effective counselor continually engages in "the-squirrel-storing-away-his-nuts" behavior and this collections of "nuts," problem-related data, is ample right after the initial session. Aside from a general knowledge of what kinds of content areas can productively occupy the group members, the counselor has been memory-banking specific data about particular members which can be trotted out whenever a natural closure time occurs. Without the leader ability to initiate, floundering and groping too frequently become group modalities, particularly at session openings. Also, an abundance of unnecessary struggle transpires, strained and pained moments, when group members seem to be imploring "Where do we go from here, O leader?"

Having initiating skills means that the counselor has a plan of action for all occasions, a preferred plan drawn from a repertoire of plans, rather than operating from a willy-nilly stance, opportunistically, hoping that everything will work itself out, putting the responsibility for productive use of time on the necks of the group members. While most times the counselor will find it unnecessary to call on his or her plan, nevertheless the plan exists, waiting in the wings of the counselor's mind for its cue. Since data collection is a precursory activity for effective initiating behavior, the counselor assiduously monitors all that goes on in the group and has an ongoing notion of who in the group needs what kinds of help, and most of the plans in the wings have a specific-person character to them. But the effective counselor is not anxious about implementing any given plan: To fall in love with a plan and make sure that it materializes at all costs is to program oneself for defeat as a leader. Whether this or that group focus and interaction is more productive than another depends on a bag of mixed variables, so effective leaders are flexible enough to go along with shifts in group movement. They engage in constant evaluation, appreciating the fluidity of the counseling process; but they are ready to help the flow of that process assume a new direction whenever their readings indicate that a spillage or a blockage or a stoppage has occurred. At such times they give the clue to the wings for this or that plan and initiate new action in the group.

There are two kinds of initiating: (a) getting the group started and (b) entering new terrain after closure has naturally taken place, after a group counseling episode has been concluded on the help given to a particular group member. Effectiveness in starting a group session means that the counselor has anticipated productive likelihoods and has plans ready. Significant ingredients of the plans include getting reports from members who have been working on behavioral change goals between sessions, making invitational statements to members to take advantage of group time to work on their concerns, and having particular strategies in mind for different individuals for providing counseling help. An example of a counselor initiation incorporating such plan ingredients is illustrated below.

This is our fourth meeting and we have seven more sessions together. After we hear from John and Adrian about how they are progressing at achieving the goals they committed themselves to work on last week, let's open the group to allow anyone to utilize our time here to work on whatever concern he or she desires. Perhaps some of you have been thinking about taking a personal risk, or you have been wishing for the right moment to come along for you to go to work on a troublesome area, and you don't want to say to yourself at the end of the group that you didn't go to work on your concerns because the time was never right. As you listen to John and Adrian, you might want to contemplate the ways in which you can use the group. We will try to program opportunities for each of you to work on yourself so that you can take advantage of the group time without being specifically asked to do so. John, why don't you bring us up to date on what's going on in your world?

If, after John and Adrian have given their reports, no one picks up on the invitation to use the group time, the counselor would move to certain individuals who have previously indicated an interest in going to work on concerns which were mentioned but have thus far gone unexplored. The kind of open-ended beckoning illustrated above allows members to work on themselves voluntarily, and after several such invitations group members will tend to become involved in the process by themselves, especially as they see how others have benefited from doing so. This is in contrast to the kind of ambiguous and discharge-of-leader-responsibility invitation, which only serves to heighten threat and create anxiety in the group, made by the counselor in the following example.

> Here we are in the fourth week and many of you haven't taken any risks at all. I want you to remember that this is your group and that if you don't take advantage of it, you will be the losers. It's no skin off my nose, if you don't want to participate. I'm going to leave it up to all of you. Either take the ball and run with it, or sit there and stare at each other.

Here the leader has indicated no sense of responsibility or commitment to making the group a productive experience for everyone: Group members then tend to become discomfitted and are fuzzy-minded about the purposes of group counseling.

The second kind of initiating involves entering new areas after closure has been brought about on a given individual. After a brief summarization, a recapitulation of counseling progress, the leader might shift by opening the group up to anyone who voluntarily wishes to use it, as is done in the example of the group session opening, or by introducing some of the data which has been squirreled away. An example of this kind of leader initiating might include a simple statement such as the following.

> Muriel, earlier you were really reacting to what Mike was saying about losing someone close to him. You didn't say anything aloud, but it was clear that it had some strong personal meaning for you. Would you like to share it at this time and perhaps go to work on it like Mike did?

Going back to the goals which each member stated on entering the group is another fertile resource for effective leader initiating. Reminding given individuals of their goals and asking them directly if they would like to work on them is a potent initiating behavior which frequently elicits goal reformulations and new goals.

Reassuring, encouraging, and supporting. Effective administration of psychological support when a group member's anxieties begin to inhibit rather than foster the personal growth process is a key group counselor skill. While providing support at critical moments is the heart of this skill, effective group counselors understand that a general posture and demeanor which includes reassurance, encouragement, and reinforcement promotes counseling goals. Mastery here has to do with timing and appropriateness. Tendering support and encouragement effectively means being able to read when it is called for and knowing the difference between helping members to take forward steps and simply reinforcing self-defeating needs to be approved or coddled.

Whenever group members begin to examine data of a personally troublesome nature, they will experience resistance to being completely honest. The resistance and reluctance are natural. People want to hold onto what has been a part of their life-support systems; their defenses have worked for them; defenses serve a purpose or they would be discarded. Giving up anything—thought structures, moral attitudes, habitual behaviors, neurotic and self-defeating relationships—means taking risks, and just because certain behaviors have not been growth-producing for the individual does not mean that giving them up, or even admitting their presence, is not threatening. Whenever an individual is asked to name and explain personal behavior and to be honest about its nature and causes, defenses can be expected, most of them ingrained and of long duration. Admitting to new, alternate possibilities for thinking and doing means entertaining the likelihood of surrendering traditional ways of thinking and doing, and, of course, abandoning these old manners and mannerisms amounts to a rejection of a part of the self. Herein lies the real threat. When I become something different, then the old me was no good, and I must admit to my inadequacy. Constantly asking group members to reject large chunks of what they have become, because these characteristic behaviors do not work as well for them as different behaviors would, is an essential part of the group counselor's mission, the core of the service that she or he provides, and here is where psychological support and reassurance is crucial.

Endorsement of a group member's ability to handle the transition from old behaviors to new, reassurance of exhibited strengths and belief in the member's capacity to take on a given program for self-change and development, providing understanding that it is extremely difficult to admit to many things and that even talking in front of accepting others about some kinds of personal concerns is a genuine struggle because it involves an admission that one has misled or lied to oneself for a long time: these are counselor support and encouragement behaviors. Without counselor support and encouragement and that which others in the group furnish, many members find it virtually impossible to change. This does not mean distributing sympathy or pity. Without counselor support, diagnostic activity and strategic planning are worth little; the plans go awry. Without convincing counselor modeling of this skill, too frequently group members do not learn it, and they engage in comforting, in giving sympathy, and in feeling sorry for a fellow member.

In the following example, Zelda has begun to squirm and get choked-up as she relates some of the details of her relationship to her father, and the counselor moves to support her over this rough spot.

Zelda, it's terribly difficult for you to even talk about your father, isn't it? You're struggling to get the words out and you're not even sure you can do it here. You have kept all your deep feelings to yourself for a long time and examining them here in the group is tougher than you thought it would be. But you've made a brave beginning. You've shown us how strong you are in many ways, and you can use this strength to work on dealing with yourself and your relationship to your father, even though these matters are painful to go into. Sharing them here is the important first step in allowing us to help you. We recognize the pain it is causing you, and we respect how trying it is for you to continue, but going through with it is worth the pain, if you can make some changes as a result. There is no reason to believe, from what you have told us so far, that we cannot be of help. We can certainly help you to handle your troublesome feelings of guilt and longing better, once we know exactly how they well up in you. You were saying that your father never finds anything of value in what you do, no matter how hard you try, and it was that thought that really choked you up.

The effective counselor sets a tone of support through voice, posture, gestures, and facial expressions, making every effort to demonstrate that he or she is with the group member who is going through so much psychic anguish, extending the hand of care and understanding in every possible way. The typically ineffective group leader becomes a dispenser of maudlin words, a sympathizer who reinforces feelings of self-pity rather than one who encourages the group member to go to work on troublesome concerns.

Zelda, you must really feel just awful. Don't cry, honey. Everyone has problems. I'm sure we can help you to feel better, can't we, everyone? When you feel unloved, it's really lonely, but you're not alone in here. We really care about you. Things will get better, so don't worry about them. We're here to give you comfort, so any time you want to talk about your dad, you know what to do. Do you need a Kleenex?

This kind of saccharine sentimentality only helps Zelda to realize she has made a mistake; it reinforces the notion that this group is not a place where genuine help is forthcoming; what can be obtained here is sympathy, people feeling sorry for the one who is already a champion at feeling sorry for herself. When group leader support is maudlin, it teaches members that the group is not a helping environment but a place where members can know how much they are liked when they feel bad.

Intervening. The group counselor as interventionist is a not uncommon concept. There is a sense in which every manifestation of counselor behavior, whatever its character, can be dubbed an intervention. Here we are separating out a group counselor skill and labeling it *intervening* because the term seems to be the most appropriate, and by it we mean breaking into or disrupting the action in the group when group time is being unproductively consumed. There is so much in this one leadership variable that we have devoted an entire chapter to the subject (see Chapter 11). Here we only briefly recapitulate its contents. Effective group counselors intervene when:

1. A group member speaks for everyone.
2. An individual speaks for another individual within the group.
3. A group member focuses on persons, conditions, or events outside the group.
4. Someone seeks the approval of the counselor or a group member before and after speaking.

5. Someone says, "I don't want to hurt his feelings, so I won't say it."

6. A group member suggests that his or her problems are due to someone else.

7. An individual suggests that "I've always been that way."

8. An individual suggests "I'll wait, and it will change."

9. Discrepant behavior appears.

10. A member bores the group by rambling.

Each of these occasions calls for an effective counselor intervention. The given list includes common cases calling for action on the part of the counselor, but certainly there are many more. The inviolable assumption here is that it is the group counselor's responsibility to help the members curtail patently unproductive use of group time. Ineffective intervening results when the counselor avoids or just plainly misses opportunities to do so, and the consequence is protracted unproductive activity on the part of one or more group members.

Dealing with silence. In the chapter on barriers to effectiveness in group counseling (Chapter 12), we state how silence in the group comprises an impediment to counseling progress. An important understanding here, too frequently overlooked when the subject is discussed in literature on groups, is that the "group" is never silent: only Mary, Tom, Bill, Carl, Jane, and the other individuals who make up the group are silent; even when there is lively interaction going on, most individuals are not talking. While one talks all the others are silent. Seldom do two or more persons talk simultaneously. For a group not to be silent, it requires only that one member talk. Always aware of this, the effective counselor need not make appeals to the group as an entity: Any individual in the group can be engaged, and therein lies the secret to limiting silent periods and promoting productivity.

Many novice group counselors find silent periods to be intimidating, principally because they have been so conditioned by their own social experience to feel anxious when the talk stops and because the expectation and desire is that talk is what a group convenes to make, be it at a party, a dinner, a committee meeting, or whatever. People talk to each other. Part of the meaning of being human means to communicate with other humans. Novice counselors feel that talk, regardless of content, is preferable to silence, and they are readily emboldened in this mind-set by group members who are similarly conditioned.

But effective group counselors simply remind themselves that silence is merely another form of human behavior, that people have a right not to talk, that this behavior, like any other, is caused, and that the causes are not necessarily the same for identical behavior as it is manifested in any two individuals. Why Sylvester is silent may have nothing to do with why Mabella is. The effective counselor is immune to the pressure to talk, however much some group members might feel anxious or oppressed by the silence, and this is a first step in dealing with silence, whether it be just short respite or a lengthy contemplative time for all the group members. To be threatened is to be rendered ineffective. The second step involves the counselor's not being the perpetual silence breaker, being free of dominating compulsion, learning to allow members to take the initiative. As silence continues, the effective counselor steadily uses the time to check out the group members. Who is nervous, tittery, semicomatose? Who seems intimidated? Who is looking for someone else to make it end? Who appears ready to say something, but can't muster the courage to let it out? The counselor is not inactive. Silence is data-gathering time. It is a time to model the notion that there is nothing inappropriate in silence; the counselor displays neither alarm nor disappointment. After the silence has been shattered by the group members themselves, the group counselor might refer to it in a statement such as the following.

That we will be silent from time to time is something that I expect to happen. Most of you are not accustomed to talking about yourselves in a setting such as this. You will need some times to think about what has taken place and to decide if and how you want to participate. I have no expectations that we will find it necessary to have perpetual noise going on in the group. Rather, I expect regularly occurring inactive times. If you find that uncomfortable, you can talk about that here in the group.

This kind of helpful statement is in contrast to one where the group leader berates the members.

If you want to waste your time by not participating, that is your business. Silence is really an unproductive way to take up group time, but I'm not going to force anyone to talk.

Such an approach increases the formidability of silent intervals and drives group members into deeper reluctance to talk: it challenges members to exercise stubbornness.

Chronic silence is a problem in some groups, and the effective counselor knows that it requires some kind of interpretation. Consonant with the group counseling goal of helping each individual in the circle to go to work on personal concerns, the effective counselor interprets silence in this light and extends an invitational hand to a given member or members.

I've noticed that whenever you seem to finish with one person's concern the group takes a silent character, almost as if everyone is contemplating if he or she wants to take a risk. Although the silence is helpful in having you think about it in your own heads, sometimes it gets drawn out and valuable time is lost. I wonder, Romeo, if this is not true for you, that you see how it helped Marty, but you're not sure if you want some of the spotlight, and so you sit quietly, and that's the way you deal with your hesitancy?

Recognizing and explaining nonverbal behavior. The group counselor who is not convinced that nonverbal behavior is an important
pool of data for advancing counseling movement is programmed for
low-level functioning. Nonverbal behavior in groups has much more
significance than in one-to-one counseling, because the stimuli come
from many more sources. The first task of the group counselor is to
recognize the existence of nonverbal behavior and to be its observer
and collector. Nonverbal behavior perpetually emanates from
everyone. Judy has involuntary facial inflections and is a head-
nodder. Sam leans forward all the time. Moe moves backwards
whenever he talks. Gary twitches his mustache and is a constant
scratcher. Harry adopts a vacuous look at key times. Gertrude never
unfolds her arms and keeps her legs tucked under her chair. Terry
either looks hurt and vulnerable or wears an insipid smile. The list is
potentially endless. Although the age-old cliche, a man is as he does,
has the most truth in it when *all* that he does is known, enough of
what people do is manifested in a group setting to give accurate road
markers to how they characteristically function if the nonverbal data
is carefully absorbed by the counselor. Effective counselors are
students of nonverbal behavior and constantly observe people in the
general society in much the same way as actors do, though actors
seek to improve their ability to convey meaning through their own
portrayals and the counselor's purpose is different.

Counselors use nonverbal data to draw someone into the group
activity, to give accurate feedback, to help a member receive reactions, to improve communication channels, to hold up a mirror and
provide valuable information to members who are unaware of the
messages they send and the impressions they create, to increase
insight, to demonstrate how they are continually servicing each
member by attentively gathering data and mentally processing it, and
to model the ways in which nonverbal behavior is observed and used.
This last purpose is constant for all group counselor skills; the more
proficient group members become in the delivery of these same skills,
the more resourceful the group becomes and the more in-charge
members become in their own lives.

Recognizing nonverbal data is only half the job. Explaining it well is
the other half and by far the harder part. It is impossible here to give a
prescription for effective explanations, since the universe of nonverbal behaviors that humans manifest is almost infinite and any particular behavior has a particular meaning in the context of its owner's
world. The effective counselor is not one who blurts out nonverbal
signals every time they are registered. (One can imagine the ridicu-
lousness of this if one pictures the counselor providing a running
commentary akin to what a radio announcer of a horse race or a prize

fight might produce.) The effective counselor has keenly observed who does what with all parts of their bodies and then uses this filed-away data at appropriate times. Timing is crucial. When the focus is on a given individual, observations of nonverbal data are added to or interwoven with feedback which relates to exploration, diagnosis, goal setting, or some other counseling dimension of interaction. The counselor explains his or her own observations and asks others to give their own. The counselor uses nonverbal data to verify a discrepancy between what an individual says and what he or she does with parts of the face, with hands and feet, with the total body. In the following example, the counselor uses nonverbal data to draw Liz into the group activity.

Liz, you seemed to react to Claude and his difficulty, but you didn't say anything at the time. You had anxious looks on your face, and you engaged in a lot of nervous activity with your hands when he talked. Perhaps there was something in what he was saying that particularly troubled you.

Here the counselor could have asked others in the group to give Liz feedback about her nonverbal signaling and what they understood it to mean. The counselor explained Liz's nonverbal behavior to put her in touch with it and to help her focus on what it symbolized in relation to what was happening in the group.

Utilization of nonverbal behavior is the most glaringly ineffective when the group counselor is not alert to it or assumes it has no significance. Usually, it is significant if it is noticed, particularly when it calls attention to itself, when it is overt or a departure from characteristic behavior in a given member. A typically ineffective explanation of nonverbal behavior occurs when the counselor operates in bulldozer fashion.

Mary, you are a bundle of nerves in this group. You shake whenever anyone talks to you; you try to hide yourself by folding your arms around you; you stutter whenever you try to talk. What's behind all this action? Why do you carry on this way?

Misinterpreting nonverbal behavioral data or attaching significance to it when there is no cause to do so is another ineffective use of this skill.

Al, when Ruth first mentioned her husband, you jutted your thumb into the air. Later, when Ruth mentioned him again, your foot moved. When Ruth just talked about him this time, you put your elbow in your ear. Now, what's going on here, Al? Your nonverbal behavior is giving you away.

Using clear, concise, meaningful communications. The counselor who consistently is not understood by group members or who continually is misunderstood hardly can hope for any success. Sending clear, concise, meaningful messages in group counseling is vital to every part of the experience. If a counselor has expertise in all dimensions of group counseling but cannot effectively communicate, his or her efforts are then self-sabotaged.

Chief offenders are those who preach, make windy orations, ramble, over-talk, complicate the simple, talk-down, intellectualize, make convoluted interpretations, indulge in jargon, monopolize, keep attempting to convince, give prolonged lectures, confuse through the multiplication of examples, use sarcasm, mumble, constantly re-explain, make fun of their own utterances or demean their import, hang back and cryptically horde, hint at but never specify, endlessly contradict themselves and never really mean or take responsibility for what they say, hesitate and then tremble their words out, think aloud instead of beforehand, fall in love with and repeatedly promote their own causes and favorite themes, insist on the validity of their own perceptions, communicate one line but live out another—a chief offender has a world of options.

How anyone can effectively counsel in a group and not be competent in the oral use of language is more than a mystery; it is a contradiction. Knowing this, effective group counselors perpetually strive to upgrade their language skills, their message-sending performances. They are constantly alert to how their communications are received by members, to quizzical looks, to requests for clarification or repetition, to member distortions of their interventions. They work at eliminating their own "uh's" and "you know's" and "I mean's." They know that producing clear, concise, meaningful communications frequently involves getting into the peculiar language and self-idioms of others. They say what they mean and mean what they say. They say what they say so it can be understood and dealt with by group members. They know their audience and could not be caught dead trying to impress some nonpresent psychology professor. They continually share their logic and background data. They check out their receivers: can Pearl, Penny, Pete, or Paul play back what I've said? They know that for every group member who asks them to clear up what they have said, because it was couched in convoluted, distorted, fuzzy, or otherwise sloppy language, there will be others in the group who lack the courage or inclination to say, "Run that by me again." In every group they lead, effective counselors teach members to become cybernetic resources, to be openly critical of the clarity, conciseness, and significance of counselor verbal behavior. Effective group counselors covet and value feedback.

Focusing. Focusing means staying with pertinent data, bringing the counseling resources in the group to bear on the concerns of a particular member who can receive the benefits of counseling at any given time. Group counselors who are effective at focusing have learned how to curb the radiation which is characteristic of most groups where there is no planned agenda. With ten members in a group, ten times the potential for digression over individual counseling exists. Any given piece of data can trigger something in an individual and, without warning, that member can seduce others into meanderings which have nothing to do with the counseling. Effective counselors know how to put focusing skills into operation to keep the entire group working on meaningful content, understanding that the main business of group counseling is counseling individuals in groups, heading off verbal expeditions which are so tempting to some group members.

Most group members have difficulty transcending themselves, and the tendency for them to take the focus off another and bring it to themselves is one that runs rampant if left unchecked. Counseling groups can easily become unfocused; in a group where everyone is bouncing opinions, observations, and self-references off each other, the effective counselor moves to promote counseling focus. "Should we be here now?" "Does this line of group activity coincide with counseling goals?" "Are we being side-tracked?" "What can I do to bring the focus back where it belongs?" Such questions fill the head of the focus-minded counselor.

Effective focusing behavior can be straightforwardly accomplished. When the counselor decides to "play the heavy," there is no need to be feckless.

Meriam, when Gaspar started talking about his relationship with his apparently senile, but definitely overbearing grandmother, you shifted the attention off of him and onto yourself. Perhaps we can work with Gaspar until he has reached some goals for himself and then bring it back to you.

Or, in the case of digressing group members, an effective focusing intervention might take the following form.

Karl, you and Freddy are really engaged in a debate, some weird kind of struggle, with the rest of the group as witnesses. This got started because Sally was talking about her own difficulties with Mrs. Fauxpas. Because both of you happen to know this woman, you are now trying to win an argument about her, and you have left Sally out in the cold. Why don't we try to get back to Sally and help her to come up with ways to deal more effectively with Mrs. Fauxpas, and you two can catch up on your argument outside of the group.

How the group got diverted to a less-than-productive focus is thus identified, and the counselor takes the responsibility for returning the focus to Sally. While a focusing intervention always has in it the element of counselor decision about where the concentration of group attention ought to be, this can be overdone, as in the following example of group reprimanding.

Harriet, you've done it again. Every time someone starts to talk about himself or herself in a personal way, you conveniently bring it around to something else. Then everyone in the group starts talking about everything but what we're here for. I want you all to stop changing the subject and to work on one person at a time, like we're supposed to.

Effective group counselors execute focusing skills in such a way as to bring about new directions in the group relating to counseling goals without calling attention to how this comes about. When group members feel that it is necessary to discuss how they got off on a tangent or to do any process analysis, the transition has not been a smooth one and the leader has more to learn about effective focusing.

Restraining, subduing, and avoiding potentially explosive and divisive group happenings. Most counseling groups take on a cohesive and helping nature very early in their tenure, particularly if the counselor has been effective in communicating understanding about group purposes, defining how counseling works in a group, and modeling helping behaviors. But some groups have members who have a penchant for stirring up controversy, who are seriously disturbed, whose personal chemistry in no way mixes with that of one or more other members, who have hidden agendas, who overreact to this or that transpiration or unpredictable phenomenon of group life. The effective counselor is always wary of the possibility that an "explosion" in a group can and occasionally does happen and that a group can be a volatile place. Heading it off is a measure of the counselor's competence and ability to read human nature.

Restraining, subduing, and avoiding potentially explosive and divisive group happenings means being able to sense when a given line of group activity is building to an undesirable crescendo. Are individuals choosing up sides and becoming hostile in their interactions? Is disagreement reaching an emotional peak? Are given members unwilling or unable to compromise? Is one person giving off sparks of being incapable of tolerating what is now happening? Do other group members refuse to acknowledge this? At such times the effective counselor calls on restraining skills and tries to cool off or refocus the group.

The counselor who functions in groups knows that there will be rare occasions when he or she must meet with a given member for individual counseling or consultation outside the group; at those infrequent times when a member's behavior has been limited or thwarted for the sake of heading off volatile happenings in the group, invitations for doing so are properly extended. Effective restraining behavior neither minimizes nor maximizes what the counselor sees: Open directness is the hallmark.

Marcia has told us repeatedly in a number of ways that she doesn't want to discuss her marriage here. While it obviously troubles her, she is not yet ready to deal with it here and may never be, and we can respect that. If you recall, we all agreed that everyone has the right to stay out of the spotlight, if that were what a person decided. Let's give Marcia her rights without pressuring her.

Or, in an example involving several members:

> Ozzy and Mel, you both seem to be heading on a collision course in which neither of you is listening to the other and both of you want to win an argument rather than help each other to listen and change effectively. Suppose you both allow everyone in the group to send you a one-way message in which neither of you speak, and you let in what others say to you. When that is over, perhaps each of you can work at setting a goal for yourself of avoiding getting worked up, which is getting you nowhere but more infuriated. Blake, why don't you send a one-way message to both Ozzy and Mel giving your reactions to what is taking place?

Should an "explosion" really occur in the group, depending on its nature, the counselor's credibility could be seriously impaired. But the incidence of such happenings is exceedingly rare, even in groups where the counselor is virtually passive, which is to say that effective counselors do not engage in restraining a group to mollify their own fears: they act upon observed and considered data. Typically ineffective restraining behavior arises when the counselor tries to deny the existence of a potentially dangerous situation or tries to sugarcoat discomfort.

> Now, Tony, you're really not getting upset just because Jerry called you a birdbrained idiot. Getting mad and yelling and carrying on will only make it worse. You're both acting like children. I think you really like each other. You didn't mean what you said, did you, Jerry?

When the leader admonishes the group for acting badly, takes on the role of referee, sides with this or that group faction, or requires individuals to apologize in order to restore civility or courtesy, he or she is not restraining effectively.

Goal setting. Goal setting is too often taken for granted by counselors and clients alike, as though this were a simple and essential process that everyone understands, so why belabor the subject and make it unnecessarily complicated? Although it can be justified on the basis that we live in a society wherein goal setting and goal achievement are a way of life and we are bombarded with injunctions to do both from every side—in the mass media; in our institutions, churches, schools, places of employment; in our social customs; in the lessons of history—such an attitude works against us if it precludes us from examining and understanding how and when goal setting is done effectively in group counseling. Productive goal setting is at the core of the counseling process and is a skill which every group counselor who becomes a consummate professional must master.

Although there are no group goals in counseling groups, as contrasted to the goals of a committee where all production is a team effort, there are two significant differences between a client establishing a goal in one-to-one counseling and doing the same in a group. The first difference has to do with trying out goal achievement in some modified or attenuated way right in the group, a safe place because no negative consequences to the individual are allowed to accrue. Practice attempts at goal achievement can be supported, monitored, and evaluated; more effective means can be modeled by the counselor or other group members. Because an individual has effectively performed some new behavior right in the interpersonal laboratory of the group, he or she has a head start in doing the same in his or her personal world between the group sessions.

The second difference is that people tend to be more responsible for taking action when a declaration and a commitment to do so has been made in front of concerned witnesses. Group members do not want to return to the group and report that they have not even tried to carry out what they have declared they would do. On the other hand, when they have tried, the support and approval which they receive bolsters their feelings of intrinsic worth in ways that are experienced in few other life contexts. A counseling group is a powerful setting in which to go to work on self-development.

Effective goal setting is marked by several characteristics. First, goals are mutually established. When a goal is foisted on an individual who does not really accept it and make it his or her own, determination to accomplish it will flag. Second, goals are specific; that is, reality steps for goal achievement are clearly laid out in detailed form and completely understood. The member who has set the goal can name exactly what she or he will do to achieve it, at what time, and in what place. Third, goals are relevant to the self-defeating behavior being replaced. Simply to cease engaging in behavior which has been self-injurious is seldom enough; effective new ways of behaving in the same life circumstance are desired. Fourth, goals are achievable. Goals that are attempted but impossible to attain because they are unrealistic result in reinforcement of the belief that one cannot change. Finally, goals are measurable. The new behavior could be observed by another; what one has gained as a result of goal realization can be pinpointed.

In the following example, the group has been focusing on Cornell to help him go to work on eliminating his shyness, and the counselor is winding up the goal-setting process.

Cornell, this all got started when you told us with great sincerity how your own fear of others has kept you from approaching and effectively interacting with people to whom you are attracted. For the past fifteen minutes you have been practicing relating to Marge and Godfrey, two people in the group you wanted to get to know better, and you have told us that your exchanges with them represented genuinely new behavior for you, and that you are pleased with the results. You got feedback from everyone, and you especially liked what Marge and Godfrey honestly told you. Now you've agreed to talk to three strangers before the group meets again. Why don't you tell us where and when, what time of the day and on what days you will do this, and how you will go about it?

When all the characteristics of effective goal setting have been included, the counselor would move onto someone else in the group, but only after Cornell had clearly fixed in his mind exactly how, when, and where he would try out his new behavior and shared this with the group. In the following example of ineffective goal setting, the counselor brings about premature closure and leaves Cornell with a vague and global intention hanging in the air.

Okay, Cornell, that's it then. We're all expecting you to be working at overcoming your shyness and interacting with everyone you can in the coming week. At the next session we'll hear how you made out. Stan, do you want to go into the business about you and your wife now?

Facilitating closure. Lingering on, having difficulty in saying good-bye, is common enough in the general society and is a pregnant area for examing typical self-defeating behavior. In counseling groups it can consume long periods of otherwise useful time, and the effective counselor takes responsibility for not letting that happen, whether this involves ending a complete session or ending a part of one.

Facilitating closure on part of a session is done when the group counselor realizes that further focus on an individual or a concern is nonproductive, when group activity has become repetitive or inconsequential and lingering continues, whether because there is avoidance on the part of some members to enter other areas or because the irrelevance of the activity is not recognized. Under such circumstances, the effective counselor mentally questions whether or not the individual who has been receiving the focus has been taken through the steps of effective group counseling (see Chapter 8): exploring, achieving self-understanding, developing alternatives, setting goals, practicing new behaviors in the group, and generating psychological homework assignments. If an individual has been carried through only a portion of this process but has become blocked in going the remainder of the way at the present time, the counselor helps to identify the nature of the barrier and receives a commitment from the individual to return to the concern at a later time. If all the steps in the process have been gone through, effective closure follows when the counselor helps the group to shift. This is best done by a cogent summary and a check-out with the individual who has been the recipient of the group focus.

Rick, I have just gone over all that has taken place up till now. You have a firm understanding of what you have been doing that you'd like to change and some new ways to go that you have practiced right here in the group, and you have declared specific goals you are going to work on between now and next week which you're going to report on at the beginning of our next session. Unless you feel, Rick, that continuing would be of some further help to you, we can shift the focus now and ask if there is someone else who would like to use the group to work on a personal difficulty. How about it, Rick? Have we left any stones unturned?

This no-nonsense approach to closure helps Rick to have a feeling of completeness and will spare him the ordeal of having to continue as the center of attention beyond a time when doing so serves no useful purpose. Ineffectiveness in facilitating closure occurs when it is not implemented even though it is obviously called for or when it happens too soon, usually out of a counselor feeling of frustration or impotency. It is also ineffective when the counselor adopts an authoritarian, moralizing mien.

We've devoted enough attention to Rick. It's time to move on to someone else. After all, we must learn to share the time so that everyone gets a turn.

Closing a session smoothly does not mean simply letting time run out. Ends of sessions are anticipated by effective counselors, and at the least some succinct summarizing is done, the mutually agreed upon psychological homework assignments are restated, and the transitional nature of the experience is emphasized.

Max, you know what it is you're going to do, now. Next week we'll begin with Myra, Gordy, and Max. Anyone who would like to get something for himself or herself at the next session can be giving it some thought before then. Remember, we'll be meeting on Thursday, not Wednesday, in this room at the same time. If anyone wants to see me individually, I will be in my office at the regular hours. See you next week.

Such a clear, concise, direct closure of the session eliminates the lingering and prattling, the kind of raggedy ending and floundering which characterize so many ineffectively led groups.

Effective closure on the entire group experience involves special activities in the final session, one which is usually devoted to tying up loose ends, evaluating the accomplishments of counseling, and determining what developmental paths members will take in the time period beyond the dissolution of the group. (Some effective group closure strategies are detailed in Chapter 10.)

This concludes our list of twenty skills for group counselor mastery. The list comprises a goal chart for counselor self-development, a model which could be expanded. For example, a given counselor might add the goal of eliminating self-references and replacing them with references which focus on the "other."

The effective group counselor is first and foremost a growing professional who is constantly working at functioning more productively in groups in every conceivable way, one who is well-grounded in a technology of highly specific group leader behaviors which can be called upon at will whenever she or he has a rationale for operationalizing them. The scale which follows is a simple device designed to help a group leader in self-assessment of current performance on the twenty skills elaborated in this chapter. They are presented in the same order as they have been presented in the chapter, not necessarily in their order of importance. The scale can be used for counselor self-ratings, by co-leaders who wish to rate each other, by trainers, and even by group members whose counselor invites and encourages their judgments. The skills can be ranked to identify which ones need the most working on, or they can be scored by placing a rating of 0 to 5 beside each and then summating all item scores to provide a total score, one hundred being absolute perfection, a goal obtained by a few masters of group counseling.

Group Counselor Leadership Behavior Rating Scale

Rating

_____ 1. Identifying, labeling, clarifying, and reflecting feeling.

_____ 2. Identifying, labeling, clarifying, and reflecting behavioral data.

_____ 3. Identifying, labeling, clarifying, and reflecting cognitive data.

_____ 4. Questioning, drawing out, and evoking material appropriate for counseling focus.

_____ 5. Confronting.

_____ 6. Summarizing and reviewing important material.

_____ 7. Interpreting.

_____ 8. Restating.

_____ 9. Establishing connections.

_____ 10. Information giving.

_____ 11. Initiating.

_____ 12. Reassuring, encouraging, and supporting.

_____ 13. Intervening.

_____ 14. Dealing with silence.

_____ 15. Recognizing and explaining nonverbal behavior.

_____ 16. Using clear, concise, meaningful communications.

_____ 17. Focusing.

_____ 18. Restraining, subduing, and avoiding potentially explosive and divisive group happenings.

_____ 19. Goal setting.

_____ 20. Facilitating closure.

_____ TOTAL SCORE

10

Group Counseling Techniques, Strategies, and Structures for the Practitioner

Becoming an expert in leading counseling groups is a professional development goal of great magnitude. Truly effective group counselors have thousands of hours of practice behind them in this most challenging endeavor. They are lifelong learners committed to becoming more proficient in the delivery of their specialized services and more in charge of their own lives. They constantly seek to refine their skills and knowledge and to increase their professional acumen and repertoire of techniques and strategies for doing their job in all of the specialized circumstances which crop up regularly in the groups they counsel. In this chapter several specific techniques and strategies are presented for the developing group counseling practitioner. All are consonant with the goal of helping each group member to change and to become self-enhancing and in charge of his or her personal world, and all have been proven useful when applied in group counseling.

Competency in group counseling often means being creative and imaginative, introducing new formats and structures. Restricting group activity to the traditional sitting-around-in-a-circle-and-talking modality can often, like any other overused structure, induce restlessness or boredom in members anticipating the same old tired business they have already experienced. By varying the action and incorporating new strategies, a counselor multiplies his opportunities for effectiveness, just as creative artists and teachers improve their service delivery by varying methods of presentation.

Nowhere is it inscribed that a counseling group must be dull, humorless, or routine. There are times in the practice of any group counselor when he or she feels lost or impotent, when the group seems to be bogged down, when the interest or commitment of some or all group members seems to have waned, or when it appears that the introduction of a new technique, strategy, or structure will revitalize group activity and still promote the goal achievements of individual members. The techniques described in this chapter are basic to a fully functioning group leader. The whys, whens, and hows are detailed. Each technique, strategy, and structure is included because it works. We know they work because we have used them on countless occasions. But what we have elaborated here only constitutes a beginning. Effective group counselors are interested in developing their own strategies and in applying their own new twists to those they pick up from fellow professionals.

The techniques presented here are deliberately brief. First the technique is described, then typical occasions for using it are outlined. Finally, a rationale for including it as a group leader strategy is given along with a brief example of how the technique might actually be employed. The list is obviously not all-inclusive. After examining the various ways we have found a technique to be useful in our own professional practice, we have made the decision to include or exclude it here, eliminating from this collection some which were too esoteric, rarely usable, or of minimal productivity.

Specific Group Counseling Leadership Techniques

Beginning a Group: Members Introduce Themselves

After explaining what the business of group counseling is all about, the leader asks each member of the group to introduce him- or herself to everyone. But members are enjoined not to use any traditional labels or any role data in identifying themselves. That is, each person is to refrain from mentioning such things as courses of study, job, vocational interests, future plans, family data, hobbies, travels, marital status, age, and so on. Instead, the introduction takes the form of having each person tell what kind of a human being he or she is. The leader asks key questions of each person to help the introductions when necessary, such as, Are you loving? Are you happy? Do you like yourself? When is the last time you cried, and over what? Are you orderly? Are you punctual? Are you frustrated a lot? The leader demonstrates the introduction by modeling his or her own introduction in the preferred style (see example below). Group members do their introductions in whatever order they choose, rather than proceeding single file around the group.

The typical occasions for using this technique are limited. It is most appropriate for an initial session, although it could appear in some modified form in a later session if the same kind of personal data had not yet been exchanged among the group members. Participants are often apprehensive about being in a counseling group for the first time, and this introductory technique is an effective ice-breaker. Members join in with little hesitancy, particularly after witnessing the leader's own introduction.

The technique is useful for beginning a group because it gives the leader and everyone else in the group a wealth of data about each person. The leader's goal is to help each person to identify some negative as well as positive characteristics in order that counseling goal formulation for all group members can begin to shape up in the counselor's mind. By helping each group member to produce a full self-description, the leader demonstrates an ability to be helpful in the earliest stages of the group, eliciting nonthreatening data in particular from members who find the task difficult because they have not thought of themselves as having worth apart from their roles or associations with others. Essentially the members are answering the question, Who am I? Who am I apart from my social roles, my relationships, my hobbies, my activities, my interests, my plans? Who am I apart from my physical appearance and characteristics? We have even tried this introduction technique in total darkness; then the members have to individuate themselves apart from their physical selves, a way which is more difficult to do. We do not, however, recommend that a group counselor attempt the darkness version until he or she is well practiced in the use of the technique since initial anxiety might be induced rather than reduced and eliminating early anxiety about what will happen is part of the rationale behind the use of this technique. The rationale is also lodged in the notion that group-grope, the members searching for meaningful content in an unstructured first session, is unproductive and "turns off" the members to the counseling process. This technique involves each person in the group at the outset, and each member is helped to overcome natural fears about participating; all individuals emerge from the first session having gotten their feet wet.

An example of a leader's own introduction, which could be expanded or altered depending on the age level of the group members, might take the following form:

My name is William, and I am essentially a happy person. I like myself very much, and I work at being happy every day of my life. I am relatively free of guilt and immobilizing worry, and I like to live by appreciating the present moment rather than thinking about the past or the future. I seldom get frustrated to the point of anger, but several specific things do tend to annoy me. I like humor and fun and create as much of it around me as I can. I am somewhat of a procrastinator, and I am vulnerable at times as well. I am basically an independent person, almost to a fault.

Beginning a Group: Members Introduce Themselves, but with a First Impressions Twist

This technique uses exactly the same group member introduction approach described above. Before beginning the introductions, however, each member is given a card or a piece of paper and asked to write down the names of all group members. Next to the names, members are requested to put down their first impressions of each other, based on whatever data they have, even on intuition. Following the noting of first impressions, the same introduction strategy is employed. As each introduction is completed, the group counselor asks if that person would like to hear what first impressions the others had of him or her. If the response is affirmative, each member reads verbatim what has been written next to the person's name.

This technique is clearly practical only in the initial session. It is an exceedingly useful data-gathering strategy, and it provides instant feedback for every member of the group from the outset. People seldom have the opportunity to discover how they strike others on a first impression basis. By structuring this kind of an introductory experience, the leader not only gives the members the opportunity to hear and evaluate how they appear to strangers, but desirable group interaction and honest communication are strongly fostered. The data emerging here, often of a mixed nature since different people have different impressions of any given person, will be useful throughout the life of the group. Members will remind each other later of these initial impressions, and they will each remeber what others thought about them. The fact that a person appears to be fearful, timid, approval seeking, or even dull is personal data which that person may find undesirable and choose to change. And a counseling group is a place where changing the impressions we give can most appropriately begin to happen.

Whether the group is composed of strangers or short- and long-term acquaintances, the leader can begin with this first impressions twist, encouraging members to write whatever comes into their minds about each other, using prior knowledge or data garnered merely from studying each other intensely for a few moments. Members may be encouraged to signify their impressions only with adjectives, as in the following example, or with brief sentences, depending on the size of the group and the time available, including both positive or negative perceived characteristics.

Mike: Strong, likable, apprehensive, curious, attractive, shy, probably moralistic
George: Tired, unconcerned, silent, somewhat fearful, intelligent, guarded

Mary: Wistful, nervous, attractive, queasy, hopeful, studious, reactive
Sammy: Egghead, thinker, bright, insecure, has trouble relating, wants to change
Ramona: Athletic, outdoorsy, wishful, funloving, impulsive, nervous talker

Beginning a Group: Group Consensus on Where to Begin

After defining the group counseling process, confidentiality, and other concerns, the leader asks the group members to write down a self-defeating behavior they would like to change on a piece of paper or an index card. The group leader defines self-defeating behavior and names several that are common among that age group. The leader also cautions that nothing should be written down that a member does not wish to share in the group. The completed cards are collected by the leader, who then redistributes them, instructing members to take any card but their own.

After assigning a number to each card, the leader directs the members to read the cards aloud so that everyone in the group can assign a rating to Card Number 1, Card Number 2, and so on, until every card has been rated by all members. Using a rating scale from 1 to 10, a rating of 5 would indicate absolute indifference to whether or not the group ought to spend time working with the member whose concern has been announced, a 6 or 7 implies a mildly positive attitude toward using group time to help that member, and an 8, 9, or 10 is a very positive rating. Conversely, a rating of 4 or 3 would indicate mildly negative feelings, and 2, 1, or 0 would indicate extremely negative feelings about using group time to work on that behavior. Group members are encouraged to rate each concern as they hear it, based on their own personal attitudes and how relevant the concern is to their own personal interests. When all cards have been rated, the leader asks that they be quickly reread in the same numerical order so that members may recheck the ratings they gave and change them if they wish. Such rechecking is important since the members had not heard all the statements before making their initial ratings.

Next, the members announce the rating they gave to each concern. The leader tallies them, gives the totals for each card, and then collects the cards in the order of the one with the highest collective rating, the next highest, and so on. The card with the highest is then read aloud, the individual who wrote it is identified, and the group counseling begins with the focus on that person's concern. Or the leader can help the group to look at the kinds of concerns which were written and judge their appropriateness (perhaps too impersonal), then give more explicit directions on what constitutes productive group counseling content and repeat the process.

This technique works because it eliminates the excessive group-grope that typifies so many initial group counseling sessions. The leader comes in with a plan, announces that this is a place where we work on becoming more effective operators in our own life circumstances, and then proceeds to demonstrate his or her seriousness by asking members to go through an exercise that is designed to have each one establish a counseling goal.

With this technique group members can talk about the concerns that received a low rating and why that occurred. Also, if a member did not rate his or her own concern with a 10, this can be pointed out. The opportunities for analyzing the data are unlimited, but the effective leader uses the technique only as a beginning, rather than proceeding through every concern to be on the agenda for subsequent sessions. The effective leader knows that other more important concerns will arise in the group, that the technique is valuable in helping the group to get started productively, and that he or she is using a method to launch the group counseling that assures that everyone in the group will feel comfortable in tackling the concern stated by a given member.

What follows is an example of how the group leader might inaugurate this technique by orally specifying self-defeating behaviors that are typical of many people. (The list is practically endless. By spelling out some of the areas that might productively be worked on in the group, the leader helps members to think about what would be the most significant to them.)

There are hundreds of things that people have trouble handling in their lives. As I list some of them, see if any of them pertain to you. If you find one that is meaningful for you, state it on your card; or you might have something in mind which I don't mention, so that is what you should write down. At any rate, some people get continually bored, or they worry a lot how others see them, or they are filled with guilt about a number of past deeds, or they are fearful or depressed a great deal. Some individuals don't get along well with key people in their lives or don't know how to get the things they want, or they get hurt a lot or feel abused, or they are overweight, or smoke excessively, or use drugs and would like to be different. Some folks live in the past, or don't know how to make decisions or plan their futures, or get angry and frustrated, or are afraid of certain things, or are vulnerable, or feel they aren't worth anything.

Beginning a Group: Providing a Sentence Stem for Getting Started

After explaining how counseling in a group works and all of the ground rules, the leader asks each member to introduce him- or herself by completing a sentence stem such as the following: "What no one has ever understood about me is . . .," or "I'm different from most people in that I . . .," or "The thing about myself that I would most like to change is . . . ."

Such sentence completions are effective in giving the group a focused beginning. Although they can be used any time in the life of a group, they work well at the start.

Since most group members are unsure about what they will be doing in the counseling experience, it is beneficial for the leader to know of exercises that will help members to become involved immediately in a businesslike fashion. The sentence completion exercise requires individuals in the group to talk about themselves and to work, even if indirectly at first, at goal setting. By having them state how they are different or what they would like to change, the leader has established an atmosphere from the opening moments in which the focus is on identifying, clarifying, labeling, and going to work on the concerns the members have. The sentence stem can be any from a list designed by the leader; a different stem can be given to each member of the group; or everyone can complete the same stem. At any rate, personal concerns and the unique data about each member receive priority attention at the first session.

As each person is completing the sentence stem, the effective leader helps by asking key questions to draw out additional data and set the stage for the development of behavioral change goals. For modeling purposes, the leader might even complete a sentence stem, such as the following two:

What I would like to change most in myself is the way I always put things off. I am a procrastinator of the worst sort, and I really am going to make an effort to be different.

The thing that no one has ever understood about me is that I genuinely like my privacy. Most of my family members and close friends find this difficult to handle, and they interpret it as rejection on my part. I would like them to know that my seeking out privacy has nothing to do with my attitudes and feelings toward them, but they get upset about my wanting to be alone.

Whenever the leader models a behavior, it is done to demonstrate the technique, not to bring the group focus on him or her. Modeling behavior, therefore, is selected for its potency as an illustration and ought to be clearly identified as such. This same point holds true for every instance of leader modeling presented in the remainder of this list of techniques.

Writing an Oral Letter

The leader asks a group member to write an oral letter right in the group. The recipient of the letter is an individual who is significant in the member's life, someone to whom the group member is having some difficulty relating or with whom the group member has never resolved a conflict. It is even possible to write a letter to a deceased friend or family member and tell that person what the group member never could say when the person was still living. The letter writer should block out the group and all potential disturbances by closing his or her eyes and actually visualizing the letter recipient. The leader explains that the letter should contain whatever the group member would like to say that has not been previously said, the reasons for any existing bitterness, and how the relationship should change. If the letter writer stumbles or has any difficulty, the leader provides suggestions, whether this is in the opening of the letter or in transitional parts of the body of the letter, being a helpful prompter who is in tune with the kind of message the writer wants to send.

When the letter has been completed, everyone in the group is requested to react and say what thoughts and feelings the letter elicited. Then the group leader rewrites the letter right in the group from the point of view of someone who is totally self-responsible and effective, given the same relational data. Any and all blaming, wishing, other-directedness, complaining, and the like are eliminated in the leader's letter to the same individual. The vital ingredient of the leader's letter is that it contains no reliance on the recipient to be different; it contains total acceptance of the status quo and announces how the writer will think and act in the future with regard to the recipient regardless of what the recipient does. Group members are again encouraged to provide feedback. The letter writer can thus see how an effective person would correspond with someone and how this communication is quite different from his or her own.

This technique is most appropriate when an individual expresses a concern about a significant other that is troublesome, agonizing, bitter, frustrating, and full of upsetting interactional demands and unreasonable behavior. The list of possible recipients is endless; they could include marriage or divorced partners, parents, siblings, current or former employers, friends who act abusively, teachers, any of the former inhabitants in an individual's life who are ghosts in the mind and still exercise some negative psychological impact. The technique is most appropriately invoked after a member has emitted considerable data about relationship difficulties and has expressed obvious frustration about the attitudes and abusive actions of the troublesome other. The leader asks the group member to write a letter with a specific purpose in mind. Talking to someone, rather than about someone, makes the communication patterns clearer and reveals much data about the relationship. From previous hurts to admonitions for past behaviors in past events, the letter-writing format provides a useful way for people to get in touch with core dimensions and feelings, even though it is on a simulated basis.

Frequently, this is an emotional experience for the letter writer. Talking directly to someone with whom one always has had difficulty communicating can be a heavy and trying venture. Opening and closing salutations are trouble spots: some individuals have difficulty saying "Dear" at the start or "Love" at the end; others voice their deepest sentiments for the first time in their lives, perhaps concluding with "May all the damnations of Hell torture you for all eternity," thus releasing the horrible pent-up thoughts they have carried for a long time in their heads; or saying aloud for the first time, "I love you." A typical letter begins with "Dear . . ., I am writing you this letter because I have always found it so difficult to communicate with you in person. You would never listen to what I had to say. Specifically, I want to tell you that . . . ." Then the soliloquy takes on its true pertinence. During the monologue, the effective leader takes notes about what is being said; this is not distracting to the letter writer, who has his or her eyes tightly shut. The notes are taken so that all the information revealed can be accurately treated in the rewriting.

Rewriting the letter is very important. Here the leader is using skills to demonstrate what the group member can say in a more positive and effective manner. The contrast in letters will actively demonstrate differences in effective and self-defeating thinking patterns. Group interaction over the letter is also important because feedback from everyone in the group helps the letter writer to learn how others view and feel about the shared personal data. The group members are each requested to give a brief reaction to what was said in the original letter and to state how they might work at becoming more effective in that particular relationship. Because the letter-writing technique introduces a first-person quality to the relationship between a member and some individual who is not in the group, everyone tends to get involved.

Oral letter writing is indeed a powerful helping tool. It should be used sparingly so that it does not become a gimmick or a game, since it can make a genuine difference in the life of a group member. In our experience, no one who has ever written an oral letter in a counseling group and had it rewritten has ever forgotten the cathartic and reconstructive nature of the technique. More importantly, letter writers later feel that there is no longer any reason to make such communications in their everyday lives.

Subdividing the Group into Dyads or Triads

The group leader brings any two members into the center. They sit facing each other and are given the following directions: "Mary, here's what you are going to do. You are going to say things to Tom based on what you have observed and learned about him in the group that you think will be helpful to him. After this is completed, you will reverse the procedure, and, Tom, you will tell Mary whatever you think will be helpful to her." The leader then assists both partners with this task, prompting them, helping them to recall specifics or to focus on particular behaviors they know about each other from their experience in the group.

The second part of the instructions involves a dialogue between the two members which results in goal setting. "Both of you have provided each other with some helpful feedback. Now, based on that feedback, try to help each other set a goal which can be attained right here in the group. Mary, tell Tom what you think he could work on in the group that would be of benefit to him and tell him how you think you could help him reach that goal. Don't give up until both of you agree on a worthy goal that is realistically attainable. Tom, you will do the same for Mary." Again the leader assists the partners to complete the task. This dialogue focuses exclusively on what each individual would be able to accomplish in the group sessions themselves, although the specified goals are ones that can be transferred to the lives of both individuals outside the group.

This concludes the demonstration part of the technique. The leader then asks all the group members if it is clearly understood how each is to function in the dyads to which each person will be assigned. The group is then either assigned randomly into pairs or triads or assigned based on a previously determined rationale. The subgroups are given a specific amount of time, 30 minutes or so, to accomplish the task they have seen demonstrated. Specific directions are given to the subgroups, and small talk and conversations are strongly discouraged. The subgroups return at the appointed time. Group members then give feedback about their own behavior in the subgroup and announce their own goal, which at least one other member is privy to and has a commitment to help them achieve. The entire group is now aware of specific new goals for each member.

The most appropriate time for using this technique is about one-third of the way into the total life expectancy of the group, although a leader could induce it at any juncture when it seems fruitful to do so. Many people find it difficult to talk in front of more than a half-dozen others, whereas dealing with one or two individuals is not nearly so anxiety provoking. In the subgroup demonstration the leader is careful to guarantee effective communication and goal setting. The small unit task is constructed to give each person something clear, pinpointed, and personally valuable to deal with and to renew each individual's commitment to derive all that is possible from the counseling in the larger group setting. When two people are checking on each other as they work toward their goals in the larger group, their sense of involvement in the process is bolstered. This subgrouping exercise helps members to become more familiar with each other and to gain a sense of trust in working together; it automatically provides witnesses to the processes of feedback and goal setting. Moreover, the counselor can use the data emanating from the subgroups at any time in the later life of the group. The counselor will find that group members are free and willing to share helpful thoughts and observations and to interact on a dyadic or triadic level provided that a clear and effective demonstration is included in the modeling of this technique.

When the members return to the group, the leader has the option of asking any individual what goals were set for achievement in subsequent group sessions. In addition, the leader can help all members to assess the feedback each received from their partner by checking with the other group members.

When the flame of productive activity in a group is dying, this technique can help to refuel it with a quick revitalizing opportunity for everyone in the group to derive safe feedback and become committed to the goal-setting process in a new way.

A Fantasy

The counselor invites a member who has had some counseling focus in the group to suspend all disbelief for a while and imagine being able to do or have anything he or she desires. The fantasy has no bounds. Anything is possible; the world is at the individual's disposal. The leader helps by telling the person to detail aloud how a few typical days will be used up, particularly eliciting who is present in the fantasy, where the person will go, roles of family members, how time is used, the part money plays, the extent to which love is present. The more involved the member becomes, the richer the fantasy. The member is given free rein—anything goes.

After the fantasizing, the group reacts and helps to analyze it. Follow up occurs in subsequent group sessions. Are there changes in the routine of the member's life or in the member's thoughts and emotions? Has a new perspective on living taken place?

This technique helps reluctant members to disclose their deepest thoughts and feelings so that the counselor and group members have a real view of their world from the perspective of looking at life goals. When offered the opportunity to engage in a freewheeling expression of personal desires, many individuals find the task difficult because they conceive of themselves as inexorably locked into their social roles and circumstances, which they have accepted as their fate. Their lives seem void of meaning and excitement; they feel stuck in their ruts. Their fantasies are frequently unimaginative, crowded with the characteristics of their own routinized living, with little or no flair introduced. The leader who uses this technique will note that most fantasies are about 90 percent attainable, given the real-world parameters of the fantasizer's existence. Few people fantasize about strolling on Uranus, being a monarch, sitting on the Supreme Court bench, being the opposite sex, or being lionized for exceptional deeds. The fantasy is usually an extension of a life that is being led in a certain mode with a few minor exceptions added. Seldom is it a radical departure, a look at a new person in wildly different circumstances.

The fantasy technique can be most productive in accelerating goal setting. When the fantasy is analyzed, it usually becomes evident that everything in it is more than remotely attainable at some level. Group members are helped to learn more about the fantasizer, and their reactions promote relational interactions on a new basis with the given member. The effective leader looks for lack of genuine love in the fantasy, living up to the expectations of others, how significant others in the fantasizer's life are treated, who goes on the trip (almost all fantasies involve travel or getting away), the extent to which power and money get attention, and how many components are currently attainable.

This is an exciting technique for helping members to discover their own most meaningful goals and how their thinking has been affected by the enculturation process, rather than seeing themselves as free agents with the power to alter their life circumstances in numerous self-enhancing ways. A miniversion of the fantasy can be employed at any time by having an individual dream aloud about how he or she would like to change a relationship, conditions on a job or in a total career or in any life segment; here the leader helps the fantasizer detail all the elements and imagine all possibilities. But again the purpose is to have the member discover attainable goals.

Role Shifting

At the beginning of a group session, slips of paper with members' names are placed into a receptacle. Group members then draw a name, making certain they have not drawn their own. For the next 30 minutes each person, without revealing the name drawn, assumes the identity and manifests characteristic behaviors of the individual whose name appears on the paper. During this time the leader engages the group in some activity which will involve everyone, perhaps asking the members to examine love in their lives, its meaning and importance, or to focus on how they function as strangers in new social situations. At the end of the 30 minutes, the leader asks each member to guess who he or she thought was impersonating him or her and why. The impersonation identities are not revealed until all the crossfire feedback, the rationale for choices, and the commentary of everyone has been brought out. After the names are revealed, further reactions are elicited.

This technique provides an excellent means for group members to see how they are perceived by others without having to deal with the resistance that so frequently accompanies more direct efforts of feedback stimulation. It is best introduced at the beginning of a session to allow ample time for post-impersonation analysis, and it should not be used until three, four, or more sessions have transpired as the members will not have collected enough behavior data to assume the new temporary roles.

The technique engenders much productive group interaction and provides valuable insight to group members on how they are being seen in the group context. Members are amazed at how they appear to others. The total involvement built into the structure allows members who have been resistant or nonverbal to become engaged in new ways, and their interaction increases. Young people take to this technique quickly, often wanting to repeat it at a later time. The group leader is careful, when giving instructions to the members, to emphasize the importance of emulating both nonverbal and verbal behavior and characteristic thinking and emotional patterns.

The Nice Thing about Being . . .

The leader asks a member who is receiving counseling focus in the group to give a specific categorical label to a self-defeating personality and behavioral dimension. Such labels as cranky, shy, short-tempered, fearful, fat, lazy, guilty, and approval-seeking are appropriate. The individual is then given the sentence stem: "The nice thing about being [cranky] is . . . ." The member is asked to repeat the stem continually and complete it with as many predicates as possible. Then the other members are asked to state the stem and complete the sentence with their own thoughts. No particular order is imposed on group members to participate in stem completion.

This strategy is best employed when the counseling process with a given individual has been moved to the step of self-understanding. The technique is designed to help a member answer the question, "What do I get out of this behavior?" By urging that member to answer the question aloud in as many ways as he or she can, the difficult work of acquiring self-understanding is promoted. Similarly, by involving other group members in the exercise, everyone begins to understand how a psychological maintenance system underlies self-defeating behavior and each member acquires some insight into analogous dimensions of his or her own living. The resources of the group are brought to bear on a member's particular concerns in a potent and focused way.

Without the self-understanding which this technique helps to bring about for each member, the counseling seldom effectively proceeds to goal setting and trying out new behaviors, the more advanced steps in the counseling process. Before members are willing to try changing current behaviors, they must know and judge what is behind them, why the behavioral patterns exist and persist.

Nothing prevents the group leader from contributing to the sentence completion exercise when the group seems to be missing some crucial diagnostic insights or when neurotic or unworthy payoffs for psychologically unhealthy behavior are not being pinpointed.

One-Way Messages

The group member who has received a prolonged period of intense counseling focus is asked to remain silent and not respond while the other members in the group send a one-way message to that person (in no particular order). When all messages are sent, the leader asks the person for reactions. This technique can be used as a closure strategy, when further focus on the individual would reap minimal returns and the time has come to shift the group emphasis to someone else.

This technique is used most effectively when the group appears to be at a standstill, when a group member is argumentative and won't consider what others are saying, or when a member denies and explains away whatever others are offering. Group members frequently are anxious to tell others how they ought to be seen and reject any picture of themselves that is different from what they want to believe is so.

Whenever the technique is employed, it is effective in helping a given member to hear what others have to say and then use his or her personal filtering system to accept or reject such offerings. It is productive in reaching withdrawn members, and it gets all members to interact with the person who is receiving the counseling focus. The person in focus receives many ideas and points of view and learns how others have been reacting to the behavior and self-disclosure data he or she has emitted. The technique serves the additional purpose of eliminating boring interchanges which often lead nowhere, although it should not become a leader device that loses its potency through overuse. The opportunities and rationale for using this strategy are limitless.

Repeat Back, then Respond

The leader joins two members who sit facing each other in the center of the group. Person X makes a statement to person Y which has been difficult to communicate to Y in some earlier group context. Y must repeat back to X's complete satisfaction what was just communicated. Y then reacts to what X said and X repeats back to Y's complete satisfaction. The procedure is repeated throughout the interchange. If the talking member does not agree that his message is correctly received, it is rephrased until it is completely understood. Understanding means that every message is reiterated to the speaker's satisfaction, not by saying "I understand" or nodding the head. When the exchange is over, the other group members give feedback to the principals, concentrating on listening and communication skills.

The leader's hidden agenda for using this technique is to facilitate more effective communication between two people in the group who have shown opposition to each other—two whose values, outlooks on life, personalities, and the like are at such odds that contention continually arises in the group when they have anything to do with each other. If two people in the group will not listen to each other or if alienation or rejection between them is running rampant, this technique is effective in breaking down the barriers. People have differences which often are extreme, sometimes permeating and affecting the entire group. Such individuals can benefit from this listening and communicating technique; it requires positive attention and allows for one's point of view to be completely expressed.

While the two principals are in the center of the large group, the leader helps them get started by reminding them of any contentious intragroup behavior which both have previously manifested. The leader functions as a helper, prompter, and monitor of the exchange, without taking either side, and takes notes about content and behavioral data. The form for the dialogue follows:

X—Makes opening statement, usually somewhat lengthy.

Y—Repeats back statement, both its essence and nuances.

X—Either gives permission for Y to react or restates the part that was missed by Y.

Y—Restates corrected part to X's satisfaction and then reacts with own statement to X.

X—Repeats back to Y's satisfaction, and the process continues.

This technique aids in bridging communication gaps in the group; pairs of members are helped to resolve differences. But the most important benefit to all group members comes from learning how tough it is to listen well and communicate effectively without letting one's ego or self-interests intervene. It can be used anytime during the life of the group.

Assistant Leaders

After inquiring if anyone in the group would like to work on leadership skills, the group counselor appoints someone to act as assistant leader for the session. During the session the appointed voluntary assistant does not focus on any personal concerns. All leader behaviors are directed toward serving the other members, and everyone in the group is made aware of this distinction.

Drawing out potential helpers and having them serve in a leadership capacity can be done any time after the group has had two or three opportunities to work together and members have had a chance to see what leaders do in comparison with what members do. Group members serving as assistant leaders practice helping interventions and simultaneously improve their own world in the process. The more one serves in the role of helper, the greater the likelihood for becoming more personally in charge of one's self. The effective counselor must constantly produce active strategies for identifying, labeling, understanding, and changing self-defeating thinking and behaving, and functioning in a leader capacity in the group enables some members to help themselves in safety by helping others.

Any time an assistant leader has been engaged, a period must be set aside for the group members to provide insightful feedback when the leadership experience has terminated. Suggestions and evaluative reactions are crucial to the volunteering leader; both support and criticism are significant for the assistant's self-development and self-confidence. Peers helping peers is certainly one of the most useful and effective strategies which can be implemented in a learning environment such as group counseling.

Promoting Spontaneity

There are two forms to this technique:

1. The leader asks a group member to act in a spontaneous manner right in the group. The leader's instructions are as follows: "When I point to someone, you are to react with whatever comes into your head, without giving a lot of thought to creating a cautious offering. I will point at random to group members, and you just react with whatever words seem fit." The leader then points to group members and helps the individual to react to them spontaneously.

2. The leader asks a group member to act in a spontaneous manner right in the group. The leader's instructions are as follows: "I am going to give you a word to start with and then you just free-associate with a list of words which come to mind. Without thinking it through, just let the preceding word elicit the next one and state the words aloud." The leader appoints someone to write the words as the individual says them to facilitate a post free-association analysis.

In using either of these spontaneous behavior-eliciting techniques, the leader is sensitive to the particular circumstances that call for such action. They are most appropriate when a member has talked about being too formal, rigid, organized, careful in dealing with others, planned, dull, lacking in spontaneity, or stereotyped as a totally predictable person in everyday living. After the counselor has helped a member through the steps of exploration, identification of self-defeating behaviors, self-understanding, and goal setting, he or she can offer the member the opportunity to try out new and different behaviors right in the group which will constitute productive change. At this point one of the two spontaneous behavior techniques or a similarly constructed exercise is appropriate.

By helping a group member to engage in some new and exciting behavior within the safety of the group, the counselor promotes and stimulates the member to initiate self-growth. When the group member sees that it is indeed possible to act extemporaneously without all of the attendant anxiety that has kept him or her from doing this before, the member gains a measure of new learning which enables more effective behavior to emerge outside of the group in his or her private world where it really counts; the member learns to act sometimes on impulse rather than restraining every harmless urge.

These techniques introduce action into the group—actually doing rather than merely talking about different behaviors. Effective counselors have action dimensions of counseling uppermost in their list of interventions, knowing that thinking which is untranslated into doing, however admirable, makes little difference in the lives of the clients they serve.

Taking a Risk in the Group

An individual in the group, who has talked about risk-taking avoidance as a self-defeating mode of operation, is asked to take a risk in the group. The member is requested to choose two or three others and to think of something to say to these members which would involve some risk. The risky communication can be either positive or negative. For some people, saying "I like you" or "I am attracted to you" is more risky than saying "You bore me" or "I've been wanting to tell you how much I tune you out." The greater loading of self-perceived risk, the more likely the individual is to benefit from the exercise. Then the group members provide feedback.

This technique is applicable at almost any time in the life of the group whenever exploration and self-understanding have taken place and an indiviudal has acknowledged that risk-taking avoidance is a part of his or her life pattern. By asking a group member to engage in risk-taking behavior in the safety of the group, the counselor helps that member to test out what it means to take risks, to enlarge his or her behavioral repertoire. The powerful lesson that a disaster does not always happen as a result of taking personal risks, that others have a healthier respect for someone who is unafraid to do so, is programmed right into the counseling activity.

In the post-risking analysis by the entire group, the member is helped to understand what has been accomplished, how the recipients of the member's risk-taking statements viewed the communications, what feelings accompanied the action, and how the activity might be productively transferred to the person's life.

The Three Most Important People in Your Life

In the exploratory stage of counseling an individual, when the leader is attempting to induce self-understanding, this person is asked to go back to a particular age, say 5 years old, and name in order the three most significant people in his or her life. Then the individual is taken to more advanced ages, say 12, then 16, then 22, at regular intervals, until the present age is reached, in each case responding to the same question. Then projection is introduced, 5, 10, 20, even 30 years in the future. "Who will the three most important people in your life be?"

This technique helps the counselor to gain valuable insights into an individual's world at various life stages, particularly in the dimension of psychological dependency. The technique can be used at almost any time in the group counseling with a particular individual, or it can be used with the total group, each member going through the exercise. The counselor seeks to determine patterns of dependency in those clients who lack psychological independence, and this technique provides that kind of insight for the client as well as the counselor.

The perceptive counselor recognizes that most people fail to include themselves in the list of the three most important people; even when projecting into the future, the self is conspicuously denied. As the lists of significant others develop, the leader gives no signs of approval or disapproval; relationships are carefully noted, and questions eliciting rationales for the choices are asked. It is a data-revealing technique which helps every member to see patterns of dependency throughout life and to make new and more self-enhancing judgments for future relationships. In any analysis of the data, the leader seeks to help members include themselves on the list, at the very top, if not now, certainly in the near future.

Project Yourself Vocationally Ten Years into the Future, then Change Sex

The group leader asks a woman who has been receiving group focus to project what her life will be like in ten years. As she projects herself into her future, the leader asks questions about her work roles, promotions, aspirations, family status, position in the world, number of children and how they are cared for, her relationship to a man or men, and so on. When this is completed, the leader then asks her to restate what her life would be like ten years from now if she were a man. The group leader and members then analyze and note differences.

This technique can be used almost any time within the life of the group to demonstrate the different expectations of women, how many women tend to have lower aspirations than men in almost every way because they live in a sexist culture. It is a particularly appropriate technique for a given group member who seems unaware of the extent to which she is lowering herself when she considers herself and her future.

Essentially the group leader is taking the member on a fantasy trip which helps that person to assess how effectively she is living her current life related to anticipated future moves. The sex shift enables the individual to see how she may be lowering her self-expectations; it is a dynamite method for demonstrating inequities. Lowered self-expectancies can then be challenged and eliminated as a part of the counseling.

Key Questions

Who listens the most closely to you in this group? Who is the most like you? The least like you? Who is the most effective? The happiest? Whom would you go to for help? Whom would you like to know better? What would you like to know?

These questions and others like them, which an imaginative counselor might think up, easily occur to a group leader in the course of counseling an individual in the group. Effective group counselors regularly involve other group members to aid in the counseling process. The process here is to have all the group members participate in the exercise of choosing other members on the basis of some criterion. The technique helps to promote productive activity in the group and can be used as a stimulus for group involvement at any time.

But promoting involvement for its own sake is not enough. These questions help to produce insights and aid the goal-setting process. When members assess whom they are most like or unlike in the group, others have different impressions; the discrepancies can be noted, reality reading can be upgraded, and goals can be set for checking impressions outside of the group. The results of informal polls can be used to help people who perceive themselves as different to learn how to deal with each other in ways that promote the acquisition of social skills and reduce fear. Often an individual who is fearful, shy, and weak will choose the strongest person in the group as the one who is most similar when in fact everyone in the group sees that such is not the case and can specify data upon which they base their perceptions. Helping members to know each other better not only provides them with the opportunity to practice important basic social skills but also results in upgrading helping competencies of members in later counseling sessions. Members give reinforcement to each other about themselves in ways they had not thought of previously, and many members are surprised and pleased by the positive statements that other members make about them.

Closing the Group: Exchanging Reactions

In the final session the leader asks each group member to list everyone's name on a piece of paper. Next to each name members are asked to write the single most self-enhancing and the single most self-defeating characteristic of that person. These characteristics are to be as explicitly stated as possible and selected because they are seen as helpful contributions. Then, proceeding around the group in random order, each member declares what he or she has written about himself or herself and then hears what every other group member has written about him or her.

This technique may be used at any time in the life of the group, but it is particularly fitting for a final meeting when evaluation of the counseling and projections for goal achievement for each member beyond the life of the group are appropriate focal areas. The technique structures the final session in such a way as to allow everyone in the group to be in the spotlight and make an assessment of where each person is and might go in the future in self-development. As each member hears from all the other group members and that person's self-data is emphasized, the leader provides a summary of how the counseling experience has been useful, reminding each member of what transpired in the group that had pertinence to the member, reinforcing gains, and helping the member to commit him- or herself to realizable goals beyond the life of the group. This provides each person with a sense of closure. Members depart from the group with their own self-assessments and that of their peers fresh in their minds; they know where they are in their lives and have made judgments about where they think they must go.

Closing the Group: Conducting a Reunion

In the final group counseling session the leader proposes that the meeting be considered a reunion of the group which is taking place in future time. "Well, here we are, just as we said we would be, on the beach at Acapulco. Exactly one year has passed since we had the last group session, and we have a great deal to tell each other about what we made happen in our lives." Each member understands the fantasy, and the members then begin telling what has happened in their lives, relating everything in the past tense. The leader helps to elicit specifics, particularly progress reports on concerns that were voiced during the life of the counseling group. How much do members weigh; are they still living with their partners; how have the qualities of their significant relationships changed; when did they do this or that; where are they vocationally, educationally, and psychologically; how do they feel about themselves now? The questions are designed to determine specifics and the answers become commitments to create self-change.

The technique of closing the counseling experience with a reunion projected a year or so into the future helps to make the final meeting a commitment session, one in which the participants make social contracts with their peers to accomplish specific goals in their lives in the coming year. The leader helps the group to close on an optimistic note by taking the reunion fantasy seriously. Members like to envision what they will achieve and to be able to state what progress they have made. Group members have grown close to each other during the tenure of their counseling experience together, and a final group meeting which is raggedy or fails to draw each member into the activity in a meaningful way would send some members away with a sense of emptiness and incompletion. Closure is always difficult, and members frequently express sadness at breaking a group, but this is averted with the reunion technique.

This concludes the list of specific group counseling techniques, strategies, and structures. Although each technique described in this chapter has limited application depending on the circumstances of the counseling process itself, they are all useful procedures which enliven the counseling process and make it more effective. Each technique has a rationale for its use, and most can be modified or adapted to many group circumstances. Although many additional fine and useful strategies could be listed, this collection serves as a beginning for the group counselor who is interested in making the group into a more stimulating and productive interpersonal learning environment.

11

Effective Group Counseling
Process Interventions*

Group counseling as a format for helping participants to become more productive and capable human beings is the appropriate *group* experience which, optimistically, will gain broad adoption at all junctures of the entire educational network, elementary through university graduate scool, and also in less formally structured educational settings. Currently there is meager agreement, if any, on the focus that group counseling ought to take and on precisely what activities are acceptable for counseling groups and which should be considered taboo. For purposes of clarification, the authors view group counseling in the school setting as a social and psychological helping activity which has as its overall objective the changing of behavior which is in any way destructive to the individuals participating in the experience and the acquisition of new behavior of a self-enhancing nature.

What behaviors are deemed negative—as being self-defeating? Without cataloging a thousand narrow specifics, it can be said that self-destructive behaviors are those which work against an individual's maximum self-acceptance, against adequate coping with or mastery of a person's environment, both social and inanimate, against being in charge of himself, his emotions, his world. Even the absence of those behaviors which most of us learn and make our own at this or that developmental stage can be construed as being self-destructive. The counseling group is seen as the safe learning laboratory in which members are committed to working on the elimination of their self-defeating behaviors; to working on their self-development formulated in highly specific, attainable ways; to working in conjunction with and reciprocation toward others likewise committed; to testing alternate ways of behaving and devising new courses of action; to exploring one's self and one's world, analyzing and assessing both in order to establish realistic counseling goals which can be achieved during the stated tenure of the group.

---

*Reprinted with permission from *Educational Technology,* January 1973, pp. 61-67.

The concepts of group counselor functioning are not universally agreed upon within the counseling profession. Those who have assumed responsibility for training "facilitators" in the encounter group movement have established a posture on the issue of group leader role which is to a great extent antithetical to the responsibilities of the group counselor in the school setting. Encounter group facilitators tend to see themselves as player-coaches, as leaders who are deeply involved in the group process in much the same way as the other participants are; they see themselves as members who happen to have "logged" a great many more hours of group inhabitation and who are willing to share what they have learned; but they still are, nevertheless, very interested, for the sake of their own growth, in becoming engaged in group happenings "on a personal level." They don't see themselves as experts, nor do they covet the responsibility implied in such a mantle for possible adverse consequences resulting from any group activity.

In contradistinction, the group counselor is the responsible professional, and the more expertness he can ethically deliver, the better off his counselees are. Nor can an adult who serves youth, which would be the case in most school situations, presume that he is in any way the peer of the group counselees. That he is paid under an occupational title (be it counselor, teacher, or whatever) additionally precludes the possibility as a matter of role identity. Nor is he a friend. Rather, he is a professional, supposedly trained and certified, a person hired to provide educational and helping services.

The group counselor's role is dominated by one all-embracing characteristic which distinguishes him from a group member: he does not permit himself to use the group or anyone in it to serve his own needs. His focus is always on the "other," or all of the "others" in the group taken together, and ought hardly ever to be on himself. He embraces, thinks and communicates in the second person singular voice, "you"; he seeks to snuff out the pronoun "I"; and he only reluctantly backs into using the pronoun "we." He attempts to serve each of the group members as effectively as possible. He therefore seeks to acquire those behaviors and competencies which will enable him to provide service, and he seeks to extinguish in himself those behaviors which tend to stand in the way of effective service to each individual in the group.

William C. Schutz, in describing intervention guidelines for the encounter group leader, writes: " . . . if I wasn't sure whether or not to intervene in a group, to consult my stomach. If it felt relaxed, do it; if it was tight, don't."* We believe a far more detailed analysis of the

---

*Schutz, William C. *Here Comes Everybody*. New York: Harper and Row, 1971, 245.

process of group leader intervention is needed in group counseling work. The *stomach as a consultant* is simply not adequate as a guide for those who are attempting to make a difference in the lives of young people. *The notion of group counseling as an amorphous activity in which one does what comes naturally is precisely why it is conducted so ineffectively by so many practitioners.*

Anyone who has ever served as a group counselor or who has contemplated that role has dealt with the conflict of knowing exactly *when* and *how* to intervene in the group action. Over and beyond any preplanning for alternate courses of action for individuals in the group or the group as a whole done for an upcoming counseling session, the proficient group counselor has ideas about what kinds of interventions he expects to make in the course of a given meeting, where those interventions will take the individuals in the group, his reasons for making them, and when particular ones will be needed. It should be noted that an intervention does not necessarily imply that the group counselor must be the one doing the intervening. That an intervention is called for should be recognized immediately by the leader. However, as the tenure of the group unfolds, the leader learns to encourage group members to become aware of the need for interventions and to actually channel interventions through them whenever possible, since many, perhaps even most, on-cue interventions are more readily accepted when capably delivered by peers, especially if other peers chime in and reinforce the meaning and intent of a member's helping attempts. The group counselor can serve as a model to the group members and actually teach them leadership intervention behaviors. Early in the life of the group the group members will observe the counselor making interventions at key points in the counseling sessions. A truly capable leader helps the pressure for actually making these interventions shift from the counselor to the group members, but he retains the responsibility for ensuring that the intervention does in fact occur.

Significant, on-target "counseling" interventions, whether made by the counselor of the group or by its members, help to keep members working on their goals and give everyone a sense of directionality. Counselees need reinforcement of their progress, and interventions which chip away at impediments to that progress provide support for group counseling as a productively meaningful process. This helps members to feel better about the struggle they are going through on their way to self-enlargement and makes them more willing to work at self-defeating behaviors and less willing to avoid such work. No work, no payoff.

What are some constantly recurring situations and times in counseling groups when an appropriate intervention is *almost always* called

201

for? Any competent group counselor who has led groups for many clock hours and who seriously entertains the foregoing question can begin to take a look at his own "break-ins," examine his counselor behavior patterns, and arrive at those propitious moments when an intervention usually seemed to be effective, even characterizing the nature of those interventions which were repeatedly productive. Reduced to their most communicable common denominators, these could be transmitted to others.

In essence, this is what we have done. The short list we offer here was compiled after carefully examining hundreds of counseling tapes, many hours of co-counseling diverse groups and distilling the results of our thinking. We observed that these specific interventions were almost always effective in promoting or in laying the groundwork for the promotion of behavior change on the part of group participants.

Ten Occasions for Group Intervention

The group counselor can productively take responsibility for initiating or causing an intervention when:

1. A group member speaks for everyone. The use of phrases such as "This is how we feel" or "The group is bogged down" or "We think we ought to . . ." is quite common in counseling groups. A group member may feel much more comfortable by stating the "we" or the "group" and assuming that everyone present feels the same, or even use the collective noun or pronoun as a ploy to muster support for a position or point of view, playing "gang up" games. This is an appropriate time for the leader to assess if everyone is in agreement. Permitting the "we" syndome to run rampant in a group can become quite self-defeating for each group member. It encourages a sense of "groupiness," an appeal to the group to engage in consensus rather than individual thinking. If it is successful often enough, group members learn to stifle themselves and only deal with group-approved material which, almost without exception in groups where consensus thinking becomes the norm, turns out to be shallow and bland. Moreover, it inhibits individual members from challenging each other for fear of upsetting the collective spirit of unanimity or equanimity.

Appropriate interventions include: "You mentioned *we* several times. Are you speaking for each person in the group? Is there anyone who doesn't agree with the position stated?" If the counselor is aware of contrary positions due to previously exposed data or due to nonverbal clues, it is effective to indicate these and ask the person associated with the data or the clues how his or her thinking differs. For the leader to go directly to another member ("Carl, is Maynard speaking for you?''), preferably a strong, clear thinker, is an effective way of derailing a wrongly scheduled "we" express train. The anti-we intervention encourages members to think for themselves, to remember that *group counseling has individual rather than group goals,* and it sets a tone in the group which permits openness by allowing each member to make his own unique contribution and establish that his perceptions are at least a shade different from everyone else's.

But more important, it teaches a counselee to read behavioral data more accurately, to *remember* the positions of others, and to judge the extent to which there is agreement with his own. It teaches a counselee to *check out* where others stand. And it teaches him to think more realistically in terms of "some" or "one other person" rather than "all." Then, too, it teaches him that the "some" can only be included if there is evidence to support such inclusions. All of these lessons, if incorporated in the self-system and translated into habitual behavior outside the group, serve to make a person more effective in his dealings with others.

2. An individual speaks for another individual within the group. It is quite common for a group member to speak for another individual in the group by saying something like "This is what she means" or "She's not saying how she feels. I can explain it."

Almost without exception, if person B takes over for person A in this fashion, usually one of two inferences can be tellingly made. First, B has made the judgment about A that A is not up to the job of sending her messages effectively, that she is inadequate or incapable, an incompetent communicator, at least less adequate or capable than B; and when B "takes over," under the guise of being helpful, B is being condescending, saying nonverbally that A has failed. A second possibility, depending on the circumstances, is that person B is worried about where the interaction is leading downstream and, sensing more emotional rapids ahead, wants somehow to avoid them. For example, leading up to B's take-over, A is experiencing frustration, confusion, tension; A's delivery of her material is tentative, garbled, wandering; B suspects that A is feeling pressured to reveal something about herself and that she is trying to steer away from it. Because B thinks A won't be able to handle *dealing* with whatever "conflict" might arise, B jumps in. This kind of "commandeering" of a situation in order to "defuse" an impending altercation is frequent in counseling groups but seldom effective.

Both of these inferences can be checked out in any given situation and ought to be. In each case what the behavioral data says about and to person B is just as important as what it says about and to A. In the latter instance, for example, person B may have taken over because *she* is ineffective in handling conflict, frustration, self-revelation of personally difficult life-data, *even when it is happening to someone else.*

But regardless of the circumstances behind one individual speaking for another, an intervention is called for. It is an opportune time for individual members to set goals for themselves. The person who is allowing another group member to speak for him might establish the goal of speaking more clearly or not allowing someone else to speak for him, whether in the group sessions or elsewhere, particularly if he discovers that this occurs all the time in his life, with all kinds of people. In addition, the "talker" can establish the goal of eliminating the tendency to rescue a person when he is not speaking effectively. Certainly the talker needs to eliminate the tendency to make assumptions that she knows how someone else feels without checking it out. Rather than allowing counselees to speak for each other, the group leader should be promoting the desire on the part of the group members to help each person become as effective as possible in their message sending and receiving. This means being able to express one's thoughts, perceptions and self-definitions so that one is understood by everyone else in the group. Anyone short-changed in this area can work on overcoming deficiencies by practicing—by struggling to change ineffectual speech patterns and habits—rather than sitting back and allowing a more lucid group member to take charge. Once the group is aware that a member has set such a goal, others can swiftly zero in on helping the struggler to work through whatever is necessary to achieve adequate communication at the appropriate times.

Appropriate interventions for elimination of people speaking for each other include: "Did Sally state how you were feeling more clearly than you were able to?" If "yes," focus on the goal for speaking more clearly. If "no," "How did it feel to have someone else rescue you?" Or, to the talker, "Did you feel that Mary needed your aid at that moment?" Or "Do you find it difficult to hold back when you think that you understand how someone else feels and that person can't express himself?" Or "Would helping Herman to make himself understood be more effective for him than your assuming the interpreter's role?"

An offshoot of this tendency of one group member to speak for another which crops up in the early stages of most counseling groups is the "third person syndrome." Group members will talk about each other to or through a third person, often the group leader, using third person pronouns. When this arises in the group acitivity, it requires only a brief intervention on the part of the counselor, something like, "You're speaking to me about Mary and she's sitting right there."

Later, only a nod of the head is required to help group members to speak *to,* rather than *about* or *at,* each other. The avoidance behavior inherent in the third person syndrome is typical of most beginning counseling groups, where some members have trouble handling eye contact, tend to seek leader approval, and engage in testing behaviors and skirmishes to determine who's who in the pecking order. The perceptive group counselor can assist the group to recognize that group counseling is most productive when counselees deal forthrightly with each other, rather than being evasive.

3. A group member focuses on persons, conditions, or events outside the group. Counseling groups can turn into "gripe sessions," particularly in the school setting, if the leader is unskilled or lacking in sensitivity. Griping about the principal, a teacher, a common acquaintance, or parents can be enjoyable, as counselees tend to reinforce and support each others' attitudes about how the world (or persons in it) tend to conspire unfairly against them, and thus a good feeling of solidarity props them up in their apparently common struggle; but this is essentially a non-growth producing exercise for group members. Talking about people, conditions, and events which are outside the counseling group tends erroneously to substantiate the notion that *they* are culpable, that the outsiders are at fault, shifting blame and responsibility outside the self.

The group counselor should be aware that this inclination on the part of the counselees occurs because it is the safe thing to do. As long as I focus on others, I don't have to deal with myself or accept any responsibility for what I do. Also, implied in the focus-on-others mien is the notion that if *they* would only change, somehow *I* would improve—false logic guaranteed to lead its user away from positive behavioral change, not closer to it.

Appropriate interventions for the group counselor include: "You keep talking about the principal as the cause of your unhappiness. Isn't it more important to be asking yourself what *you* can do to improve yourself or your happiness?" Or "Focusing our attention on someone who isn't here keeps us from having to look at the people who are really responsible for our own shortcomings." Or "Does complaining about the way someone else acts really mean that if only that person were more like me, I could be happier?" Or "You keep mentioning your mother as the source of your being miserable. But what can you do to make yourself happier in this world?" Or "Are you interested in becoming a critic or a doer?"

Any intervention should have as its central purpose bringing the group members back to themselves. Talking about *them* or *they* in the group can do nothing but reinforce a group member mentality of believing someone else is to blame. While venting gripes may be a necessary prelude to getting down to work in some groups where the frustration tolerance levels over institutional conditions are too high to ignore, the gripe session should not be construed as constituting an effective counseling practice. Long-winded complaints about others or the state of the world which no one can do anything about rarely serve the complainer in any positive way.

Interventions here ought to be designed to teach counselees that they must assume responsibility for themselves, that they must be able to handle themselves more effectively in encounters with the complained-about other, and that focusing on the character of behavior of the other is self-defeating avoidance behavior. They ought to learn from these interventions that group counseling deals with the present and the possibility of new behavior in future moments and not with historical events, that making one's happiness contingent upon other people changing their behavior is basically the thinking of a fool, and that griping about the behavior of others is wasteful of time and energy.

4. Someone seeks the approval of the counselor or a group member before and after speaking. Approval-seeking is one of the most common forms of unhealthy human behavior; and, when it is done in the counseling group, this is no exception. The group leader should become aware of such a proclivity on the part of a member and be prepared to intervene when such behavior surfaces. Some individuals look for constant nonverbal acceptance by the leader—a nod, a glance, a smile. Such persons may be intimidated by personal strength or by significant or authority figures or have such a poor sense of self-worth that they are always going outside of their own resources for support and self-endorsing approval. It is essential for the leader to point out approval-seeking behavior so that the individual is made aware of it and recognizes that the counseling group is an experimental laboratory for working on this behavior in safety.

Approval-seeking may take many forms. Often a group member will look directly at the leader both before and after speaking to assess if he has the leader's agreement. An appropriate intervention in this case is for the counselor to deliberately look elsewhere, scanning the faces of the other members, forcing the speaker to appeal to others and change the direction of his delivery, the leader thus taking care not to reinforce the client's neurotic need. If the behavior persists, identifying it to the individual is most appropriate, along with setting up individual goals which might include working on understanding why the need for approval exists, as well as alternate behavior to be practiced in the group.

Approval-seeking might also take the form of asking for group consensus or for various group members to agree with a certain position. Once again it is important to point out the approval-seeking acts and to ask if the individual is interested in working on eliminating this essentially nonproductive behavior. In school counseling groups, students frequently talk about feeling bad because someone (a friend, parent, teacher) doesn't agree with them about a position they have taken. Here again, approval-seeking behavior is present. The group leader can confront the student with why it is important to have others agree with him. Such interventions as these are appropriate: "Do you think that your need for Mike to agree with you is based upon a strong desire for him to like you?" Or "You always look at Maryanne before you speak, almost as if you're asking permission." Or "Why is it so important for other people to share the same opinion as you?"

If the leader provides a model for these kinds of interventions, the group members will begin to ask each other similarly vital questions as the group gains maturity. Interventions designed to point out approval-seeking behavior in counseling groups will aid participants in improving their own self-awareness and self-concepts. In addition, it teaches counselees that they will always encounter disagreement in life, that being psychologically healthy means being able to accept one's self when others have contrary opinions and to have a solid rationale for one's point of view which puts one in a position of not needing others to be on one's side.

5. Someone says, "I don't want to hurt his feelings, so I won't say it." This is a common practice in the early stages of counseling in a group. When a leader observes this kind of sentiment in a group, he can suggest that two alternatives are responsible for such a mind-set: (1) the recipient is so fragile that he would collapse if you shared your honest perceptions about him or (2) you're afraid to say what you think because of your own self-doubt (i.e., "Someone might not like me if I don't say nice things, and I can't chance not being liked"). Either choice is inhibiting to self-growth, and therefore a leader intervention is proper. If the group member who is reluctant to share heartfelt feelings and perceptions fears the brittle composition of the potential recipient, he ought at least to be sincere enough to check out his concern with the individual, especially as such an assumption almost always turns out to be apocryphal. The perceptive group leader would be cognizant of the resistance to being candid and of the dynamics behind the reluctance. Pointing out reasons for the fear of being forthright will contribute to destroying the barriers and will encourage group members to share perceptions and feelings which they see as a contribution to the welfare of another member.

6. A group member suggests that his problems are due to someone else. There is some overlap with number 3 above, but this call for intervention has unique overtones. So often do counselees suggest that their problems are caused by others that the counselor needs to be aware of how to intervene when this defensive phenomenon crops up, as it inevitably will when one works with students. Adolescents particularly enjoy making others responsible for their own nonproductivity. When an individual intimates that if someone else (my teacher, mother) were different, then I would be more effective, the group must be made aware of the discrepancy in this kind of self-defeating thinking. Such interventions as these get the therapeutic process started: "Who is really in charge of you?" "Why should someone else change for you?" "Can't you be what you choose to be, despite the way others are?"

A productive group counseling program will help students to cope effectively with these kinds of questions and to examine how they can personally take charge of themselves to become more effective human beings. The authors are not suggesting a nonsympathetic counseling posture; the group, however, is an arena for effectively coming to grips with how each person can assess what he can do for himself to become all that he wishes to be, rather than providing just one more futile environment where the student assigns the responsibility for his failures to someone else and continues to function at less than optimal levels. The group counselor must be constantly alert for the manifestation of member behaviors which imply or assign responsibility for personal effectiveness on "others," and he should search to build an arsenal of interventions geared to refute such self-crippling thinking.

7. *An individual suggests that "I've always been that way."* When a counselee mentions that "I've always been that way," or "That's just the way I am and I can't help it," he is engaging in self-defeating thinking of the first order. This becomes a propitious moment for the leader to intervene and help the group member to see that a person is really what his choices make him, rather than someone over whom he has little or no control. Group counselees frequently plead that they can't really help the way they are, sometimes supporting each other, Greek chorus-like, in the perniciously fatalistic idea that they have had no (and won't ever have any) control of their development and destiny.

Appropriate interventions for the group counselor include: "Do you feel that because you've always been ineffective, you are destined to remain that way?" Or "You're suggesting that someone else is in charge of what you are and always will be, and you can't help it." Or "Do you feel that everyone has certain areas of his life over which he has no control?" The group counselor has the responsibility for seeing that the group helps each member to deal effectively with the areas of his thinking which inhibit growth. Believing that one's past necessitates one's future is fallacious thinking which encourages people to function at lower levels than what they could attain. Learning that all of the self-defining "I'ms" (I'm shy, I'm lazy, I'm lousy in math, I'm . . . *ad infinitum*) are really choices that individuals make which allow them to keep from working at self-development is an important lesson one absorbs on the way to psychological health. The "I'ms" result in some highly circuitous thinking which in turn determines self-defeating behavior: (a) I'm shy; (b) I think I'll approach that attractive and likable person; (c) Oh no, I can't. I just remembered that I'm shy. Thus we live out our self-fulfilling prophecies.

Interventions of the type described in this section will help group members to identify the thinking and behavior which leads to their being ineffective in specific areas of their lives. They will also learn that they are not doomed to repeat the mistakes of their past if they will take constructive action to become different. In addition, they will soon recognize that all people have a list of self-descriptions which they conveniently bring into their consciousness when they want an excuse for not working hard at changing. The effective group leader is aware of this tendency in group members and makes the appropriate intervention. If the interventions do not occur, it is most likely that the group will reinforce the inert, nonproductive thinking simply because it is a safe approach: Everyone can remain comfortable, do nothing, and stay the same.

8. An individual suggests, "I'll wait, and it will change." This posture is one that members commonly assume in the early goings of a counseling group. The faulty thinking goes something like this: "I want to be different. But I don't want to do anything, so I'll postpone action and things will get better." Group members are often willing to talk about their self-defeating behavior patterns. The competent group leader should be aware that talking about a problem is only the beginning step toward becoming more effective. When any group member suggests that doing something about it is impossible or very difficult, then the counselor needs to intervene in a way that will put the group member onto an action path leading to a resolution of the difficulty. All interventions of this type are designed to teach group members that inertia is not the strategy for eliminating any self-destructive behavior, and that until some striving, at least, occurs, only a piddling change can be expected.

9. Discrepant behavior appears. A group leader intervention is essential when discrepancies occur in a member's behavior in the group. Discrepancies take many forms, but the following appear with regularity:

(a) A discrepancy between what a member is currently saying and what he said earlier. (Obviously, the group counselor must be aware of what counselees say throughout the life of the group.)

(b) A discrepancy between what a member is saying and what he is doing. The discrepancy between what he says he does and what he actually does is important, and a group counselor must be willing to point out any obvious gaps.

(c) A discrepancy between what a member says and what he feels. Here the counselor can intervene with a facilitating description of how the member is coming across, how he is unconvincing, how his nonverbal behaviors (the indices of his feeling states) betray and contradict the content of his utterances.

(d) A discrepancy between what a member is saying and what the counselor is feeling in reaction. The group leader may be incorrect in his assumption that his own reactive feelings point to a discrepancy, but his checking it out helps a counselee to clarify where the psychological truth lies. The intervention is appropriate, regardless, and the skilled group counselor will find that the majority of his feelings about the group members are usually "right on." Helping counselees to learn the extent to which their interpersonal actions are affect-laden, and the character of such emotional loading, is an important first step toward psychological congruence of thought and action.

(e) A discrepancy between how a member sees himself, according to his own data, and how others in the group have been seeing him, according to data they have at one time or another proferred. Again, it is important here to signify the fact that effective professionals pay hard attention, have long memories and excellent recall of specifics, and can muster forth a therapeutic feedback reference swiftly.

The interventions which identify discrepant behavior are confronting in many ways. The group leader who is professional, however, remembers that the road to trust-building in counseling groups is strewn with open, forthright confronting, rather than a warm accepting approval of everything a member says or does. It should be made clear that group members are never on trial in a hostile setting and that anger and hostility are not in the repertoire of the effective group leader's interventionistic mind. With the identification of the discrepancies which arise in counseling groups, the group members see for themselves that here is a setting in which being plain and direct is a way of life. The name of the game is seeing and naming what constitutes the intrapersonal and interpersonal reality as a condition of counseling movement. Moreover, the path to being self-actualized or self-fulfilled is one in which an individual learns how to be direct and unabashedly candid in dealing with himself. If the group counselor provides the environment which accepts less than honesty, then he does a disservice to each counselee in the group.

10. A member bores the group by rambling. Seeking approval through overtalk or simply being unable to facilitate self-closure on a verbalization is a widespread typical behavior in counseling groups. A possible intervention would be to turn to another person and say: "Mary, repeat what Duane just said." If she is unable to do so, then a goal of Duane's to speak more succinctly is in order. If she can repeat it, perhaps a statement which approximates the following is in order: "How come it took you two sentences to say what it took Duane three minutes to say?" This intervention can be handled most tactfully by involving the other group members with helping people to avoid turning the group off with their rambling and groping. A corollary to this issue involves the overly intellectual member who is attempting to impress the group with his or her knowledge, acumen, discerning perspicacity, or stunning ratiocination. The counselor can ask other members to react to what the "intellectual rambler" has just said and to suggest that they provide the rambler with feedback about his ability to be long on obfuscation and short on present moment meaningful message sending, particularly when his real intent is clearly not communication, a meeting of minds over bloody ideas, but a desire for strokes.

Final Thoughts

This elaboration of ten occasions for group counseling process interventions, the rationale behind the need to intervene, and the explication of specific leads and counselor behaviors concludes a presentation of suggestions for more effective group counselor functioning which is by no means exhaustive. It barely scratches a bulging surface. But it does present a model of the kind of group process analytical thinking which the counseling profession can surely use more of—an antidote to "stomach consultancy" for group leader functioning.

The ten areas we have covered are general enough to be taken as an umbrella of guidelines from which a myriad of specific differential interventions can flow. But the number of umbrellas could be increased a thousandfold. What effective leader interventions are possible at the beginning of a group session which have an anchor in theory, a rationale, and a predictability record to recommend them? Or at the ending of sessions? Or when and why and how should interventions occur which serve to recapitulate, to take stock, to assess and re-evaluate particular kinds of progress for this or that group member? Practically all of the tried-and-true group counseling practices are still out there waiting to be drawn together and effectively communicated to the interested professional membership. Effective counseling in groups is a complicated business, and hardy hunters, practitioners in pursuit of an ever-higher level of functioning, those dedicated to their own professional development, need help from every source they can find.

12

Barriers to Effectiveness in Group Counseling

Group counseling, when skillfully conducted, is an exceptionally potent activity which focuses on the elimination of self-injurious thinking and behaviors of individual group members and promotes, facilitates, and reinforces personal growth. This assumption rests on the skillful conduct of the counselor for its validity. What frequently occurs in actual practice is that participants emerge from a group counseling experience feeling that it was a barren, nonproductive exercise. Many well-intentioned counselors organize and institute counseling groups only to become disillusioned when their groups do not "get going" or do not serendipitously materialize into a helping experience for the group members. Novice group counselors in particular are commonly disconcerted with the lack of progress in their groups.

After supervising countless numbers of group counselor trainees, analyzing and evaluating the endless specific details of their in-group performances, and studying the process variables manifested in their groups, we have concluded that the same counselor errors are repeatedly committed and that the troublesome impediments to group member growth are most often directly attributable to the leader's not recognizing barriers to effectiveness. A large percentage, if not the majority, of these trainees possessed high-level counseling skills which they effectively exercised in one-to-one counseling sessions; yet befuddlement and ineptitude became characteristic of their in-group behavior. They consistently engaged in misdirected or even obstructive interventions or failed to recognize the need for telling interventions when the happenings in the group called for them.

Admittedly, counseling in a group is a complex activity, and there are a multitude of learnings for a counselor to acquire in order to become an expert in the delivery of genuine service. Recognition of barriers and skill in overcoming them, therefore, is crucial to effectiveness.

Categories of Barriers

The concept of a "barrier," as the term is used here, presumes that strategies exist for either overcoming it, eliminating it, rendering it impotent, or recognizing it as a limiting reality factor. Barriers to effectiveness in counseling may be classified in a number of ways, and their numbers are legion. It is not our intent here to address ourselves to the efficient handling of every last one of them, but rather to help the reader to become aware of what constitutes a barrier and to provide specific methods for dealing with a cluster of the most common ones.

There are five principal group counseling barriers: (a) those inherent in group preselection conditions; (b) those which are situational; (c) those residing in the minds of the group members; (d) those in the mind of the counselor; and (e) those which are a part of the group counseling process.

Group Preselection Conditions

The effective group counselor is attuned to the fact that a set of conditions, any one of which may impede his or her productively conducting a counseling group, exists prior to the group's formulation. These conditions exist in the context of the environment surrounding the group. If the group is conducted in a school, a prison, or an agency of a different character, for example, administrative policy might constitute a barrier. Group member selection procedures and group composition variables can produce built-in barriers. For example, excessively large or small groups, involuntary groups composed of hyperactive resisters, or homogeneous groups where the price of admission is advanced behavioral pathology in a given dimension all contain some incipient barriers to effectiveness for a counselor untrained or unskilled in dealing with them; these all tend to be absent in heterogeneous, middle-sized groups where members are appropriately prepared for the experience.

Frequently, counselors unsophisticated in the knowledge of factors outside the group which can impinge on what goes on within the group charge ahead, formulate the group, begin group sessions, and then learn that meddlesome others interested in what is going on are having an impact on in-group member behavior or creating conditions which mitigate against continued counseling. Thus, parents might stop a school counseling group if their cooperation had not been earlier engaged.

Situational Barriers

Environmental conditions account for barriers to effectiveness in some groups. These refer to conditions in the setting where the sessions are held: furniture arrangements, noise levels, temperature, lighting, size of room, frequency and type of interruptions, and a gamut of other possibilities. A counselor seeks to have a group meet in a place where optimally positive conditions exist, but usually this means making the best of one of several undesirable options. The key to effectiveness here is that the counselor anticipates all complaints and the propensity of members to become fixated on unpalatable characteristics of the setting as a means of avoiding becoming engaged in the counseling process. Effective group counseling can proceed in a cold dank dungeon or in a garbage dump, if all members are helped to become committed to the counseling process in spite of, or having a high tolerance for, negative environmental circumstances.

We once successfully conducted a group counseling session in a "fishbowl," with twelve members in the group and some seventy observers seated around the circle, in a large room where a sparrow was flying loose. The bird had flown in a window and could not find its way out. The extent to which group members were helped to ignore the bird and remain intensely involved in the group member interaction became a positive status variable to which all twelve members responded.

Barriers in the Group Members' Minds

Unless these are anticipated and effectively dealt with early, barriers which group members carry into the experience can endure over countless sessions. They take the form of expectations which are not consonant with group counseling. Some members thus preprogrammed vainly strive to turn the group process to their liking. Some members come to the group fearful of the process because of what they have heard and believed about negative happenings in small groups. Some come with hidden agendas, seeing the group as a place to rap, to find support for a point of view, to make converts to a political or religious ideology, or to advance a relationship with one or more other members. Whatever the concealed or erroneous expectations, the effective group counselor is on guard and succinctly defines and acts consonantly with what the counseling process is, in order that such barriers can be worked through quickly or eroded.

215

Barriers within the Counselor

The counselor who lacks expertise, who has an erroneous conception of what constitutes effective group counseling, who is anxious and fearful about what might happen, who is constantly seeking approval of his or her own behavior by the members, or who serves his or her own needs in any of the infinite ways that are possible tends to create barriers which are insurmountable simply because the counselor is blind to them and finds it personally devastating to attribute them to his or her own doing. The solution to the elimination of such barriers lies in the counselor's awareness that they may be present, constant vigilance for their appearance, and commitment to working on overcoming them through revised thinking and follow-up behavior.

There are ways to discover what such barriers are. Anticipating their likelihood and establishing a workable contract for feedback is a powerful reason for having a co-counselor, but not the only reason. In the absence of a co-leader, consulting with a knowledgeable and willing colleague over taped records of sessions helps in the identification of such barrier-producing counselor behaviors. But the prime source of identification is in the group itself: The trained group counselor teaches every group to question leader behavior at every turn. Whenever any member fails to understand what is going on, he or she is helped to call the counselor on the intent of his or her behavior; such teaching of members gets reinforced throughout the life of the group as standard operating procedure in effectively conducted counseling groups.

Barriers Inherent in the Group Process

Most barriers which occur as part of the group counseling process are outgrowths of the four preceding categories. Suffice it to say that any such barriers can be effectively hurdled or removed by appropriate counselor activity, provided the counselor recognizes them and accurately diagnoses their essence, because it is the leader in a counseling group who has the responsibility for orchestrating what occurs.

The group leader conducts intake interviews, explains the procedures and ground rules, organizes time schedules, guides each group session, and brings to the group a model of expertise in effective living. Virtually all barriers to productivity in group counseling can be traced directly to the behavior or absence of behavior on the part of the group leader. That is, the competencies, the skills, and the perceptions of the group counselor in leading the sessions are the final tests in assessing the ongoing effectiveness of any group counseling activity. Many a beginner has arrived for a first counseling group session hoping to have talkative and risk-taking group members, so that fears of acting upon or missing significant happenings within the group will be mollified. Aware that leading a counseling group is as many times more difficult than one-to-one counseling as there are group members, the fledgling group leader frequently overlooks or is unaware of the omnipresent obstacles that surface in virtually all counseling groups.

What follows is a short list of group counseling barriers. They are not presented in any systematic or rank-order way. They are by no means intended to exhaust all the possible barriers. Rather, they represent common outcroppings, areas where the group counselor can go to work to increase effectiveness by behaving in productive ways. They represent a sharing of our experience.

Common Barriers In Group Counseling

Reinforcing Neurotic or Self-Defeating Behavior

The Putneys, in describing normal neurosis in Americans, assert: "The adjusted American does not recognize the neurotic nature of much of his behavior, because this behavior is normal" (Putney & Putney 1964, p. 12). The implication is that neurotic behavior is normal because it gets accepted and reinforced repeatedly within the culture. This is a danger within the group counseling setting, and an effective counselor is sagaciously aware of this at all times.

The group leader is a reinforcer. This is not a choice he or she makes. Counselor choices relate to what to reinforce and when. In discussing the best methods for goal achievement in counseling, Krumboltz (1966, p. 15) addresses this point: "The question is not whether the counselor should or should not use reinforcement—the question is how the counselor can time his use of reinforcement in the best interests of his clients." Learning not to reinforce self-defeating thinking and behaving in the counseling group is a step in the direction of eliminating this pervasive barrier to effectiveness. Some specific examples of neurotic behavior in counseling groups and appropriate counselor behaviors are discussed below.

1. At the beginning of many counseling groups, members will display resistance by discussing topics not related to the group. In school groups frequently silliness and giggling behavior are manifested at the beginning of group sessions, as well as discussions about weekend parties, the upcoming football game, and the like. The

effective group counselor can recognize this kind of activity as normal passive resistance to seriously engaging in the business of group counseling. If the group counselor encourages such conversational chit-chat, he or she is teaching group members that this kind of activity (resistance) is appropriate for the group, and this kind of group behavior can be expected to persist at the beginning of every session. Often the best strategy for dealing with this phenomenon is to ignore it and thereby lend no credence or support to such behavior.

If the group leader simply introduces the business of the counseling group and devotes no attention to the unrelated conversation, it becomes clear to all that the counselor perceives counseling to be a serious enterprise. If similar resistance persists in the group, then labeling the behavior as reluctance and allowing the group to react to such an intervention is an appropriate tack. The group counselor who is determined to be effective will question whether or not evasive behavior is being encouraged by his or her interventions or lack of them. Certainly no effective leader wants to reinforce the very thing that has become an impediment to progress in the group.

2. The overly intellectual or explaining group member can become an obstacle to movement in the group. By condoning such behavior the counselor reinforces it and indirectly invites similar behavior from others who have the propensity to follow suit. Simply identifying rambling verbalizations and suggesting that the group counseling setting is an inappropriate place for such behavior will often put the skids on it. Also, an interpretation that this behavior is occurring and that it is a barrier to effective interpersonal communication will provide each group member with a goal for lucidity in member exchanges and thereby discourage the practice. Effective counselors often go to others, when rambling overtalk comes from one member, to check out their understanding of what the message really was. Intellectualizers and ramblers are usually unaware of their true motives, and interpretations relating to these become penetratingly helpful to them. For example, overtalk is often the result of approval seeking; intellectualization frequently stems from a desire to be seen as super-intelligent. Both behaviors are seldom effective, and members manifesting them can be helped to set goals for their replacement.

3. Frequently the members of a group will attempt to "fill in" an absentee from a previous session and take up a chunk of valuable group time. If the group counselor allows this practice to become an established ritual, he or she is inadvertently reinforcing self-defeating behavior in both the absentee and the other members. The counselor thus teaches everyone that it is perfectly permissable to miss a session because the group will take the time to bring the absentee up

to date in the next session. This obviously encourages, rather than discourages, absenteeism. Moreover, group members who recognize that risk taking is a part of the counseling group have a ready "out" when they feel discomfort cropping close. The group leader can ask that the absent member listen to the taped record of the missed session or have another member "fill in" the absentee at a time which does not encroach on the allotted group counseling time. This strategy eliminates the possibility of reinforcing absentee behavior on the part of group members. The same, it might be said, applies to the tardy member.

4. A common reinforcement of neurotic behavior occurs when the group counselor overlooks obviously defensive or "excuse-building" behavior on the part of any group member. If the leader is aware that a group member is clearly fooling himself or herself, particularly when the verbalized commentary fails to be in congruence with other behavior manifested by the same person, and other group members spot this as well, not having it pointed out is tantamount to setting defensiveness as a norm for the group. This is not to suggest that every single incident of the employment of defensive mechanisms must be picked apart and exposed; but any group which functions at a level of nonconfrontation and acceptance of repeated defensiveness has a leader who is reinforcing, albeit inadvertently, neurotic group member behavior, which becomes a potent barrier to effective progress in the group.

5. Counseling groups generally have members who assume a variety of roles. When any member takes on a role that is debilitating to him or her, having it overlooked encourages the individual to stay in that role. This includes the classic showoff, the boisterous clown, the confessor, the agreeing head-nodder, the supporter of every struggler, and many others. If a person has set as a goal, as every group member might well do, not to be seen in a strictly limiting, monomorphic capacity, such as the joker, then each time that member lapses into such role behavior, labeling it and getting an acknowledgement of recognition from the member is helpful in extinguishing compulsiveness. Simply ignoring the role behavior or laughing at the joker who is seeking attention and approval encourages self-defeating behavior to persist. In counseling, unlike in other life arenas, few if any role behaviors are advantageous to their owners. The leader who encourages neurotic role behaviors through passivity helps to maintain a barrier to effectiveness in the group.

6. Blaming others or finding fault with them in order to justify personal shortcomings, the undesirability of life-space conditions and limitations, emotional states, or any lack of development is a neurotic activity which is seldom, if ever, productive in counseling. If the

group counselor reinforces such activity on the part of one or more members, setting a tone in the group which encourages talk about outsiders (parents, teachers, cops, the "system"), he or she is reinforcing some of the most self-destructive thinking imaginable. This amounts to teaching counselees to look to sources outside themselves for answers and explanations of their plight rather than working intensely on making themselves more effective managers of their own lives. Groups frequently want to engage in carping and caviling about the system, the institution, or various tyrannical others because members find comfort in knowing they are not alone in their miseries, that their self-defeating perceptions about being "locked in" are shared. The leader who erroneously endorses such activity on the grounds that "catharsis" has an inherent value helps a group to become cohesive in a way that constitutes a barrier to effective counseling. Group comfort or feelings of belongings have low worth; the proper measure of effectiveness is the acquisition of self-enhancing behavioral change in any given member in his or her own life outside the group. Groups convened for any other purpose are not counseling groups.

It is possible to catalogue an interminable number of specific examples where the reinforcement of neurotic behaviors in counseling groups might take place through the passivity or misdirected efforts of an insensitive leader. With the illustrations above we are endeavoring to send one message clearly: When the group counselor spots behaviors which are neurotic or self-defeating in any way, she or he ought not to be yet another person in the life of each member who reinforces such behavior, either passively or directly, thereby encouraging its survival. The avenue to effectiveness has the opposite character: The competent leader pinpoints such neurotic behavior, labels it for what it is, helps members to understand what neurotic gains account for its persistence, helps them to learn about self-productive alternate ways of thinking and behaving, and helps them to work at acquiring these.

Endorsing Silence in the Group

There are many individuals who are self-punishingly incapable of being silent in the company of others and this very incapability frequently reveals a network of neurotic thinking and behaving which can be altered once it is manifested and understood. Thus, a long period of silence in a group might provide an onerous endurance test having the result of bringing certain kinds of unwanted behavior to the surface which can be productively worked on. But beyond this there is little value in all group members being simultaneously still. Any given member who requires time for reordering his or her thinking, for mulling over this or that, or for whatever reason, can choose not to participate verbally in the group activity. At any given moment in a group *most* members *are* silent; it hardly takes an all-be-silent test to flush out a compulsive talker.

Silence as a test device has no more creditability than does any similar conditional factor induced into the group environment which might flush out other kinds of behaviors debilitating to some individuals. Ought a counselor to conduct sessions in complete darkness in order to learn which members deal ineffectively with darkness? Or in a sauna? Or in a walk-in refrigerator? Or in a room where loud noise continually grates from a record player? Most members are aware of life conditions with which they have difficulty coping, and these tend to come out during the course of the group counseling.

The group counselor who takes no responsibility for breaking the silence promotes this barrier. Similarly, the counselor who attempts to rupture the silence by asking, "Why are we silent?" misses the point and reinforces a notion that, when perpetuated, constitutes an even more formidable barrier to effectiveness, one we discuss below. Briefly stated in this context it is that no member is responsible for the group or anything "it" does. As a matter of simple truth, the "group" is never silent: only Mary, Tom, Carl, Jenny, or Casey is, one by one. Thus the effective counselor goes to this or that particular member with his silence-breaking interventions: "What's going on in your head right now, Tom?" Or "Casey, earlier you indicated that you wanted to go to work on overcoming your compulsiveness to be super-organized. Now might be a good time for you to go into that."

Over-Emphasizing Feelings

To the extent that emotionalism is promoted as a goal unto itself, the leader is erecting a barrier to productivity within the group. Too often group counselors are able to elicit emotional expression by group members ("Let it all hang out, Emily. Get it out and you'll feel better.") by focusing on feelings and then find they have reached a blank wall. Such comments as "But how do you feel?" or "Get down to gut-level feeling" are common group counselor ploys. The effective group counselor realizes, however, that the unfolding of emotions is a means to an end, not an end in itself, and in any given case of his or her intervening to focus on feelings he or she is seeking a window on the thoughts which are their cause. It is inevitable that group members will confront each other on a variety of levels; they can productively do so without becoming "emotional" or "gutsy." The competent leader constantly keeps in mind the overriding goal for each group member: to become as personally masterful in as many life areas as is possible. This might involve group members or the leader modeling other more effective ways of thinking and behaving, role-working activities, or specific feedback to a group member about how he or she is behaving within the group. Admittedly, feelings are an important component of effective counseling. It is not intended here that such observable physiological reactions to deeply entrenched thoughts ought to be considered taboo.

The counselor whose competence is judged on the basis of how much "feeling" was elicited in the group is having his or her behavior analyzed with inappropriate measures for assessing effectiveness. Far more significant than inquiring how many people are expressing their feelings are such questions as: To what extent are individuals within the group gaining greater self-confidence through specific skill-building, through the acquisition of higher levels of performance in life areas important to them? How many group members have reached stated goals for becoming more in-charge human beings in specifically delineated ways? How many group members have partially or wholly eliminated self-defeating behaviors?

In one counseling group led by a counselor in training the leader was insisting that members were evading expressing their feelings. A group member confronted this leader with: "What do you mean by feelings? And why is it so damned important to you that we all express them?" The novice counselor was at a loss for words, and his authority as an expert was thoroughly discredited. He had not thought through precisely what it was that constituted a "feeling" nor what was important about "getting them out." He had inadvertently constructed a barrier in his group by placing the emphasis on a component of counseling that is an aid to effectiveness rather than any indication of successful leader behavior.

Many group counselors also fallaciously assume that there is a clear, measurable distinction between feelings and thoughts and that, somehow, the latter are less palatable for counseling focus than the former. Not so. Feelings are quite impossible without thoughts. Essentially, feelings are physical reactions to cognitive processes. To attempt to separate them is to induce confusion. To insist that group members express their feelings as if they were separate entities to be called upon at will is folly.

Making the Group into a Confessional

Experienced counselors who have logged hundreds of hours in leading groups soon learn that confession for its own sake is seldom productive. When it is reinforced in members, its frequency increases, and another time-consuming barrier to effectiveness is installed. As Ernest Beier (1966, pp. 158–159) notes: "An emotional climate will always constrict the communicative process of the group, and the constriction will distort the interaction. By giving confessions special attention the group counselor communicates approval to the group and is likely to reinforce cathartic confessional behavior." The point is that although confessions are usually laden with emotional overtones, and therefore of high interest to others, they seldom advance individual behavioral change goals, unless the counselor is effective in focusing on what a confessor can do to alter debilitating thinking which surrounds a past event.

In one of his novels, Truman Capote has one character remark about another, "If she had such a lousy childhood, why does she talk about it all the time?" (quotation not authenticated). Why, indeed? It may be assumed, when a group member brings up such material, that a present moment gain is sought, albeit often neurotic in nature, and the effective counselor looks for what that might be. Whether a member is trying to be seen by the members in a different light, revealing what a cargo of guilt he or she carries, seeking support and justification for past actions, or wanting the good feelings which result from "washing the soul," the knowledgeable counselor in each case labels the confession for what it is and helps the confessor to move back into the here-and-now implications of such action, to evaluate its consequences, and to redirect thinking and behavior surrounding confession content toward more productive ends.

Every individual has a past which contains mucky private elements which are no one else's business and ought to remain so. If some members neurotically confess, trading personal information for its shock value or to gain attention, their motives ought to be exposed. The group counselor who helps confessors to flourish heightens group pressure on those who are threatened by any invasion of their privacy. The counselor who fosters a climate of confession for the purpose of "getting down to feelings," or for any other nonproductive reason, is unconsciously raising barriers within the group.

Any individual who enters a counseling group has the same right to privacy that exists in any other life circumstance. This right ought to be protected by the group counselor at all costs. If a member voluntarily chooses to pour forth personal stories to gain the sympathy or endorsement of the group for past actions, the leader must ask some vital questions. How will this person benefit from releasing skeletons from the closet? Is the person seeking sympathy or approval for past behavior from the group members? If so, will group support and sympathy do more harm than good? Is the group counseling arena the appropriate setting for this confessionary behavior?

Essentially the psychology of the confessional is debilitating to the progress of the confessor as well as those listening to the confession. Each member is in group counseling to work on individual goals which relate to changing current behavior. Consuming group time to hear confessions of past sins or stories with emotional overtones is basically an interesting but unproductive activity. When the counselor lends support to this kind of group activity, the neurotic need of the confessor is reinforced, if the focus remains on *past* behavior. The effective group counselor will ask those members who are prone to emotional story telling, "How can we be of help to you now?" This shifts the emphasis from the past to the present. The counseling group is more appropriately a safe laboratory for analyzing thinking and behavior and practicing new modes of both than it is a forum for cathartic confession. Clearly, the group counselor can assume responsibility for dismantling this troublesome barrier to productivity.

Misunderstanding the Leader's Role

The effective group counselor makes it clear at the initial session precisely what his or her function within the group will be. Moreover, the leader's behavior in all sessions substantiates this given position. The group counselor is not a member of the group. This always means that the counselor does not use the group to disclose problem areas in his or her life or seek help in working at becoming more personally effective. The group counselor's charge is to help others, not to be helped. To the extent that the group counselor uses the group or any part of the experience to gratify personal needs or desires, group members are being cheated or abused. (See Chapter 11 for a more detailed statement of group counselor role and function.)

If the group members are confused as to leader responsibility, they will use group time to repeatedly ask for clarification. Beyond this, they will attempt to draw the leader into areas of personal self-disclosure and other unrelated functioning. Group counselors who do not state their responsibilities and demonstrate their credibility by behaving as leaders also invite challenges to leadership. Obviously, any group contains a barrier to effectiveness if members spend time and effort in attempting to usurp leadership or in challenging the credentials of the leader.

The group counselor is the unquestioned leader of the group. He or she is the expert in analysis of human behavior, and his or her job is to assist all group members in working on themselves in a helping environment. Persistent efforts by dominant group members to gain leadership or to cajole the leader into group member status are distractions, and such activity is done at the expense of each group member who could be using the time to gain from the counseling process. A clear statement of leader function, along with continued concomitant leader behavior, works to obliterate this barrier in group counseling.

Making Cohesiveness a Group Goal

Few people knowledgeable about group dynamics will argue the advantage of a cohesive over a noncohesive group. However, many beginning group counselors unwittingly spend an inordinate amount of time and effort in attempting to build cohesiveness into their groups. This is generally wasted time.

Groups become cohesive as a result of their prolonged existence. Time and being together are the two not-so-mysterious components of cohesiveness. The important consideration is: What makes it important to deliberately work on the attainment of cohesiveness? The rather peculiar aim of the counseling or therapy group is that it moves toward its own dissolution. Time spent working at becoming closer together, when in effect the group must eventually dissolve, is a blatant squandering of precious group counseling moments. Cohesiveness and movement toward unity will undoubtedly take place. But whether it does or not is unrelated to individual behavioral change goals of the group members. Cohesiveness is observable in almost all groups that meet for any duration of time. It is a factor of group life, something that investigators of group dynamics have grabbed onto as a measurable entity.

Cohesiveness is also a mysterious concept that defies quantification. Groups are not any one thing, including cohesive, at all times. Hostility, confrontation, argumentation, elation, divisiveness, and a host of other descriptive terms can be applied to a group at any given moment. During periods of open hostility, cohesiveness is minimized, yet moments later the group may be operating on a high level of affectionate togetherness. All of this is essentially unrelated to the measurement of effectiveness within the group. Are individuals changing? Are they learning about themselves? Are they being helped? These are the important questions of the effective group counselor. Do they like each other? Are they warm? Cold? Is this a closely knit group? These are less important questions by far. Working at making a group close, when the overriding objective is ultimately to disband the group and send the individual members back into their own worlds with new armaments for effective living, is analogous in a hyperbolic way to bombing villages and then sending in teams of workers to repair the damages. The group counselor who is desirous of eliminating barriers to effectiveness will eliminate activities generated for the bogus purpose of bringing members closer together.

Using Group Time to Establish Group Goals

Committees have group goals. Task groups have group goals. Athletic teams have group goals. In groups where a group end-product is the group's reason for existence, the individual member does not matter. In such groups an individual's behavior is subordinated to and enlisted in service toward the ends of the group as a group. Such is not true of a counseling group: It is each individual member who matters most. Counseling groups have individual member goals. Each person in the group is unique in his or her behaviors outside the group. Each member of the group is at a different stage of development in any given behavioral dimension, even in a homogeneously composed counseling group. Therefore, each member of the group has individual work to accomplish in the achievement of a number of personal goals related to becoming a more effective, in-charge person in a life context different from that of any other person.

The group counselor who sets the formulation of group goals as a task throws a snag into the group activity. In many counseling groups led by inexperienced counselors, literally one-third to one-half of their early sessions are spent in a struggle to come up with group goals because such leaders foolishly request them. The activity is loaded with travail because group members then tussle and agonize to create something which can never exist in a counseling group. By asking each member to set personal goals and by helping individuals to set new goals as the group progresses, the group leader removes the obstacle of group goals and all the time-consuming effort discharged in such an elusive enterprise.

Excessive Group-Grope

Most counseling groups are slow to get underway, and many never do, largely because the group leader has been an ineffective model for demonstrating the activity of group counseling. A group leader can avoid the lengthy periods of time which are wasted in getting down to the business of the counseling group by demonstrating early what the process is all about. Asking group members to set goals for themselves, even to have them written out and read aloud, is one helpful technique. Identifying observable self-defeating behaviors manifested

226

by members right in the group and helping members to focus on these and go to work at eliminating them is another way to get the ball rolling and avoid long, tedious struggles within the group.

Group members ought to leave the early sessions of group counseling with a profound sense of participating in a worthwhile activity. The counselor who allows the group to grope for problem areas and activities often pushes some members to view the experience negatively, and such a leader thereby delimits his or her own credibility as an effective determiner of group productivity. If groping is considered a healthy experience in the group, then limiting it to the first thirty minutes or so will provide group members with an opportunity to "experience" it and still leave much additional session time for valuable counseling practice. If a group spends one-half of its allotted life struggling to identify areas of concern, it is apparent that the amount of time remaining for effective group counseling for each of the members has been reduced by half. The proficient group leader is alert to the predisposition of many members in beginning counseling groups to avoid problem areas and devises individual goal-setting strategies to eliminate this barrier.

Nonclosure on Rambling, Boring, and Irrelevant Activity

Most counseling groups tend to contain one or more members who monopolize group time by rambling on about nothing of importance to the other members. Tiresome lecturettes and irrevelant observations inhibit members from working on personal goals. Earlier we discussed the propensity of some members to over-explain or to intellectualize. Here we are emphasizing that any extended verbal activity which has nothing to do with the reasons for the group's existence can constitute a barrier to effectiveness, if the counselor does not initiate closure in some manner. Counseling groups are not discussion groups. When members indicate that they are "contributing to the discussion" or "adding to the topic," interventions by the counselor are called for. Nor are counseling group sessions a time for "brainstorming" or a place for opinion poll-taking. "Carl, what has this activity to do with each member's stated purposes?" the effective group counselor will inquire of an obviously bored member and, with this move, begin to reteach errant group members what more appropriate directions are. Group members who are bored or amazed by the tirades or mastications of irrelevant material by others thus become important resources for eliminating barriers to effectiveness caused by the introduction of extraneous data.

No Follow-Up from Session to Session

When a group member has had an opportunity to gain self-insight and to see alternate modes of behavior, he or she then sets goals for new behavior outside the group. This is a regularly recurring phenomenon in effectively run counseling groups. Furthermore, reports made back to the group on the success of such extra-group efforts are not only encouraged, they profitably become a way of life in the group. If group members agree to attempt new behaviors outside of the group and are given no opportunity to relate their new learnings back to the group, then a barrier to effectiveness has been instituted. Follow-up is a crucial element in any helping enterprise, and group counseling is certainly no exception. Each weekly session can begin with a report from group members who are working on new behaviors. Support for successes is encouraged and group members are given the opportunity to provide feedback. This is a vital principle in learning theory, and since the counseling group is primarily a learning laboratory, positive reinforcement close to the time of success is a potent part of effective group counseling process.

Barriers Are Endless

So ends our short list of common barriers. Surely we have not exhausted the genre. Rather, we have made a case for the creation of one. Every counselor who seriously sets out to become more competent in plying his or her services in groups can hardly afford to ignore modes of thinking and organizing an ever-enlarging repertoire of techniques, strategies, skills, knowledge, or experience which enhances productivity in actual performance. Our objectives included not only the sharing of knowledge about particular obstructions to effective group counseling and some ways for the leader to go in causing their removal, but provided a model, as well, of a system of categorization which gives any group counseling practitioner a means of ordering and remembering his or her own learnings. By being alert to possible barriers, identifying them, establishing hypotheses for their elimination, testing these, and evaluating results, a group counselor productively directs his or her own behavioral change toward increased professional effectiveness.

References

Bier, E.G. *The silent language of psychotherapy: Social reinforcement of unconscious processes.* Chicago: Aldine, 1966.

Krumboltz, J.D. (Ed.) *Revolution in counseling: Implications on behavioral science.* Boston: Houghton Mifflin, 1966.

Putney, S., & Putney, G., *The adjusted American: Normal neurosis in the individual and society.* New York: Harper & Row, 1964.

13

A Group Counseling Experiment with Chronically Obese Students

The following text presents a special instance of group counseling which was first reported in the *Michigan Personnel and Guidance Journal* (Fall, 1970, pp. 5-10) and is reprinted here with permission. It details how a school counselor proceeded with the formation of a special group, one convened around a single selection criterion, obesity. It is a success story. The group participants all benefitted from the experience.

Organizing counseling groups on the basis of a common pathology among the members, however, raises serious questions which are not yet resolved by practitioners. It is questionable, for example, whether a group composed entirely of drug addicts, nonreaders, truants, pregnant girls, underachievers, alchoholics, or whatever comprises the most therapeutic combination of individuals. Individuals who manifest a particular kind of "losing" behavior find support from others who have the same ingrained losing behavior and frequently succeed in cementing such behavior with new logic (albeit, neurotic) garnered from members more advanced in the psychological maintenance of the behavior, often superloaded with personal self-depreciating payoffs. A more heterogeneous group would contain members who would have incorporated more self-enhancing alternatives to the losing behavior, perhaps even able to model the more desirable behavior in effective ways.

The question of having special purpose groups composed of members homogeneous in selected ways needs much research. Perhaps certain kinds of human behaviors are self-enhancingly more modifiable than others. For example, although it may be unproductive to group hard drug addicts, grouping pregnant girls may result in productive benefits for each participant. Such was the case in the group experience which is described in this chapter. But it is noteworthy that the counselor did not focus on the remediation of the common "loser" dimension which was the chief criterion for admission to the group.

Group counseling has been rapidly gaining popularity as a viable process for helping young people in the school setting. Eleven years ago, Wright reviewed the literature and concluded, "The attention given to group counseling was accompanied by a greater acceptance of this procedure as a valid concept of counseling *per se* and by the recognition that the group process might provide some benefits which individual counseling does not" (Wright 1963, p. 205). More recent reviews have also indicated a profession-wide acceptance of group counseling both as preventative mental hygiene and as an educative group experience for students at all levels.

The criteria used to determine membership in counseling groups has also been the subject of considerable discussion. For example, the notion of organizing counseling groups on the basis of common problems (underachievers, discipline problems, attendance difficulties) is thoroughly discussed in Ohlsen's book. He comments, "When clients share common problems, the counselor also can more readily identify affiliation responses. For the adolescent period, when they cherish being like their peers, it is very supportive to discover that fellow clients have similar problems. To identify students with similar problems a counselor may have prospective clients complete a problem check list" (Ohlsen 1970, p. 109).

The majority of school counseling groups in which the students share a common problem are established on the basis of a behavioral or academic difficulty. Bennet (1963) devoted a section of her text on group counseling to experiments at the high school level. She briefly described one attempt to provide group counseling for seven obese girls who presumably had no endocrine involvement in their overweight condition. She further indicated that this experience was beneficial to the counselees in that they showed more adjustive behavior both socially and in Rorschach patterns of emotional and ego development. We believe that physiological maladies as criteria for participation in a counseling group in which members share common concerns are equally as valid as emotional, behavioral, or academic areas of commonality.

Forming the Group

Based on the research and convictions cited above, a special group counseling project was inaugurated at Mercy High School in Farmington, Michigan. Six chronically obese girls (a minimum of 75 pounds overweight) convened for ten weeks of group counseling on a twice-weekly meeting basis. Two girls were in grade ten, three in grade eleven, and one in grade twelve. Before the program began, each family was contacted and the parents were asked to accompany their daughter to an orientation meeting in the evening. At this meeting the objectives of the project were discussed, and questions regarding the entire process of group counseling were answered. The twelve parents were able to interact with each other over their own common problems related to raising an obese daughter and in most cases their own weight problems as well. The group counselor explained carefully why he was organizing such a group and that he had discussed the matter individually with each of the girls. This initial explanatory meeting also provided the impetus for the building of a close relationship between the counselor and the six parent couples. (This parent/counselor relationship was responsible for helping these students with a host of difficulties in a spirit of trust while they were in high school, even eighteen months after the termination of the group counseling.)

Immediately preceding the first group session, the following letter was sent to parents to extract written permission for participation in the project:

Dear Parent:

Beginning next week I will inaugurate the new group counseling project which we discussed at our meeting. I would like very much for your daughter to participate in this program. I have discussed the objectives of the sessions with her, and she has indicated that she is willing to be a member of this group. It is important for you to recognize that these group counseling sessions will in no way be considered as therapy, nor will any prescriptive medicinal or dietary advice be administered.

The counseling sessions will take place during the school day and will be confidential in terms of the general student body and faculty. If you have any questions please feel free to consult with me at any time. Please sign below and have your daughter return this letter to me, if you consent to her participation.

Sincerely,
Wayne W. Dyer
Guidance Counselor

Signature: _____

Establishing Group Goals

As explained to the students, the objectives of the group sessions were not necessarily to show a weight loss at the end. The goals of the group were to be set by the girls themselves in the incipient stages. The process and some specific objectives of group counseling were explained to each participant in an individual meeting, and each was administered the *Mooney Problem Check List*. The counselor found Mahler's explanation of the goals and purposes of group counseling to be of help in developing student expectations:

Group counseling provides an opportunity for students to examine in a friendly and permissive atmosphere their feelings and attitudes, and the ideas they have about themselves and the world. Each member of the group is encouraged to think for himself and to learn how to share his own perceptions, whether or not they are in agreement with those of other members of the group. Gradually he learns to accept responsibility for his own behavior. Members are encouraged to deepen their understanding of behavior and to learn not to be satisfied with a mere surface view of their own or other people's actions. (Mahler 1969, p. 14)

Mahler also indicated several global objectives for counseling groups. Those listed below were most applicable to the group of obese girls and are in harmony with the goals the girls set for themselves:

1. Developing greater confidence in one's own perceptions.
2. Learning to really listen to others.
3. Providing a safe climate for healthy exploration of feelings and control of them.
4. Learning how to be more responsible for one's own behavior.
5. Learning to better understand other people. (Mahler 1969, pp. 15–16)

Goal number 4 (above) was particularly relevant to the obese students in that they spent much time talking about accepting responsibility for their obesity.

The initial session encompassed an entire afternoon, or a total of two hours and forty minutes. All subsequent sessions lasted sixty minutes. At the first meeting ground rules (adapted from Gendlin & Beebe 1968) were distributed to the group. These rules were discussed and members were encouraged to come up with specific objectives related to why they had consented to participate.

The objectives agreed on were almost identical to those listed by Mahler and cited above, although there was considerable discussion regarding how the group would know when these objectives had been fulfilled. Several of the girls wanted to start weight charts and plan diets, but this was discouraged because of the need for medical supervision. It was decided, however, to have a medical doctor and a nutritionist visit the group and discuss the physiological implications of obesity, but not until the fifth week.

How the Group Proceeded

In the second group session, the leader presented the following summary of the problems the members had most frequently checked on the *Mooney Problem Check List,* the twenty (out of 300) which received the most attention:

1. Being overweight.
2. Sometimes wishing I'd never been born.
3. Not very attractive physically.
4. Trouble with mathematics.

5. Wanting to improve my appearance.
6. Worrying about grades.
7. Having dates.
8. Confused on some of my religious beliefs.
9. Worrying how I impress people.
10. Forgetting things.
11. Feelings too easily hurt.
12. Afraid of making mistakes.
13. Too little social life.
14. Being watched by others.
15. Wanting to be more popular.
16. Not getting enough exercise.
17. Slow in getting acquainted with people.
18. Being ill at ease at social affairs.
19. Not mixing well with the opposite sex.
20. Not attractive to opposite sex.

In addition, a chart was compiled showing the individual responses to each item and the frequency of item selection for all 300 items. Although too lengthy to reproduce here, it was helpful in providing insights into common concerns.

In final evaluations the six girls reported that the twenty sessions were productive. Attendance was excellent, and the girls were most enthusiastic about the project. They found it easy to be open and honest with each other after the third or fourth session. They confronted each other with the fallacies of their defenses for staying overweight, and they were comforted to realize that they all shared a great many feelings related to their obesity. A sense of camaraderie developed, and each meeting found them more and more able to interact on a feeling level. The leader was amazed at the willingness of the group members to share with each other how they felt about themselves. Such comments as, "I feel that people are always staring at me" and "I don't even know what it's like to date a boy, and I wonder if I ever will?" were common in the early sessions.

The counselor would write notes on the just-completed group session and present a review to each student prior to the next meeting. The girls became willing to confront each other as the counseling progressed; there was considerable embarrassment, however, at talking about one's self. This was pointed out to the group, and they related to the leader that "fat" girls use one of two available devices to cope with social situations: they make themselves the butt of jokes and allow themselves to be laughed at by peers in order to gain status, or they say nothing at all and live alone with their feelings of being peculiar. They talked at length about these two strategies for social acceptance and revealed that they had assumed both postures regularly, particularly in school. They related how they were often reluctant to answer questions in class for fear of bringing more unfavorable attention to themselves, since this was something that they experienced almost daily. They talked of an almost paranoid notion that people were always staring or laughing at them. Each member was surprised to learn that the others felt the same way. Sensitivity to insult was discussed in detail: each told how she had learned to bear insults as a condition of growing up fat, but that they still hurt, nevertheless. They unanimously agreed that a person becomes sensitized to derogatory comments as a result of being fat.

The group spent much time considering the paradox of remaining overweight while desperately wishing to shed 75 to 100 pounds. One member joined Weight-Watchers after a session in which the girls bemoaned their fate for a full hour. She ecstatically reported on the merits of this club and how she would show them that just wanting to be thinner was not enough. She extolled the virtues of the organization and cajoled two others to attend with her on a guest basis. At the end of the ten weeks four of the girls had joined and were showing appreciably decreased waistlines as well as the determination to make their physical self-concepts more closely aligned to what they imagined for themselves.

Occasionally the group leader brought in summaries of medical journal articles on the physiological and psychological implications of obesity. One such article (Snapper 1955) theorized that food appearance was a primary factor in food consumption by the obese; chronically overweight people make eating a ritual, and food must be colorful and appealing to the eye. The girls gained considerable insight in realizing that they all made eating a ceremony and how important a role food actually played in their lives.

At the conclusion of the twenty sessions the girls wrote extensive evaluations and made recommendations for future counseling groups. With genuine fervor they endorsed this kind of experience for obese students. They felt they had gained the strength to pursue a weight-losing program, and they recognized the need to muster the courage to change. Gratifying was the fact that four of the six had sought out medical help and were actively engaged in a supervised weight loss program.

Conclusions

The counseling profession needs to re-examine ways of helping those most in need of counseling services in the schools. Chronically obese students receive a significantly disproportionate amount of love and attention as they proceed through their various developmental stages. Peer ridicule, lack of attention from teachers, and often parental disgust are customary responses to this self-perceived outcast. As counselors, we ought to provide more services for those students who are the "hardest to love." Young people who live constantly with bruised egos and twisted self-images are sure-fire candidates for neuroses unless someone intervenes. The counselor is often the professional best equipped to help youngsters to actively do something to change the source of their discomfort or at least to help them incorporate rational coping mechanisms.

The group leader discovered that the six obese girls were befuddled at the concern shown them. It was hard for them to believe that someone genuinely cared for them, and consequently they were unable to cope with this "new love" in a regular way. They bombarded the counseling office almost daily to talk about every little concern imaginable, even manufacturing problems just to tell someone who cared. That counselor attention elicited such a dramatic reaction is a dour commentary on the fact that they had not incorporated as a part of their normal development the typical cultural response patterns for coping with a caring person. The girls openly admitted that outside of their parents, they didn't know of anyone who genuinely loved them. Moreover, three of the girls seriously questioned the love of their parents.

On every count the group counseling experiment for the six obese girls can be regarded as successful. As in this case, group counseling is frequently the answer for effective intervention into the lives of students who are not "making it" on one level or another. More of us need to be trained in the theory and methods of groupwork; we need the opportunity to lead counseling groups in a supervised training laboratory to develop efficiency as group leaders. Hopefully, we will be able to look to the universities for such leadership training. (For a description and analysis of one such training program implemented at Wayne State University in 1968/69 for guidance and counseling doctoral students, see Dyer 1970.)

References

Bennett, M.E. *Guidance and counseling in groups*. New York: McGraw-Hill, 1963.

Dyer, W.W. Group counseling leadership training in counselor education. Unpublished doctoral dissertation, Wayne State University, 1970.

Gendlin, E.T., & Beebe, J. III. An experimental approach to group therapy. *Journal of Research and Development in Education*, 1968, *1*, 19-29.

Mahler, C.A. *Group counseling in the schools*. Boston: Houghton Mifflin, 1969.

Ohlsen, M.M. *Group counseling*. New York: Holt, Rinehart & Winston, 1970.

Snapper, I. Food preferences in man: Special cravings and aversions. *Annals of the New York Academy of Science*, July 15, 1955, *63*, 92-106.

Wright, E.W. Group procedures. *Review of Educational Research*, 1963, *33*, April, 205-13.

14

Role Working in Group Counseling*

In a counseling group with college graduate students, a 34-year-old black woman talks about her feelings of inadequacy because, as it turns out, she was hired by a local college to serve as a "black statue." Assigned the title of assistant dean, her major job responsibilities include guiding the cheerleading team, answering the telephone, and recording minutes at weekly department meetings. She has come to feel used, only a token giving visibility to racial quota filling, a featherbedder rather than a vital contributor in an important position.

After she has related her concerns and frustrations, explaining how thwarted and underrated she feels, the group counselor suggests conducting a simulated departmental meeting in which she actively confronts her "colleagues" about one aspect of her job, her secretarial role of minutes-taker at the weekly meetings. She describes each member of her department, and then selects a group participant whom *she* feels could portray that person with sufficient fidelity. When all roles are assigned, she is required to talk about her previously customary conduct at the departmental business meetings which is objectionable to her and to set as a personal goal a presentation of her dissatisfaction at the next staff gathering.

The leader sets the scene, and a contrived departmental meeting gets underway. She struggles to make her position known to her ersatz colleagues, who all attempt to deal with her as she would be treated in the genuine setting. After working through the scene, in which she is successful in making her point, and evaluating her experiences with the members of the counseling group, she leaves the session determined to have an effective confrontation at the upcoming departmental meeting. She returns for the next group counseling session having implemented her plan and having insisted that she will no longer demeaningly serve as a secretary to a group in which she is designated a co-worker, unless it is done on a rotating basis. Thus she has actively begun to redefine her job status and functions: she is working at being more in command of herself in her world.

*Reprinted with permission from *Educational Technology*, February 1973, pp. 32-36.

A 15-year-old boy has talked about his many brushes with disciplinary officials because he is afraid that his friends "won't like him" if he assumes a conforming posture. In the safe experimental climate of the counseling group, the boy proceeds through a variety of exercises in which he tries out simulated new behaviors with his friends. Group members assume a mixture of roles in a number of scenes realistically characteristic of the young man's life, all designed to demonstrate to this counselee that he has alternatives and that most of the fantasies of impending events he has created for himself are based on false assumptions. As the enactment unfolds, group members take turns being his alter ego, being spokesmen for what he feels as contrasted with what he thinks and says, or doubling as more aggresive versions of a possible self. He has the opportunity to observe others acting out his role, to hear his doubles put into words and actions what he would genuinely like to get across to his friends. After working through his conflicts with the helping group members who have assumed the identities and behaviors of his real-life chums, he tries out his newly discovered alternative ways of dealing with his friends, and he learns that being what he chooses to be makes him feel better and that his peers continue to accept him after his forceful insistence on his position.

An eight-year-old girl, obviously shy and lacking self-confidence, quietly tells her group that she doesn't know why she is a nontalker; she usually is just afraid, and that's that. She is able to tell that she really would like to be different, more like Suzy, a spontaneous talker and an easy mixer in most social situations. She is given the opportunity to act for a few minutes with other children in the group who assume the role of (a) a favorite person and a person who always scares her and makes her hangbackish and tentative. She shows the group members how she characteristically behaves in situations with such people, and the group counselor assumes the role of her "real feelings," saying aloud how the girl really feels (or what she would like to say) each time after the girl speaks. Thus the reticent child has the opportunity to practice new and more effective behaviors, and to observe firsthand a skilled person verbalizing those inner feelings and fears which have seemed to imprison her in a mysteriously internalized shell of timidity and, at times, panic.

These actual accounts, taken from the case files of the authors, and an unlimited number of group member concerns, life conditions and situations, troublesome or neurotically debilitating relationships with significant others, many of which lend themselves to therapeutic recreation in dramatized forms, are the typical stuff of focused group counseling activity. It has been traditional in psychological and educational literature (see Corsini 1966 as an important instance of the former and Shaftel 1967 as a knowledgeable instance of the latter) to refer to the practice of spontaneously dramatizing situations and relationships in a person's life as roleplaying, what the "playing" part of that term connotes mitigates against its significance as a vital, highly productive counseling strategy.

Actors play their parts for the sake of an audience, for love or money, not so that they can live their lives in a more personally rewarding way. The play is a work of art, created for its own sake as an enduring entity; it is not life. When a youngster says, "I was only playing," this is understood to mean that he is defending against real intent; what he did is not supposed to count. In this sense the word *play* carries with it a loading pejorative to counseling purposes.

Also, the sense in which *play* means having fun, passing time in an amusing or delightful game or make-believe activity, is hurtful to the ends being sought for a member's sake when the strategy is employed in a counseling group. In a counseling group such play is too serious to be so misnamed: it is not play at all. It is work. It is testing activity, the trying on of new (albeit, uncomfortable) behaviors. It is not a substitute for life; it is a practice ground, a precursor of life. In many cases it is life; what many a counselee works on in a dramatized episode constitutes an experience in and of itself. The action in the group is not fun and games, meaningless, unreal. Rather, it is group members working together in an assortment of role techniques using the personal real-life data of one or more of their number, recreating scenes for enactment which will result in specific self-enhancing gains to that person.

Psychodramatic procedures are an exceptionally powerful category of the armamentarium available to group counselors, and if they are to be executed tellingly, they require the manifestation of skill and expertise on the part of the group counselor and hard work on the part of everyone in the group. Labeling these procedures *roleplaying* ought to be considered the product of a profession in its infancy, one struggling in hit-or-miss fashion to find its proper voice; it is time for a more mature professional stance, a consolidation of gains. We suggest a shift of emphasis, roleplaying to *roleworking*. Roleworking connotes a working through of difficult psychological material while in a role. It is safe, because it is an experience not yet actualized in one's life in a "counting" sense—a cushioning, precursory shakedown cruise. Roleworking connotes professional seriousness. It suggests a technology of dramatic methods, a well-planned and tested battery of group counseling strategies which can be set to work. Group members working in roles can-help themselves to eliminate self-defeating behaviors in a psychologically therapeutic environment where co-helpers are supportively hard at work at their side.

What Is Roleworking?

Roleworking in a group counseling session is a deliberately, though spontaneously, contrived helping structure in which group members receive assistance by working through old behavioral patterns and trying out previously unselected alternatives in a snug social enclave minimizing risk and maximizing involvement, feedback, and openness. The group members seeking help are provided with an opportunity to check their own defenses, reactions, strengths, and weaknesses in a simulated environment and to develop insights into their own behaviors in given settings. Roleworking is a total group process in which a variety of methods can be used for the purpose of helping individuals to observe and feel, on the spot, how they characteristically comport themselves in troublesome circumstances and to learn fresh approaches to handling themselves in the presence of significant others in their lives which were not previously incorporated into their repertoires of behavioral alternatives.

Roleworking involves the creation or re-creation of dramatic episodes out of the real-life (often visceral, almost tangible) data from the personal world of a particular member, which are then enacted within the counseling group. The procedure is happenstance, spontaneous, arising out of the present moment needs of a group member or members seeking greater behavioral effectiveness and freedom, understanding, three dimensional feedback, or the enriched opportunity to communicate volatile person-to-person material to other group members through demonstration. (Roleworking is brought into being in a counseling group because of some such rationale, one which is either remedial or growth promoting for a particular member or members.) Helping the group to decide on a script, deciding which role-working techniques to employ, directing the episodes and members of the "cast," selecting or collaborating with the protagonist to select the role workers, modeling many of the role-working behaviors—all of these functions and more require a skilled and competent group counselor trained and experienced in group psychodramatic technology. In addition, the group counselor helps to establish the climate in which the roleworking occurs, protecting each member of the group by assuring voluntary participation in each role and by careful monitoring of what is going on to make certain that in no case are the ego-strength limitations of group members exceeded.

Some Specific Role-Working Principles, Structures, and Techniques

Although there is an extensive literature of psychodrama and enough qualified regular practitioners of this method of

240

psychotherapy to comprise a school, psychodrama is often miscon-strued or ignored by counseling professionals as being inappropriate, too specialized or esoteric, for incorporation in counseling groups. Group counselors who take such a posture reject out of hand a fertile and important resource for adding to their storehouse of effective group counseling techniques. Illustratively we present here some specific role-working structures, principles, and techniques which, while not unknown to psychodramatists accustomed to working on a stage, are adaptively suited to the purposes and milieu of counselees working together in groups.

In one-to-one counseling, role working succeeds most productively when the counselor takes the role of the counselee and the client in turn assumes the role of the significant other, be that person the counselee's mother, girlfriend, teacher, or whomever. The counselor can mimic his counselee's actions accurately for he has accumulated the necessary behavioral evidence, but he usually fails in portraying accurately any important figure in the counselee's life because he can know that person only through the prism of his client's distorted perceptions. By having the client work in the role of the other, the counselor learns more poignantly how the other is seen by the client, something about the quality of the relationship, and what kinds of emotions arise in his client. When the counselor works in the role of his client, he is able to mirror back behaviors which his client has been manifesting in the counseling sessions, which, if judciously selected and properly analyzed, promote therapeutic movement.

The same principle applies in groups; if group members work as other group members, they are more successful than if they attempt to work in roles of people not present. Of course, it is not always possible to have group members working exclusively in each other's roles. Whenever it is appropriate, under such circumstances, the counselor coaches a group member in working in the role of the missing figure, helping the counselee whose life circumstances are thus being dramatized to flesh out and bring into the group the pertinent behavioral variables of the newly introduced character, to show the group members in a more tangible fashion what there is that is important for them to know for the sake of the scene that is to be worked through. Such a demonstration then allows a different member to facilitate accurate roleworking when roles are later re-versed. After a counselee has shown how his "others" behave, the roles can be reassigned, the new roleworkers being enabled to per-form more capably in their efforts to achieve the desired outcomes.

The use of doubles allows for a variety of role-working strategems in group counseling. If a member has difficulty in handling or express-ing his feelings with another person in his life, a spouse or a sibling,

241

for example, the leader can assume the role of his double and another group member can work in a second-double role. The protagonist sits in the center of the circle with the counselor on his left and the second-double on his right. Sitting opposite the protagonist is the significant other in his life (in role) with whom he has understanding, communicating, and relating difficulties. Each time the protagonist speaks, or every second or third time, the group counselor verbalizes what the protagonist would like to say, and the second-double verbalizes how the protagonist really feels at the moment he is speaking. This extended double technique allows the counselee to actually hear the discrepancy between what he says, what he would like to say, and what he is feeling. In the evaluation session following the roleworking, the dynamics behind such discrepancies can be pointed to and alternate ways of behaving can be considered.

As here suggested, the number of double possibilities is endless. One double could do the work of portraying any and all negative emotions, another simultaneously portraying the positive emotions of a group counselee who is filled with ambivalence. Doubles could be assigned roles of id, ego, or superego (or child, adult, parent, in the framework of transactional analysis—see Berne 1964). A skilled group counselor, aware of the potential in this technique, learns to apply it creatively and helps side-by-side double arrangements arise in the group for any number of given client concerns.

Doubles can be assigned productively to roleworkers in roles other than that of the protagonist. A double in such a situation, for example, might be used as a pump primer, as a collaborator in more effective role portrayal.

Allowing a group member to be a mentally but not physically involved observer of his own life problems being worked on by others is a potent role-working method. The group counselor and a group member demonstrate a more expedient and satisfying way to work through a trying social situation while the member observes. This technique permits the observing counselee to watch two people who are working in his role and that of a significant other in his life deal with each other on a higher level of effectiveness than he has experienced in his own living. Group members are prone to suggest that a protagonist behave in a certain way and he will be much better off, but the natural tendency is for a counselee to believe that such would be impossible, given the circumstances and people in his real life. After he has demonstrated how each of the others in his life behaves, he then observes as a skillful group counselor works in the role of the protagonist and literally adopts new and effective strategies for working with the troublesome others. When it is demonstrated, the "if I were you, I would act thus and so" approach to helping takes on a credibility that it lacks in advice-giving form.

The scenario role-working technique is described in the opening paragraphs of this chapter. Here several or all of the group members assume roles which are given in the context of the presented problem. Perhaps a family or a classroom subgroup is involved. The group counselor stays out of the action as a roleworker, preferring to function instead as a director, perhaps now and then sliding into a double-like relationship with this or that roleworker to facilitate in pump-priming fashion more effective ways of working. The protagonist assigns the group members to the various roles as he sees fit. New behavioral alternatives are stressed by the group counselor, and those working in roles are encouraged to help the protagonist in trying out more effective methods for working in this social setting.

In every counseling group there are certain members who, in their customary interpersonal transaction. styles, more nearly resemble significant others in the lives of some participants than do certain other group members. This is to say that although Pete is forty years younger and the wrong sex, he behaves in a fashion remarkably similar to Mary's grandmother, a person she has trouble dealing with; at least Mary sees an obvious resemblance in ways important to her. When such a connection is noted, a productive role-working structure can be instituted by having Pete work in the role of grandmother and help Mary to work out new behaviors and communication patterns.

When conflicts arise, or counseling blocks, or any of the possible logjams which tend to occur in counseling groups, whether they involve the group as a whole or develop just between a few or two of the members, roleworking is fruitful in helping to surface the causes and psychopersonal dynamics of the discontent. Group members exchange member roles. The role-working script comes from the interaction of the group itself.

Even without discontent or group logjams being present, role reversals among members constitute a productive technique. Having each member work in someone else's role for a time period of thirty minutes or so provides a kind of feedback which, for some members, tends to be as meaningful as anything else they experience in the group. With this exercise, as with most of those cited, post-role-working analysis by the group becomes crucial. Elizabeth finds it hard to ignore when the entire group agrees that she was accurately portrayed by Carl, even though she herself thought that Carl's work in her role was too ridiculous to be an honest reflection of her behavior.

In addition to scenes constructed out of the real-life personal data of a group member, imaginary scripts of high therapeutic value can be improvised and worked through in the group. Getting-into-Heaven scenes enacted at St. Peter's Gate, courtroom scenes (group member witnesses testifying for each other), wedding and funeral scenes, even scenes in which abstractions such as death, ectasy, guilt, or justice are given roles in the manner of the morality dramas of the Middle Ages, any one of these and more can be brought appropriately into the group counseling process in order to help a member work through self-defeating behavior or learn to contend more effectively with life conditions.

Finally, the simplest and most easily effected role-working technique ought not to be overlooked. Skillful group counselors put members into roleworking behaviors by becoming a significant other in spontaneous show-me-don't-tell-me-fashion. This, as noted earlier, is most effective when the counselor slides into the role of another member in the group whom he has studied and can imitate with fidelity. For example, "All right, Monica. Now I'm not me. I'm Sam. And I've been sitting here thinking that everything you've said in the last five minutes is absurd, that you're just trying to protect yourself . . . ."

Suggested Role-Working Precautions

The above delineations of some structures and techniques in role working hardly begin to exhaust the known technology nor the possibilities. They are presented here to give the reader a flavor of how role working can be introduced effectively into the group counseling process.

Beyond this, it is important to note that competent group counselors who employ role-working structures and techniques exercise principled cautions and controls, tried and tested operating guidelines to more effective role-working behavior in counseling groups:

1. A group needs to be prepared for the frequent or occasional introduction of role working. The most appropriate time for this is during its initial use. The first role-working experience in the group, therefore, should be carefully brought into being and handled supportively, with nonevaluative reactions to member efforts.

2. Effective role working depends on cooperation, not coercion. A worker ought to assume a role willingly, even if he has not volunteered, as may be the case when he is chosen by the protagonist. Similarly, a protagonist ought to endorse the transformation of his concerns into a script or scenario to be worked through in the group. Counselees know themselves and are the authorities on their limitations, and to push them into possible areas of hypertension without

their consent and considered agreement is to invite irreconcilable difficulties, perhaps even chaos, which may be more damaging to the group counseling process than any role-working gains could offset.

3. The role-working setting, the direction the plot will move, who the characters are, and what they are trying to achieve in the scene—these ought to be made known clearly to all participants.

4. The presence of a group counselor trained in role working is vital. What strategies he employs in the group depend on his level of professional functioning. When he is venturing onto new role-working turf, it ought to be in the presence of a more highly trained group co-counselor whose expertise is adequate to the demands of the situation.

5. A competent group counselor is the decision maker (or final endorser) about what role-working activity takes place in the group. As such, he is clear about the goals of the activity and helps the counselee whose script is being enacted, if not all of the group members, to understand beforehand what outcomes are expected and exactly *why* the role working is a desirable part of the here-and-now counseling process.

6. Problem areas, interpersonal relationships, and social situations to be worked out in role should not, in the considered judgment of the group counselor, be beyond the capabilities of the group participants.

7. Allowing discussion to occur prior to the rendition of any conjured role-working episode is particularly important in counseling groups; and in earlier role-working episodes in the life of the group, such is essential. Every group member has an equal right to understand what is going on in the group and to partake of its beneficial effects. All questions which relate to the reason for role working at this particular time in this particular instance, or to reservations of any kind, should be dealt with in a forthright and nonevasive manner by the group counselor.

8. Role working is a spontaneous enterprise. A group counselor who evaluates the action of previous group sessions as calling for the introduction of a role-working episode for the sake of the growth of a particular member or members always does so, if he is realistic, on a tentative basis.

9. Reluctance to role working is common, and competent group counselors see this as normal rather than as surprising. A statement such as, "I really don't think it will do any good" is typical. But even given such reluctance, the working in roles will usually be beneficial if the participants are not fearful of the process. No group member should be cajoled or forced to do role working against his will. Group members tend to join in when they see the process as being of genuine help.

10. Avoid dull, nebulous, wandering, inconsequential scenes which serve no purpose other than to turn off group counseling members to this technique.

11. Don't kill the efficacy of the technique by role working every concern raised by group members. Role-working techniques and structures are powerful counselor protocols inviting free and frequent usage, but not to the exclusion of other group counseling resources. If a group counselor, at any given moment in the life of the group, makes role working the number one treatment process over other choices, he ought to have rationale to justify his choice to himself and the group.

12. Inasmuch as a role-working episode usually grows out of the real-life data of a particular member, it is possible that some group participants neither identify with any part of the activity or with the goals, nor are they even willing to pay attention when role-working events transpire. Such a situation can be the cause of a group rift which works against what happens in the group as a therapeutic process for the service of all. Therefore, a chief counselor objective ought to be the involvement, on some level, of everyone in the group, whether in roles or post-role-working analyses and evaluations.

13. Role working that ends when a group counseling session ends is not effective. A group needs time to evaluate what has gone on, to understand and profit from the experience. Then, too, many experiences are highly emotional and require an unwinding time, a return to homeostasis for many role workers.

14. Post-role-working evaluation ought to answer the following questions: Was the experience effective? For whom, in what ways? Was this the most productive way for the group to spend its time? What conditions, procedures, roles, or whatever ought to be changed in the next use of this procedure? What was learned, socially, behaviorally, emotionally? By whom? In what context? Why did the group decide to enter into this activity? Did it achieve what it set out to do?

The Need for Training in Role Working

Virtually all counselee problems, concerns, and discovered objectives that materialize in counseling groups are amenable to role working. The presence of many willing co-helpers committed to common goals who can participate in an array of episodes and roles makes the counseling group format a consummate one for this potent behavioral modification methodology.

The key to successful role working is the training and expertise of the group counselor in psychodramatic skills and structures, in his directorship. As we have indicated, when working in roles is taken seriously and is executed effectively, the training and acumen required of the counselor are considerable. A call for the inclusion of courses in role working, where counseling students can receive the needed varieties of experiences actually working in roles to develop the necessary expertise, ought to be heard throughout the counseling profession.

References

Berne, E. *Games people play: The psychology of human relationships.* New York: Grove Press, 1964.

Corsini, R.J. *Role-playing in psychotherapy: A manual.* Chicago: Aldine, 1966.

Shaftel, F.R., & Shaftel, G. *Role-playing for social values: Decision-making in the social studies.* Englewood Cliffs, N.J.: Prentice-Hall, 1967.

15

So You Want to Help People: Notes for the Nonprofessional Counselor

Many people who are not employed nor paid for such services would like to help others. Although they have little or no training as counselors or psychological helpers, they wish to help another person, perhaps several others to become happier, more effective individuals in charge of their own lives. Perhaps they have a talent or a propensity for helping and have experienced some success at helping in the past. Others may seek them out. They have lots of drive, like people, and are good listeners. They engage in straight talk about realities and possibilities. They are level-headed, full of common sense, and dispensers of good advice.

Since they feel rewarded when they truly help others, they want to go beyond well-intentioned efforts. They want to get results every time. Frequently in the past there were few or no changes in their "clients" as a consequence of their efforts. Perceiving their lack of effectiveness as a lack of knowledge and skill, they are drawn to a book such as this. They want to learn. They want to enlarge their collection of helping behaviors that work.

While this book was originally intended for professionals, we discovered that many nonprofessionals were finding it useful for helping others in a variety of relationships and situations. We began recommending it to parents, married couples, supervisors, teachers, those engaged in training for helping professions and in special helping group activities, and especially to our own clients and group members. Readers of the book, from whatever walk of life, found its contents applicable to the specific realities of their daily social life. Laymen as well as mental health professionals—whether counselors, trainers of counselors, psychologists, psychotherapists, social workers, psychiatrists, medical doctors, or academic advisors—discovered that the techniques in the book worked.

On the basis of past evidence, then, this is a book for everyone. In this chapter, however, we address ourselves to the nonprofessional, to that person who seeks to become more proficient in helping others but who has little or no counseling training other than what he has picked up along the way as a result of being alert and alive. We do not see the lack of formal training as an overwhelming handicap. In fact, as we have become more experienced in counseling, we have discovered that much of what we had been professionally trained to do did not work, took too much time, or only confused us. There is much we have had to unlearn. In this sense, coming to this book with no background in the theories of counseling is an advantage.

Any Helper Can Use This Book

Although, as we have said, this is a book for everyone, users will tend to fall into several categories:

1) *The reader who is seeking self-help.* Such a reader will find this book full of practical, workable ideas easily translated into action. Throughout the book we speak of behavior that a counselor develops to become more effective. We discuss specific helping strategies to be used with clients who are dealing with certain situations, relationships or self-defeating behaviors. Someone seeking better ways of functioning in life can absorb the instructions for effective counseling and apply them to himself. Thus the reader actually becomes his own counselor.

For example, we discuss how an effective counselor is forthright and doesn't unnecessarily take up valuable counseling time with chitchat about the weather or some other unrelated subject and, instead, gets right to the business at hand by stating, "What brings you here?" Noting this, a reader can examine his own characteristic ways of relating to others and practice eliminating small talk or overtalk in favor of dealing directly with what is important between himself and another person. There is practically nothing that an effective counselor learns how to do that is not also an important part of becoming a personally masterful, in-charge individual. Readers will learn how and why not to give advice, how and why to keep confidences, how to be more open, take meaningful risks, attend to others, control their own thoughts and eliminate negative feelings, and a hundred other vital strategies for more effective and productive living.

2) *The reader who is a client receiving or intending to get individual counseling or therapy.* Such readers can learn about any given effective behavior used by a psychological helper and apply it as a criterion to the professional help offered them. By actively confronting and questioning

their professional helpers, client and counselor can decide upon realistic goals. The client always determines the behavioral changes; the professional can only assist. Therefore, the first way for a client to be effective in counseling is to help the counselor behave in helpful ways to the client. This book details what they are.

If a reader is in a counseling or therapy group, he will want to know both how he, as an individual, can get more out of the group and how he can become a more effective member of it. This book will help the group member realize both objectives. In fact, the entire second half of the volume is devoted to effective group counseling.

The aim of every group, of course, is to help each member of it function more fully in the world outside it. In the chapters devoted to group counseling, we discuss methods that will help counselors help the group members to this end. A group member need only read these methods from the other point of view—that of the client rather than the counselor—to make new decisions to act differently and become a more productive, effective member of the group.

3) *The nonprofessional reader who wants to help someone else.* This is just about everyone but we list here some typical examples of people who have already found this book to be of practical value in their helping efforts. Each example is an actual case taken from private practice, consulting, lecturing, or counselor training.

• The mother who helped her high-school daughter to make her own decision to attend a particular college.

• The wife who helped her husband to think differently and be happy while working at a job he thoroughly disliked.

• The businessman who helped a stranger, a young woman who sat next to him on a three-hour airplane trip, to quit seeing a boyfriend she only tolerated in spite of the fact that he was the only prospect she had.

• The father who helped his son to behave differently so that he did not upset himself in the presence of his critical, domineering grandmother.

• The housewife who helped her neighbor to find absorbing personal interests and generate meaningful activities instead of worrying (which had never changed anything in the past) about her husband's unhappiness and constant badgering of her.

• The boss who helped his secretary to be effective in handling the individuals she encountered daily on the phone and in person by helping her to master the risky business of speaking directly, saying no when necessary, and needing to please only herself.

• The worker who helped a co-worker to quit playing the self-defeating game of "ain't it awful," wasting time making herself unhappy by telling herself she was a victim of stressful working conditions.

• The lover who helped his girl friend to have realistic expectations in their relationship.

• The friend who helped a recently widowed woman take charge of her altered life, feelings, and steps to an uncertain future.

• The paraplegic septuagenarian inhabitant of a nursing home who helped five other inmates, one by one, to stop brooding on the fact that family members did not show up or care about them and start making their lives more meaningful within the context and conditions of their present situation.

These are only a few brief examples. Individual cases from our own experience could fill a book. The point is that these people and hundreds like them have found concrete help for helping others in this book. The information is neither esoteric nor complicated. The recommended behaviors can be grasped by anyone and applied in almost any interpersonal relationship, provided the helper is aware of some preconditions and operational principles we will discuss below.

4) *The reader who is a professional in another field and constantly deals with customers, clients, or patients who ask for psychological help.* Many such professionals, be they physicians, dentists, lawyers, hairdressers, insurance salesmen, accountants, brokers, bartenders, nurses, or whatever, find that they have been chosen to be the recipients of personal problems and confidences. The lawyer, bartender, or hairdresser may try some elementary advice-giving. The professional often makes a referral to a professional counselor or psychologist. Both responses frequently fail, especially if the client is unwilling to seek professional help. Assuming the nonprofessional wants to take the time to help, what can be successfully accomplished? This book provides many answers to that question.

5) *The reader who is either a member of a leaderless group or who has taken on the responsibility of providing leadership to a group convened for interpersonal helping purposes.* This might be a consciousness-raising or rap group or even some sort of brain-storming or task group. (We'll talk more about kinds of groups below.) Such a person will find many useful techniques in this book, but all presuppose and build upon the expertise required in one-to-one counseling. This is to say that in group counseling individuals receive counseling in a group setting. This setting provides the advantage of special structures and practices not available in a one-to-one setting, but it does not replace steps in the core process. Although there are certain advantages to group counseling, the structure may get in the way of individual helping efforts. Therefore, the effective nonprofessional group leader profits from knowing how to function as a one-to-one helper as well as a group leader.

The following are crucial considerations for nonprofessionals who wish to improve their helping efforts. First, we call attention to those principles vital to one-to-one helping, then we discuss matters essential for group leaders.

A Checklist of Helping Principles for Nonprofessionals

The first two chapters of this book present an operational definition of one-to-one counseling with some of its underlying assumptions and the essential components of an effective initial interview. The information in both chapters applies to the professional counselor. Now we recast that information for the nonprofessional. And perhaps even more important, in addressing ourselves to the nonprofessional, we correct many common misconceptions the lay public has about psychological helping. In the principles of counseling effectiveness outlined below we refer to the helper as the counselor and to the individual being helped as the client. Wherever necessary we distinguish between the professional and the nonprofessional helper.

1) *The counselor has no vested interest in the outcome of the counseling.* This aspect of counseling is perhaps the most difficult for nonprofessionals to understand. More than likely the impetus for helping originates in a vested interest. Relatives, friends, lovers, mates, workers, and neighbors who want to help ascribe their feelings to love or concern for the valued party, but the truth of the matter is usually that if the client changes, their own lots would improve. Who wants to be around a depressed person, a bumbler, a complainer, someone who moans, groans, and acts out his misery? A friend's or loved one's thinking goes something like this: "You whine and cry all the time. I don't like to be in your company when you are like this. I know you've got it tough. You really hurt. I want you to stop hurting so much. I even feel guilty being happy, knowing you're so miserable. Let me counsel you."

In the case of a co-worker, the self-interest may be even more blatant: "Damn! Because you have all these troubles you can't do your job. I have to hold up your end and I'm getting tired of it. Let me counsel you."

Counseling that arises from such motives is often doomed to failure. One difference between the professional and the amateur is that the pro gets paid for his services. This is an enormous advantage in counseling. The client assumes that whatever the counselor does is for the client's sake since the counselor has already profited. The lesson in this for the nonprofessional is that the more remote from the counselor, the greater the likelihood that the counseling will be effective.

In counseling someone who is close, someone with whom the counselor has an on-going relationship, the nonprofessional can best proceed by: a) getting all the possible payoffs which might accrue to the helper if the helpee changes out in the open; b) suspending the role relationship during the period when the counseling actually takes place; and c) convincing himself that he has no vested interest in the outcome of the counseling, and communicating this to the client. This last point means complete acceptance of the client as he now is. It also means unconditional acceptance of any client change.

For the counseling to proceed productively, the counselor might make a statement like the following and function accordingly. "I have talked about all the ways I can think of that I would benefit, if you changed your behavior. And you have pointed out some more. And they are all true. I *would* like to see you change. I can't deny it. But that is mostly because I care for *you*. When this is no longer true, I'll do something about it. In the meantime, I'll be all right no matter what happens, whether things stay the same, get better, or worse. You own your life, your feelings and behavior. You are the one who must decide what you want to do and set goals for yourself. I can only help you think things through. Every time it seems I am going beyond that to influence you for my own sake, call me on it.

"Whenever we meet to work on your concerns, for those periods I am only a helping person, and I'll try to think and behave like one. I'll put aside the fact that I'm your mother (sister, boss, friend, grandson, colleague, neighbor). Later, when we're through, I'll act like your mother again. But I won't confuse the two roles, objective helper and mother. You don't think I can do it, but I can. Test me on it. Remind me when I start to slip. Since I have decided to try to help you, it's important that I learn to separate the two roles. I have committed myself to that because I understand how important it is.

"Now. Can I have your reaction to these statements?"

2) *If there is no true commitment to help on the counselor's part or commitment to change on the client's part, the counseling won't get out of kindergarten.* The effective nonprofessional knows that he cannot unilaterally decide to counsel. Who hasn't experienced the person who grabs him and says: "Sit down. I'm going to talk to you. You need help."? That isn't counseling; it's meddling.

The client must actively seek help, sincerely want to change. Similarly, the nonprofessional counselor must really want to help, not simply offer advice about what he thinks the client ought to do.

The nonprofessional counselor ought first to decide, on his own, how much time he is willing to devote to the counseling and what special conditions he feels he would have to invoke, then communicate these specifics to his prospective client. From the client he must get a similar commitment and the declaration that the client will work hard at self-change. Without both parties declaring to themselves and each other their responsibilities and intentions, neither can rely on the other. The best method is to contract for a given number of meetings, then evaluate progress and reaffirm or renegotiate the contract. "So, Carl, it's agreed, then. We'll meet for five sessions. At the fifth session we'll decide if these meetings are making any difference for you, whether we ought to change anything, whether we ought to quit or continue. Prior to that time we won't ask that question. We'll get together no matter what, no matter how tough the going might seem. OK?"

3) *Change takes place over time, not instantly as a result of the counseling.*

Professional counselors do not allow themselves the luxury of impatience. They know that such feelings can negatively influence the client. Clients find new ways of functioning at their own pace, according to their readiness to try out new behaviors, ability to learn, and capacity to handle the discomfort of something new. The professional doesn't forget that it took a number of years for the client to become the way he is and a few quick counseling sessions won't reverse everything or cause miraculous rebirths. The professional doesn't allow himself to have *any* expectations; thus, there will be no disappointments. The lay person tends to think one good heart-to-heart talk will make a big difference. On rare occasions, this will occur, but the odds are overwhelmingly against it. New behavior is acquired one painful step at a time.

The nonprofessional who thinks that counseling someone means a one-shot, high-powered dose of potent interaction, a cataclysmic event where two people "get down" to one person's nitty-gritty, is mistaking counseling for something else, perhaps a "you-shape-up-or-I'll-boot-you-out-of-this-organization" scene. Counseling means providing help for another according to the other's timetable. If the professional is in a position of power and can apply leverage, he might effect helpful change, but he is not counseling.

4) *Counseling is most effective when it is scheduled and there are no interferences.*

The nonpro would do well to imitate the pro and make a schedule of appointments. By deciding to meet for a scheduled time block, at least an hour, in a quiet setting free of interruption and distraction (this could be in a car, in the woods, on a porch, in a bedroom, but not in a bar or restaurant), the business takes on the dignity and seriousness it deserves. When the two parties agree to set aside some specific time and to go somewhere special for these sessions, they are demonstrating commitment to the process.

5) *Personal data a client shares with a counselor is strictly confidential.*

Professional counselors are not the only ones who understand the "sacred trust" they hold when their clients confide in them. Reporters protect their sources. Physicians and attorneys refuse to tell. Confidence

254

is the bylaw of the service professions. And anyway, breaking a confidence helps no one, but may hurt a good many people including the one who talks.

In counseling, without confidentiality, no client can risk revealing what is most important to work on, those private thoughts and feelings, too awful to even talk about. When a father counsels a daughter and later tells his wife what he learned, he is a spy, no matter how he justifies himself. Whatever the daughter feels the mother ought to know, she can tell her. When a supervisor learns what's behind an employee's behavior, and later the worker hears his secrets from the lips of another employee, he is demoralized as well as betrayed. The importance of confidentiality in counseling cannot be overstressed. If it does not exist, the activity might better be called conversation, not counseling.

But how is confidentiality effectively established? Just as the client may be reluctant to be counseled by the nonpro, because that person could have a vested interest in the outcome, so too he will be less likely to confide in the nonpro because that person has a presence and a role in the client's world. Confidentiality does constitute a limitation. But effective counseling can proceed if the limitation is named and its character explored. This client question, spoken or unspoken, needs clear answering at the outset of the counseling. "Who else will know about anything I might say to you?"

During some part of the first meeting the effective nonprofessional counselor outlines the conditions. "In order for you to get full value from our sessions, you must know that I won't tell anyone else anything I might learn about you. At this point you don't know if you can trust me or not. All I can say is that I won't tell anyone anything. Right now, all you can go on is my word, but let's look at what's involved. To whom do you think I might say something? Why? What might I say? And if I did, then what? Let's look at your concerns in this area."

6) *The counselor doesn't count as a person when the counseling is going on. Only the client does.*

When two people are engaged in the act of counseling, the service, the payoffs, everything, is for the sake of the client. The personal pronoun to use is "you"; seldom, if ever, "I," and only occasionally "we." The counselor must lose awareness of himself as a person because he is focusing on the client; he must develop the counselor's mien, the mental set of using himself as an instrument to service another. The effective professional knows this. He operates out of an emotional neutrality. The counseling is centered on the client. Personal anecdotes are out. References to self are expunged. Instead of uttering "I believe you're trying to . . ." or "I think I understand what you're saying," the pro says, "You're trying to . . ." or "What you're saying is . . ."

7) *Counseling is not advice giving.*

"If I were you," most advice givers begin, "I would try to . . ." and the advice receiver thinks, "But you're not me," and shuts his ears. The trouble with advice giving, the reason it seldom has any impact on another's conduct, is that it is a cheap way to dismiss another person. It takes time and effort to know how another human being really functions. It's often easier to pass out pat advice.

Because advice is I-centered, not other-centered, the recipient understands it to be a negative commentary on his behavior. "Quit being such an ineffectual dummy and be like me." That's the message. Advice givers seldom examine their own motives or rewards, but the chief rationalization is the notion, "I can't help you because you're different from me. Here's the way I go about running my life. That's what I know. If it will work·for you, take it and begone. If it won't work, begone anyhow. Helping you, getting into your perspective, is too tough for me. And giving you my advice is a socially accepted way of getting rid of you."

The President has advisors. Lawyer A goes to Lawyer B and buys his expertise for a consultancy fee. The practice is common in our society. Buying a consultant's time is often the quickest way to acquire knowledge, and knowledge is what we all want. Therefore, if I have the knowledge, why not lay it on my client?

The client needs more than the knowledge of what successful functioning is. The client must learn how to take those first difficult steps toward what he wants. That is why it behooves the counselor to go back to his own beginning struggles toward self-realization, to remember what it was like, then *lead* the client. Though the counselor can draw on his own experience for understanding, the leading and the direction in which it goes must stem from the client's struggle, not from his own. Rather than advising, a counselor might better proceed in this fashion: "You say your shyness gets in the way and you would like to be more outgoing. When is the last time it got in the way? What did you do in that situation? What thoughts did you have? What else might you have tried? Would that work? Why wouldn't it? You say the other party might bring up something you couldn't discuss? Give an example of what that would be. How would you handle that? What responses could you make?"

8) *The client needs to understand what to do in and between sessions and what the counselor will do.*

Self-enhancing behavioral change will occur in the client only as a result of his own efforts. There is probably no activity more trying than self-change. Until now, the client has behaved in a certain way. If the client knew a better way, he would behave accordingly. The client's characteristic level of functioning represents the most he has learned. To learn more and put that knowledge into action is hard work.

First and foremost, counseling is client work. It is not simply a warm time for comforting. If the client has other expectations, they must be brought into the open and discussed. Once the counselor recognizes the distortions, they can be corrected. One way to get at client expectations is to examine the former helping experiences he has had. From whom has the client sought (or been forced to endure) help before? What was the nature of the help? Was it effective? Once these questions are answered, it is possible for the counselor to state clearly in specific terms how the counseling will compare.

Counseling is essentially a verbal process in which the counselor does a number of things best described by the following verbs. "What can you do to help me?" a client wants to know. The counselor's response may go something like this: "I can help you *to examine* where you stand in this or that aspect of your life, *to clarify* your thinking, *to evaluate* what you have been doing, *to decide* on alternate ways of behaving, *to set goals* for doing new things. I can *provide support* as you work on changing yourself. I *can encourage* you and *give you feedback*."

We have discussed various aspects of counselor behavior, including reflecting feelings, diagnosing, interpreting, and hypothesis-testing. We have provided even a self-rating scale for judging counselor performance. The important point is that whatever goes on between two individuals in counseling must be specific. Unless both parties understand what they are doing, much unproductive groping around, however warm and friendly, will be the predictable outcome.

In defining counseling, one additional factor must be emphasized. The professional understands that client dependency is easily fostered. Independency, however, is the goal. Therefore, the counselor must stress that whatever gains are made are due to the client's efforts, not to the counseling or the counselor. A client must feel and know within himself that the new behavior resulted because *he did the work to bring it about*. The effective counselor does not take over and do anything for the client. "Give a man a fish and you stave his hunger for a day. Teach him to fish and you stave it for a lifetime."

9) *In effective counseling, straight talk is vital.*

Professionals know that absolute honesty is necessary in counseling. Any beating around the bush creates distrust. When the counselor is evasive, the client thinks: a) "my counselor is judging me but won't admit it; b) he sees me as inadequate or sick and thinks I can't take it; c) he can't deal with the stuff I'm laying on him. He's got his own hang-ups."

In order to talk about anything a client presents, a counselor must be open. This means nothing the client says will shock or sway the counselor from a position of complete acceptance of the client as a person. It means that the counselor can deal with the client in the client's language, using the client's metaphors or swearing, if need be, and handle the client's personal data in a neutral way. It means that the client can have any outburst of feelings in the session and the counselor will not try to cover it up, approve, disapprove. When a client feels totally safe with a counselor, anything might come out, including revelations of crimes committed; self-abuse; abuse by others; intentions to commit suicide or murder; vile thoughts about others; confessions about dope, alcohol, money, and sex; nightmarish fears and woes the like of which no human has seen since Pandora opened her box.

Effective counseling means that the counselor can accept anything and will not withhold anything in return, providing revealing it would enhance the counseling. Every client thinks justifiably, "How can I confide in you, if you withhold from me?" Effective counseling requires that the counselor is "together" enough not to be threatened by anything a client might reveal, not to identify vicariously with the client, nor to project onto the client personal values, biases, or feelings. The counselor must, like Albert Schweitzer, feel, "Nothing human is alien to me."

10) *Where to begin? Effective counseling focuses on an exploration of the present.*

People determine what goes on in their heads and lives. They are also in charge of their own thoughts and the resultant feelings and behavior, however self-injurious. There is much they might not understand about why they think, feel, and act the way they do, and they feel frequently that if they knew the why then they would automatically change or accept themselves. As a result, they may want to search around in the dark pockets of their minds where all the old movie reels of life as they once lived it are stored and run these over and over again for the clues they might contain. Effective counselors know better than to attend these private screenings.

While it is true that most self-defeating behavior began at some point in the past and grew with reinforcements, this behavior persists in the present because there are still rewards, however neurotic. For example, if I can blame my mother for my behavior, I don't have to take responsibility for my own actions or try to change them. The effective counselor, on the other hand, thinks and says: "Who cares how it all started or grew to maturity in a cruel world? The only important question is why is it continuing?" The search for why the behavior persists takes a specific counseling form. "Let's see what you do, with whom you do it, where and when you do it, and look at what you get out of doing it. You're the person who knows the answers to these questions. You know what you think before and after you do it. You say the last time it happened was yesterday? Where were you and who else was around?"

11) *Counseling which does not focus on specifics gets lost in fog.*

Earlier we gave some examples of how nonprofessional helpers used what they learned in this book to help others successfully. In each case the client changed particular behavior. That is effective counseling. The client doesn't become a different person. He is the same person but now does certain things differently. While a client's concern or difficulty may contain many parts and it may be necessary to explore every facet in the end, the changes, the new behaviors required for more effective functioning, boil down to particular thoughts and actions in a specific time and place. These particulars are real and can be discovered and named. Identifying and labeling, the hard work of specifying, is what the effective counseling process comes down to in the end. In the beginning there is data gathering, an exploratory process, and in the middle there is priority establishing. In the end there is action.

12) *Acceptance and understanding are the keynotes of counseling. To state that one cares a lot or feels sorry for someone means nothing.*

Bleeding for another person who is bleeding doesn't staunch the flow of blood. To say, "I know how you feel" is to invite the question, "How do *you* know?" If the answer is "Because I've been through it too" the focus is merely taken away from the client. The professional doesn't do this. Instead he says, "You're having a terrible time right now. The pain is so excruciating you can hardly stand it. You wonder if it will ever end," and communicates these words with posture and face and every fiber of his being. But most important, the professional counselor demonstrates care by giving attention to what is going on in the client, by concentrating every energy there rather than on pity. An effective professional would never say, "Oh, honey, I feel so sorry for you." This only highlights the fact that "I'm okay and you're not," and is a commentary on the hopelessness of your situation. It is also a denial of what can be done now, and something can always be done. A person can change his thinking. To provide the kind of help that enables that to happen is the aim of counseling.

Just as we said above, the counselor must not condemn the client, but accept everything about him, so the counselor must be willing to make the effort to understand the client as a separate and equal individual. Understanding is a rare commodity in this world. Who hasn't cried, "Nobody understands me"? To be completely understood by another person, even for a short time, is a phenomenon many people live a lifetime without experiencing. Operationally, in counseling, as in other human interaction, understanding is being able to state to the client's satisfaction what the client is experiencing.

Some Thoughts for The Nonprofessional Helper in Groups

Groups may be convened for fun, work, or both. In work groups—such as juries, platoons, committees, or sports teams—the group goal is what matters. In a helping group, an encounter, counseling, or therapy group, there is no group goal, only the individual goals of the members to get something from the experience. They join the group for themselves, not to contribute to a group result or product.

Groups are formed in homes, community centers, churches, even businesses. They include single adults meeting to discuss the likelihood of finding partners; neighbors concerned about the neighborhood and what they want from each other; married couples sharing problems to try to get more from their marriages; pregnant women exploring what lies ahead and their feelings about it; assertiveness training groups; interested rap groups, and scores more.

In many lay groups where members get together to share experiences and work on self-improvement, the individual benefits frequently fall far short of expectations because self- or group-appointed leaders lack the knowledge to orchestrate or facilitate group functioning. The participant in any group who wants to take on a leadership role will find many helpful ideas, structures, strategies, and practices in the second part of this book. Beyond these, here is a short list of important considerations for the nonprofessional group helper:

• Help the participants to decide and clearly label what the purposes of the group meetings are and what each member can and cannot expect to derive from the experience. Later, when some activity occurs that doesn't seem to have any relationship to these purposes, the leader can intervene with: "I don't quite understand what this has to do with why we said we are here?"

• Discuss confidentiality. What goes on in the group belongs only to the participants, not to any outsider.

• With the help of the group define what will go on, what behavior is appropriate and inappropriate, and who will do what. In a counseling group, the leader cannot use the group to help himself; he is there to service others.

• Give the members some notion of the kinds of concerns appropriately worked on in the group by providing a large number of typical examples.

• Use the resources of the group. Encourage everyone to participate. Having others to call on or to provide feedback is the big advantage that group counseling has over one-to-one counseling.

• Help members to practice new behavior in the group. When they declare they are going to behave differently in their personal worlds from now on, have them show the group how they'll do this by getting members to take roles. Act out the new behavior and have the group evaluate it.

• Check out how people are feeling about the concerns at hand by studying them and reflecting and interpreting their feelings. Help them to get at the thoughts that engendered these feelings.

• Study nonverbal behavior to see if it agrees with verbal behavior. Confront members with any contradictions.

• Don't discount anyone's contribution. Anything is behavior and behavior is neutral, neither good nor bad. It is what a person knows how to do.

• Join groups. Get all the experience possible wherever possible. A leader cannot know too much about how people behave in groups.

• Read all you can on group work. There are plenty of books in the field.

A Trio of Final Thoughts

When we say counseling, we are referring to a helping process for normal people who are growing and developing in various ways; that is to say, everyone. We view psychological abnormality as referring to behavior, not to a whole person. People *behave* abnormally at times. People are not abnormal. Life is lived in the here and now, and in any given moment anyone's behavior can be viewed as abnormal, uncommon, even bizarre, assuming it was different from that of prudent people. Such a definition of abnormality can include exceptionally productive behavior as well as self-defeating behavior. Therefore abnormal behavior is not necessarily undesirable. Behavior must be perceived from the point of view of the person from whom it emanates, not in comparison to the behavior of others.

But what of neurotic or psychotic behavior? What about insane behavior? Here, again, the important focus for an effective counselor is on the *behavior* itself. The concept of insanity can be operationally understood, if one knows what to look for. A person would be acting more or less insanely, depending on the extent to which that person lacks control over his behavior and the extent to which he distorts reality. By this definition all of us are insane when we sleep and become progressively more insane as we continue to consume alcohol or some other drug. Similarly, we are less able to correctly perceive reality if we are in a state of extreme fear, anger, or depression (having our consciousness turned inward), because we have denied ourselves the full use of our senses to absorb the reality of our surroundings. Under such circumstances an effective counselor does not try to counsel a person. Other helping tactics are necessary, perhaps physically helping the drunk person to get home, or helping a fearful or angry person to work through the fear or anger. What we are saying here is that the effective counselor does not try to counsel at the time the client is behaving in a manner that demonstrates that he is out of control or distorting reality.

So much for our special notes to nonprofessional helpers. We have presented what we consider to be the most salient considerations. Of course there are others, and this book is full of them. What the nonprofessional who seriously tries to grow and develop as an effective helper of others will discover is that he will first learn to be more fully functioning in his own right. Counseling others is an enormous impetus for self-development.

The helper-denigrating aphorism, "Those who can, do. Those who can't, teach" is mostly false. Counselors are teachers who inform in especially potent ways. The best ones can perform in every dimension they counsel in. The civilization of our species has depended on teachers, on passing on to others what we know. It is a sacred and worthy undertaking.

Appendix:
Group Counseling

The following are three very different kinds of guidelines for the production of writings related to group counseling for particular individuals. In each, the individuals are identified, purposes are delineated, and specific directions are given. Following the three sets of writing guidelines, we present a practical instrument for use by group counseling members, "Group Counseling Scale for the Analysis of Fully Functioning and Self-Defeating Behaviors."

The first, "Personal Masterpiece Construction: Log-Keeping Guidelines for Counseling Group Members," was originally created for university student counselors in training who were required to keep a log of their experiences as members in a counseling group as a scheduled part of their master's degree program. We have found that the guidelines are an effective device for increasing the potency of the counseling experience in other settings as well. They have been used in other group counselor training settings, in our own private practice groups, and even with adolescents in schools. Just as any strategy which helps group members to extend and enlarge upon what happens in the group and contributes to personal growth is welcome, keeping a log provides a structured goal and does not consume group time.

The second approach, "Guidelines for Analysis of Group Counseling Tapes," was conceived for students in an advanced group counselor training program who were themselves co-leading groups of adults and tape recording their sessions. They were required to analyze their own taped sessions and those of other group counselors and to write their analyses. Each student was interested in and committed to developing personal group counselor skills. These burgeoning group counseling leaders found the analytical process to be of special value and a major contributing factor to their learning, which helped them to consolidate competency gains accrued during other phases of the training program.

The third approach, "My Behavior in Groups," guidelines for analyzing and reporting on personal case data related to one's group membership and behavior, was developed as an assignment requiring individuals to look on themselves as more than isolated or separate entities in the human community, as people who inhabit life groups in which they manifest characteristic or uncharacteristic behaviors. In a first course in a counselor training program, which focused on group counseling principles and practices, students were required to look at themselves experientially and to examine where they had been and where they now were as members of significant groups. The assignment proved to be far more meaningful to those students than group literature examination and evaluation assignments. For many it became a new window on their own worlds.

The "Group Counseling Self-Evaluation Scale for the Analysis of Fully Functioning and Self-Defeating Behaviors" is an instrument developed by Kottler, Vriend, and Dyer to help members of their counseling groups assess their own behaviors in crucial, personal mastery dimensions of effective living. We are currently in the process of further refining the scale and establishing reliability and validity norms, so at this time the scale must be considered an experimental tool only, one that may be used operationally by a counselor to foster group member growth but not for purposes of scientific research.

The scale has internal consistency, and all of the items are adapted from the logical theoretical model which the authors have presented in their tape series, *Counseling for Personal Mastery**, an empirically based and unified counseling approach to help individuals become more effective, in-charge determiners of their own living.

The scale is essentially designed to enable group members to make a personally practical determination of where they stand in a number of personal mastery dimensions and provides them with baseline data against which they can measure their progress as they work on their own self-development goals during the period they are in group counseling. We have used the scale as a group counseling pre-post evaluation aid and had the group members keep the results themselves, not sharing them with other group members or the counselor; we have used it in a particular session in the middle of the life of a group, the members discussing the items and formulating counseling goals as a result of their own scoring profiles; we have used it as a counselor tool, the counselor rating group members and the members comparing their own ratings to those of the counselor; we have used it as a counselor evaluation device, co-counselors rating each other; and we have used it with clients during individual counseling. In all of these areas the scale has been found to be productive in accelerating the counseling process. Individuals who agree that it is a significant use of their time to work at improving themselves in the personal mastery areas that the scale measures find that it helps them to accomplish their goal.

---

*John Vriend and Wayne W. Dyer, *Counseling for Personal Mastery*, an audiotape series published by the APGA Press, Washington, D.C., 1973.

264

Counselors, group counselor trainers, counselor educators, and others wishing to use the scales or any of the three guidelines described in their own professional operations are welcome to make reproductions without written permission as long as proper source credit is given. If they are to be reproduced in a publication of any kind or used commercially or for any research purpose, written permission from the publishers *is* required.

Personal Masterpiece Construction: Log-Keeping Guidelines for Counseling Group Members

Keeping a log (journal) in conjunction with a learning and self-development experience, such as being a member of a counseling group, provides the learner with a unique opportunity to enlarge and enhance that experience. By actually writing down the thoughts one has about self and the others involved in the experience (behaviors, feelings, new learnings, plans, goals, evaluation, interaction patterns, etc.), one is forced to crystallize and articulate what would otherwise remain vague. A counselee in a group is exposed to what seems like a jumble of stimuli, both internal and external, and it is difficult at best (a) to acknowledge and sort out what is personally valuable, (b) to absorb what seems like a mountain of new insights and learnings, (c) to remember them all, (d) to integrate them into the self-system, (e) to translate them into new behavior through selected practicing, and (f) to make them permanently one's own. Log keeping aids immeasurably in this process.

The log becomes a repository, a place where the fresh insights and ideas, self-analysis summaries, notes from related readings, in short, all important data and thoughts, can be chronicled and stored. The log provides you with a mechanism for thinking through whatever has begun to stir in you as a result of what has gone on in the group.

The log furnishes you with another avenue for communicating with your group counselor and for sending and receiving personal messages which you did not send or receive during the counseling sessions themselves. Inasmuch as the log is private and will not be shown to other counselees in the group unless you choose to do so, you have the opportunity to communicate with your counselor that which, for some reason, you have decided to suppress during the group time.

The log is a means by which you can speak to a future self. Who you are and how you behave now will be of immense importance to you later, provided you do a comprehensive job of recording. Individuals who use the group productively learn to examine their life situation, their current thinking, feeling, and behaving, their relationships with significant others, and their efforts to take charge of more and more aspects of their daily living.

The log is a place where goals and plans can be worked out, stated,

266

and restated. To specify goals and solidify the rationale and intent behind them is to make a commitment to action and serves to reinforce a decision that is too frequently only tentative or a will which is too often weak.

Finally, the log serves as an exercise book for practicing and developing writing skills. And who doesn't want to know how to write better? What you write you tend to remember, especially if you go back and read it again and again. Nor will you run out of material. What more important and interesting subject matter is there than you and what happens to you? You are the center of your world. Who else is or could be studying you as authoritatively or as intently as you can study yourself? Who else is in a position to take the results of such study and do something with them of consequence to you? Write your heart out! The payoff accrues to you in every way.

Directions

Write on only one side of 8½" × 11" binder sheets of paper which can be detached from your binder and handed in. Fold these sheets, the fold running from the top of the page to the bottom. Then make your entries on one-half of the page, leaving the other for responses, reactions, and comments from your counselor. Date your entries and include the actual time of the day you begin to write and the time you finish.

You are required to write for one hour between group counseling sessions each week, but you need not restrict yourself to one hour. Write as much as you please, but write only what has meaning for you. Quantity is not your purpose.

Use ink or the typewriter, but don't bother to rewrite. What you write is for yourself, and it ought to be readable. Since you are not being graded, your errors, poor sentence construction, or lack of grace will not be penalized in any way. If there are errors, exposing them in order to work on correcting them can become a part of the self-regimen.

You are being exposed to a variety of ideas about how people function in counseling groups, about group counselor behaviors and interventions, and about group counseling structures, strategies, and processes. Although many of these ideas are interesting relative to what is happening to you and others in your counseling group, these ideas cannot appropriately be discussed in group sessions unless they have a bearing on particular aspects of personal behavior. You can and should log them, however, since they have a meaning for you which transcends the counseling experience.

Do not write anything in your log to impress your counselor. To your counselor, your writing is just additional behavior to view neutrally and react to objectively. The log is a personal record, which should become your most valuable document, the one item that should be saved above all other personal belongings.

Guidelines for Analysis of
Group Counseling Tapes

The task of analyzing the taped record of a group counseling session is admittedly difficult. It takes time to associate voices with names and with the characters and life data of the group members who are being identified. Besides, there are many ways of approaching the task. An analyzer could, for example, single out one group member and study exclusively that person's contributions and reactions, his or her influence on the group as a whole or on particular others, and the influence of the group as a whole or particular others on that person. An analyzer could focus exclusively on group counselor behaviors, or group process variables could be inferred and concentrated on, as though they existed independently of the behavior of the individuals who make up the group.

Group counselors in training, however, have the clearcut goal of self-help toward more effective in-group leader performance and are looking for any insight or model which might accelerate that end in any specific behavioral fashion. They continually seek to add to a personal storehouse of skills and competencies. Studying the life of a group, what specifically happens to each member, and what each member causes to happen, therefore, is related to developing one's own ability to perceive what is actually going on in any particular group member or between participants at any given time, how the action in the group got to where it is, where it is headed, and how leader interventions might benefit its progress for any given group member. These guidelines are presented as aids to building the analytic skills so important to group counselor expertise.

Each person in the seminar, besides co-counseling a group, is monitoring a group co-led by two others in the seminar. It is expected that each monitor will produce four copies of his or her (typed, double-spaced) analysis of each group session: one for each co-leader, one for personal use, and one each for the seminar instructors. Seminar time will be provided for monitor and co-leaders to discuss these analyses and compare points of view, exchange insights, and minimize ambiguities and discrepancies. In their own analyses of each session, the leaders are directed to use these guidelines to facilitate the employment of a common language with their monitors.

Monitors are urged to approach their task with either or both of two mental sets: a spirit of scientific inquiry (objectively: What is happening? What can one learn about group member behavior which might benefit a person setting out to lead groups? Which points might be extrapolated to all such groups as this?), and "If I were the co-leader, what would I do at this point and why?"

Format

Each analysis should have a heading that includes monitor's name, co-leaders' names, date of counseling session, and number of session (e.g., third, fourth, fifth, etc.). Analytical remarks should be organized (perceptions, conclusions, interpretations, insights, evidence) into the categories below, using direct quotations where meaningful. There is no minium or maximum length.

Analysis Categories

a. Counselor Behaviors

What kinds of counselor behaviors result in what kinds of group member behaviors? Leader behaviors may be highly deliberate and calculated, spontaneous, or even totally involuntary—as an automatic response might be characterized. Some of the following verbs can serve as shorthand tags for leader behaviors: identifying, clarifying, reviewing, interpreting, restating, connecting, advice giving, reassuring, supporting, encouraging, intervening, goal setting, causing closure, hanging back, etc. (Many of these verbs need objects; they make sense only in the context of the specific group activity. The list given is far from exhaustive and includes only those behaviors which might be construed as positive. Leader behaviors construed as negative might include such verbs as: insulting, putting down, ignoring, etc. But whether a behavior is positive or negative depends on what results from it and how that result is related to group member goals and outcomes.) Certainly leader behaviors will be manifested in group members. A significant goal of the designated leaders, for example, would be to reinforce positive leadership behavior on the part of any group member.

b. Communication Structure

What is being communicated? While A talks to B about A's involvement in a political activity, for example, the message A might really be sending is simply: judge me as trustworthy and important, as a good guy who is on the right side. Messages are sent by whom and to whom? Messages are received by whom from whom? Who participates in the communication? What affect levels exist in the communication? Every message has an affect loading: it could be loaded with anger, intimacy, bitterness, result in an altering of the affect level (emotional climate) of the entire group, exchanges containing mounting doses of anxiety, for example.

c. Group Movement

What shifts in group movement are discernible? Groups frequently engage in cyclical behavior, living through a series of incidents and then returning to them again. What patterns or themes occur and recur, both in process (group member behaviors) and content (topical material)? How do individual members react to certain repetitive events? Who causes the group to return to that which it has already worked on? Is the movement of the group toward greater cohesion and intimacy or toward divisiveness (splintering into factions), toward resolving conflicts with authority, or does the desire to avoid such resolution determine its movement, to give some examples.

d. Power Structure

Who talks? Who listens? Who tries to influence others? Who responds to whom? Who tries to control? Who does control, and how? Where do the leaders stand? Is there evidence that group members are trying to use one leader against the other? Does the power shift, or does it remain localized in the hands of a few? Do the leaders completely dominate what happens? Occasionally, frequently, intermittently? What events seem to bring out such behavior? Are the influencers and controllers in the group helping or hindering movements? In what way?

e. Group Norms

What kinds of behavioral group norms are established and tend to prevail? What kinds of behaviors are tolerated, accepted, or rejected? Who tolerates what, permits what? What leader behavior is tolerated? What behavior gets rewarded or punished, and how does it? Does the group permit some members to remain silent, for instance? Is physical contact allowed? Is the expression of intense feeling allowed, encouraged, banned? Using the "game" metaphor, what kinds of games has the group decided are appropriate to play?

Cautionary Note

Remember, in all analysis and write-ups, that the word "group" and anything ascribed to it is an abstraction, a convenience for ordering certain kinds of thought. There is really no such thing as a group, a group goal, norm, stage, or pattern. The group truly does not exist, however much we need the word and concept in order to discourse about what it is that people do when they are in the company of others for a structured experiencing. Individuals exist and behave in specific observable, meaningful, self-initiating or responding-to-stimuli ways. A counseling group, taken as an entity, is meaningless. Any meaning it might have is in the head of the labeler. No one person can own the behavior of a group; nor need a member own the behavior of any part of a group other than his or her own.

To talk of a group as though it were human, had a mind of its own, had a life of its own, a self-determined direction, character, or predisposition is folly, an exercise in self-mesmerism. When a group counselor asks, "What does the group think about Jack's statement?" he or she is being ineffective by definition, for no group thinks. People, one by one, think, play, eat, make love, or blow their noses; groups do not.

In analyzing the events in the group sessions, therefore, one must be concious on two levels: to see behavior as located always in this or that individual, and to see the individual behavior as being manifested before and in relation to witnesses, some, if not all of whom have a relational, if not a vested, personal interest in what that behavior is.

When analyzing or reporting on what went on in a given session, one should not lapse into thought or communication which has the group as the subject and something later as predicate without qualification for the recipient of the thought or communication. For purposes of discussion, a group "norm," when properly described, might fit a reality but only for communication to another for special reasons. Actually, a "norm" is an unreal mental construction having no existence outside of two or more minds which decide to concur: such is what mental abstractions are all about.

My Behavior in Groups: An Assignment in Observation and Introspection

Writing and Format Directions

The final draft of your essay (which can carry a different title than *My Behavior in Groups*) should be: a) typed and double-spaced on 8½ x 11 inch white paper, b) no longer than 3,000 words, and c) include all references in the *A.P.A. Publications Manual* format. Quotations are discouraged, but the use of reading resources to stimulate and help generate thinking is encouraged. Write as clearly, crisply as possible. Support your contentions, themes, and conclusions with logic, convincing data, and authorative backing. Tell it "like it is," not how "it should be." Organize your material according to your own sequential and categorical rationale.

General Guidelines

Purposes

The thrust behind this assignment is to help the student, who is open and eager to learn more about how people function in groups, focus on pertinent experiential variables. Such students:

1. Seek to learn principles of human behavior in groups (group dynamics) and how these pertain to themselves.

2. Desire to become proficient diagnosticians, understanders, and interpreters of the meaning of human behavior.

3. Want to know what causes people to behave in certain ways in groups.

4. Look for similarities and differences between kinds of group membership.

5. Seek to understand the effects of group characteristics (such as leader behavior, setting, composition, structure, etc.) on themselves and others.

6. Desire to explore the pertinent scientific resources for practical help in applying groupwork knowledge and practice to their own professional behaviors and settings.

7. Seek to empirically know and evaluate their own behaviors as members of various groups.

8. Are capable of adding a dozen more similar purposes for undertaking such a study.

Content

Essentially the content of your essay should be a description, analysis, and evaluation of your behavior as a member of assorted groups, a delineation of group operating variables in relationship to such behavior, and, particularly in those currently ongoing groups, an evaluative progress report of attempts and successes in personal behavior modification. Be certain to include a description, analysis, and evaluation of your behavior as a member of the following groups:

1. Family group in which you are an offspring.
2. Family group in which you are a parent.
2a. (If you are not a member of a family group in which you are a parent, substitute the social group—friendship circle—of which you are a member.)
3. Your adolescent peer group. Choose a particular group from a particular adolescent period in your life.
4. Your childhood (below grade 8) peer group. Choose a particular group from a particular childhood period.
5. The staff group (professional colleagues) with whom you work.
6. Class groups. These include subgroups as well as the entire class as a group.

Overall Suggestions

All groups are defined as such according to certain criteria, and your behavior is related to some, if not all, of these. Be sure to consider such ideas as pecking order, communication patterns, group task, membership requirements, structural limitations, leader and member roles, power structure, and other conditional aspects of group life.

Continually question the "why" of all human behavior in groups, particularly your own. Look for, be able to identify and name, and trace the mental causes of emotional behavior. Look for motivation and intent, especially one's own. (What are particular members trying to accomplish? What is standing in the way of reaching my goals? Why am I not being as effective as I want to be? In what specific ways am I the least in charge of myself? The most in charge?)

Keep a written progress report of yourself as a behaving person in the ongoing groups. In a journal or log, write up the pertinent happenings of each session as they relate to your interaction or lack of it. This log will be of inestimable value when you begin to draw all your ideas and data together for your essay.

Finally, in the conclusion of your essay be sure to include a synthesis of your behavior as a member of assorted groups, a profile of yourself as a behaving group member. Be sure to include whether your study of yourself has resulted in any behavioral shifts, whether you now behave differently than when you began your study, in what specific ways, and what your behavioral intentions are for your future group living.

Group Counseling Scale for the Self-Analysis of Fully Functioning and Self-Defeating Behaviors

Jeffrey Kottler, *John Vriend and Wayne W. Dyer*

This self-evaluation device has been constructed to help you identify, look at, and analyze some important personal life dimensions. Effectively going to work at improving behavioral skills which promote more personal mastery and increasing the extent to which one is more in charge of his or her life circumstances is a chief task of every client in the counseling process. It makes sense to identify and diagnose areas of strength and weakness in one's repertoire of mental, emotional, and physical behaviors before one can work to improve skills of functioning in these dimensions.

This scale will help you to identify those behaviors which are self-defeating and ineffective as well as those which are self-enhancing and fully functioning. You will be able to trace your development in these specific behavioral dimensions by assessing yourself now, and again upon completion of the counseling experience. In knowing exactly where you stand in relation to where you could be, you will feel a greater responsibility for being a productive client. You will create an extensive portrait of the ways you characteristically behave in your world, one that you can share with your counselor and the other group members to heighten the effects you can derive from the group counseling sessions.

This device is only as accurate as your honesty makes it. There are no appropriate, inappropriate, good, bad, right, or wrong responses. Rate yourself as you really think you are, not how you think others see you, nor how you would like to be.

Instructions for scoring your profile are given at the end of the scales. There are two responses required for each item on this scale:

1. Rate the following statements according to your own behavior by placing the appropriate number, 1, 2, 3, 4, or 5 in the space immediately to the right of the statement.

2. Rate the accuracy of your response to each statement by indicating your level of confidence decision with the corresponding number, 1, 2, 3, or 4 in the space to the right of your first response.

Make sure you respond to the statement *first*. Then rate your level of confidence in your response.

---

* Jeffrey Kottler is an assistant professor of counselor education at the University of North Alabama in Florence, Alabama.

Extent Statement Characterizes My Behavior

% of time I engage in this behavior	0%	25%	50%	75%	100%
	never 1	seldom 2	sometimes 3	usually 4	always 5

Level of Confidence in My Response

1 I haven't thought about this.
2 I have thought about this, but I'm still unsure of where I stand.
3 I have thought about this and have a general idea of where I stand.
4 I have thought about this and know exactly where I stand.

Example: I answer questions honestly on questionnaires. <u>5</u> <u>4</u>
(I always answer questions honestly on questionnaires and know exactly where I stand on this issue.)

Statement	Extent Statement Characterizes My Behavior	Level of Confidence in My Response
1. I feel free to be or do anything I want.	⎯⎯	⎯⎯
2. I end up in arguments and fights that I know I can never win.	⎯⎯	⎯⎯
3. I use "should" a lot to describe the way things ought to be rather than accept the world as it is.	⎯⎯	⎯⎯
4. I like to be in love intensely with total involvement.	⎯⎯	⎯⎯
5. When I'm depressed, frustrated, or anxious, there is very little I can do about it.	⎯⎯	⎯⎯
6. What I have done in the past has nothing to do with what I do now and can do in the future.	⎯⎯	⎯⎯
7. I feel lonely.	⎯⎯	⎯⎯
8. I feel guilty about things that I've done in the past that I shouldn't have or things I didn't do that I should have.	⎯⎯	⎯⎯

Statement	Extent Statement Characterizes My Behavior	Level of Confidence in My Response
9. Nothing another person does is bad, wrong, immoral, disgusting, or anything else except human.	_____	_____
10. I love the way I am.	_____	_____
11. I feel inferior to people around me.	_____	_____
12. Although I may *prefer* things and people who are close to me to be a certain way, I don't *need* them to be so.	_____	_____
13. I enjoy experiencing the new, mysterious, and unknown in my daily life and actively seek such opportunities.	_____	_____
14. I am careful not to hurt anyone's feelings, even if it means watering down the truth.	_____	_____
15. I do things that others might regard as crazy and am not concerned with what others might think.	_____	_____
16. I enjoy and seek out privacy.	_____	_____
17. No matter what risks are involved I aggressively seek what constitutes the truth and reality of my world.	_____	_____
18. I have a difficult time changing my views or admitting that I'm wrong.	_____	_____
19. I find fault in others rather than myself.	_____	_____
20. It upsets me if I lose, fail, or am unsuccessful at something I try.	_____	_____
21. I feel there are other people I answer to for my actions besides myself.	_____	_____
22. My present moments are too important for me to think about the pleasurable and painful moments of the past.	_____	_____

Statement	Extent Statement Characterizes My Behavior	Level of Confidence in My Response
23. I spend time worrying about things that could happen in the future over which I have no control.	_____	_____
24. I enjoy the natural world without boredom and accept all things as they come.	_____	_____
25. To myself, I am the most important person in the world.	_____	_____
26. There are things about myself that I don't like or am ashamed of.	_____	_____
27. I tend to use the existing alternatives and options when I work on a problem because they have already been proven right.	_____	_____
28. I obey only those laws, rules, and societal expectations that are personally meaningful.	_____	_____
29. I feel that if I wait long enough a problem will go away by itself.	_____	_____
30. I fight crusades to make a difference in things that matter to me and help those who need me, but I quit the moment I know I can't make a difference.	_____	_____
31. I sense the sublime, ridiculous, or humorous in almost any situation or person, including myself, and bring it into my life every chance I get.	_____	_____
32. I feel impotent by my inability to cope with certain situations and panic because of these circumstances in my environment.	_____	_____
33. I consistently come up with creative and original solutions to problems that concern me.	_____	_____

Statement	Extent Statement Characterizes My Behavior	Level of Confidence in My Response
34. I feel uncomfortable and insecure when I am unexpectedly confronted with someone or something new or mysterious that I don't understand, and I tend to avoid such situations.	_____	_____
35. I don't *need* the formal institution of religion.	_____	_____
36. I cope with tragedy in my life without remorse, incapacitation, or lingering side effects.	_____	_____
37. If I choose, I have no problem telling people exactly what I think of them.	_____	_____
38. I take over and speak for at least one other person in my life without his or her consent.	_____	_____
39. I fantasize about the good times and would like to change many of the past experiences that I've had.	_____	_____
40. I feel it is a losing cause to fight society's rules and laws that don't make sense to me.	_____	_____
41. It is impossible for anyone to affect me with words unless I allow them to.	_____	_____
42. I don't consider postponing gratification for something I can get now and have seemingly endless energy to get what I want.	_____	_____
43. I tend to use statements like "I've always been that way" and "That's the way I am" to describe myself.	_____	_____
44. I am open-minded and flexible in my thinking and have no vested interest in hanging on to ideas.	_____	_____
45. When I act below my standards of perfection I don't condemn myself for failing or feel I have to finish a task just because I started it.	_____	_____

Statement	Extent Statement Characterizes My Behavior	Level of Confidence in My Response
46. I criticize people who act differently than I would.	————	————
47. I find others' admiration and approval more important than my achievements.	————	————
48. When things go wrong in my world, I don't argue about whose fault it was, but accept the responsibility and try to do something to change it.	————	————
49. I only feel at ease when everything is organized, ordered, or in its place.	————	————
50. I use a number of negative statements to describe myself such as: "I'm dumb," "I'm quiet," "I'm not a swimmer," "I'm not good at Math," etc.	————	————

Scoring

You can obtain a numerical value for each item by multiplying the two numbers (rating response times confidence level) and entering the product in the margin next to the item. Example: If the rating response was 3 (sometimes) and the confidence level was 1 (I haven't thought about this), then the score for that item is 3 (3 × 1).

Identify each item score with either a Fully Functioning Behavior (FFB) or a Self-Defeating Behavior (SDB) shown in the "Delineation of the Major Areas of SDB's and FFB's" given below.

Study the individual item responses. Compare matched pairs (one SDB and one FFB from the same behavior category) for the reliability of your responses. Note any gross inconsistency between paired responses. Total the item scores of SDB's to obtain a Self-Defeating Behavior Index (SDBI). Total the item scores of FFB's to obtain a Fully-Functioning Behavior Index (FFBI). Underline the extreme scores, those that are fifteen or above. These are your most prevalent indicators of behavioral skill strengths and weaknesses. Subtract your SDBI from your FFBI to obtain your Personal Mastery Index (PMI).

Just before completion of your counseling experience, use the scales again to determine areas of growth as well as areas of stagnation. Each self-evaluation profile has value only to the person whose level of personal mastery is being assessed. It cannot be meaningfully compared to that of another individual. Self-development can only be measured in relation to the point where an initial assessment was made.

Delineation of the Major Areas of SDB's and FFB's

SDB items: 2, 3, 5, 7, 8, 11, 14, 18, 19, 20, 21, 23, 26, 27, 29, 32, 34, 38, 39, 40, 43, 46, 47, 49, 50.
FFB items: 1, 4, 6, 9, 10, 12, 13, 15, 16, 17, 22, 24, 25, 28, 30, 31, 33, 35, 36, 37, 41, 42, 44, 45, 48.

Score

Am I in charge of my world? or Is it in charge of me?
#1. FFB—I feel free to be or do anything I want. _____
#32. SDB—I feel impotent by my inability to cope with certain situations and panic because of these circumstances in my environment. _____

Truthfulness and Evasiveness
#37. FFB—If I choose, I have no problem telling people exactly what I think of them. _____
#14. SDB—I am careful not to hurt anyone's feelings, even if it means watering down the truth. _____

Pursuit and Avoidance of the Unknown
#13. FFB—I enjoy experiencing the new, mysterious, and unknown in my daily life and actively seek such opportunities. _____
#34. SDB—I feel uncomfortable and insecure when I am unexpectedly confronted with someone or something new or mysterious that I don't understand, and I tend to avoid such situations. _____

Creativity and Conformity
#33. FFB—I consistently come up with creative and original solutions to problems that concern me. _____
#27. SDB—I tend to use the existing alternatives and options available when I work on a problem because they have already been proven to be right. _____

Resistance and Compliance to Societal Inculturation
#28. FFB—I obey only those laws, rules, and societal expectations that are personally meaningful. _____
#40. SDB—I feel it is a losing cause to fight society's rules and laws that don't make sense to me. _____

Internal and External Control of Emotion States
#41. FFB—It is impossible for anyone to affect me with words unless I allow them to. _____
#5. SDB—When I'm depressed, frustrated, or anxious, there is very little that I can do about it. _____

"The way I am" vs. "The way I was"
#6. FFB—What I have done in the past has nothing to do with what I do now and can do in the future. _____

#43. SDB—I tend to use statements like "I've always been that way" and "That's the way I am" to describe myself.   _____

Action Toward Self-Gain and Procrastination

#42. FFB—I don't consider postponing gratification for something I can get now and have seemingly endless energy to get what I want.   _____

#29. SDB—I feel that if I wait long enough a problem will always go away by itself.   _____

Self-Worth and Self-Pity

#25. FFB—To myself, I am the most important person in the world.   _____

#11. SDB—I feel inferior to people around me.   _____

Living Now and In the Past

#22. FFB—My present moments are too important for me to think about the pleasurable and painful moments of the past.   _____

#39. SDB—I fantasize about the good times and would like to change many of the past experiences that I've had.   _____

Acceptance and Rejection of the Natural World

#24. FFB—I enjoy the natural world without boredom and accept all things as they come.   _____

#3. SDB—I use "should" a lot to describe the way things ought to be rather than accept the world as it is.   _____

Democratic Fights and Hopeless Battles

#30. FFB—I fight crusades to make a difference in things that matter to me and help those who need me, but I quit the moment I know I can't make a difference.   _____

#2. SDB—I end up in arguments and fights that I know I can never win.   _____

Aggressive Truth-Seeking About the Reality of My World

#17. FFB—No matter what risks are involved I aggressively seek what constitutes the truth and reality of my world.   _____

Guilt

#8. SDB—I feel guilty about things that I've done in the past that I shouldn't have or things I didn't do that I should have.   _____

Understanding Love

#4. FFB—I like to be in love intensely with total involvement.   _____

Worry

#23. SDB—I spend time worrying about things that could happen in the future over which I have no control.   _____

Unhostile Sense of Humor

#31. FFB—I sense the sublime, ridiculous, or humorous in almost any situation or person, including myself, and bring it into my life every chance I get.   _____

Speaking For Others

#38. SDB—I take over and speak for at least one other person in my life without his or her consent.   _____

Psychological Dependence and Independence

#12. FFB—Although I may *prefer* things and people who are close to me to be a certain way, I don't *need* them to be so. _____

#21. SDB—I feel there are other people I answer to for my actions besides myself. _____

Privacy and loneliness

#16. FFB—I enjoy and seek out privacy. _____

#7. SDB—I feel lonely. _____

Focus on Self and Others

#48. FFB—When things go wrong in my world, I don't argue about whose fault it was, but accept the responsibility and try to do something to change it. _____

#19. SDB—I find fault in others rather than myself. _____

Approval-Seeking and Indifference

#15. FFB—I do things that others might regard as crazy and am not concerned with what others might think. _____

#47. SDB—I find others' admiration and approval more important than my achievements. _____

Freedom and Fear to Fail

#45. FFB—When I act below my standards of perfection I don't condemn myself for failing or feel I have to finish a task just because I started it. _____

#20. SDB—It upsets me if I lose, fail, or am unsuccessful at something I try. _____

Ethnocentricity

#9. FFB—Nothing another person does is bad, wrong, immoral, disgusting, or anything else except human. _____

#46. SDB—I criticize people who act differently than I would. _____

Flexibility and Rigidity of Thinking

#44. FFB—I am open-minded and flexible in my thinking and have no vested interest in hanging on to ideas. _____

#18. SDB—I have a difficult time changing my views or admitting that I'm wrong. _____

Self-Love and Self-Shame

#10. FFB—I love the way I am. _____

#26. SDB—There are things about myself that I don't like or am ashamed of. _____

Index